Get the Picture?

THE MOVIE LOVER'S GUIDE TO WATCHING FILMS

Jim Piper

ALLWORTH PRESS
NEW YORK

for Carol

04 03 02 01 00 99   5 4 3 2 1

Published by Allworth Press
An imprint of Allworth Communications
10 East 23rd Street, New York, NY 10010

Cover design by Douglas Design Associates, New York, NY

Page composition/typography by Sharp Des!gns, Lansing, MI

ISBN: 1-58115-081-4

LIBRARY OF CONGRESS CATALOGING-IN-PUBLICATION DATA
Piper, Jim
Get the picture?: the movie lover's guide to watching films / by Jim Piper.
p. cm.
Includes index.
ISBN 1-58115-081-4
1. Motion pictures—Appreciation. 2. Cinematography. I. Title.
PN1994 .P619 2001
791.43'01'5—dc21
00-53123

Printed in Canada

Contents

I CINEMATICS

    Frames
    Angles
    Moves
    Optics
    Composition
    The Long Take: High Art or Playfulness?
    Film Stock

    Lighting
    Set Design
    The Same, Only Different

    Dialog
    Music

Sound Effects
Sound Mix
Sound to Picture

Basics
Grammar
Time
Space
Art

The Great Divide: Realism versus Formalism
Elements of Style
Ones, Twos, and Threes
Eights, Nines, and Tens
The Rise of the Stylistic Middle
Classic Hollywood Style
Five Practitioners of Classic Style
New Cinematic Style and the Move to Formalism
Four Formalist Directors
Truth's Beauty

II STORY

Types
Conflict
Resolution
Believability
Point of View
Cinematics and Drama

Main Characters
Protagonists and Antagonists
Round and Flat Characters
Thematic Characters
Mythic Characters
Epic Characters

Characters Who Change for the Better
Characters Who Change for the Worse
Good Characters under Pressure to Change
Characters Who Should Change
Character Relationships
Cinematics and Character

Season
Era
Setting as Journey
Settings in Foreign Films
Cinematics and Natural Settings

Up Tones
Down Tones
Mixed Tones
Cinematics and Tone

From Tone to Meaning
Genre Movies
Subtext
Micromeaning
Symbols?
Macromeaning
Countermyth
Theme
Arriving at Large Meaning in Two Contemporary Films
Triangulation

LIST OF *TRY THIS* EXERCISES

Acknowledgments

I met a guy who had written a novel about Viet Nam. Maybe he was a little shell-shocked. He said by God no editor is going to change one word of my book. I looked at a few pages and understood that he will always remain an unpublished amateur.

All writers need editors, even professionals. *Especially* professionals. That's how they got to be professional. A writer without an editor is like a guitar out of tune. You wouldn't want to hear the music or read the book. I've been writing professionally for over twenty years and not only do I still need editors, I *crave* them.

When a person writes a book, he is exceedingly self-absorbed and self-contained, trapped in his own arrogance and limited by his shortsightedness. He is, in fact, a little mad and out of touch, as I have been before my editors brought me back to reality. Nicole Potter and Elizabeth Van Hoose, both linguistic psychologists, helped me break through the shell and look back at the mess I had wrought. Without their assistance, these pages would be neither readable nor marketable. Nicole kept me steering in a good and true direction, to switch metaphors. Elizabeth helped me attain final-draft sheen. Both provided invaluable, sane other-sensibility.

Still, do not blame them if you read things you don't like, because the availing duo nearly always gave me final say in rhetorical matters, usually after several exchanges of emails, which in themselves were humane and respectful, making the process enjoyable. I can't imagine having a better editors-writer relationship.

Then there is Carol my wife, for whom profuse thanks are in order. Carol is not a book editor but a terrific movie-watcher. She is better at staying awake than I am, plus she never, never walks on bad films. I try not to doze. I have learned so much from her, about staying awake *and* about films.

Fresno, November 21, 2000

Movies and Films

T he purpose of this book is to help you get more out of the movies and films of your life. Movies and films? We Americans don't use those terms interchangeably. We seem to want to save "film" for motion pictures that are more serious somehow than mere movies, which are just for entertainment. This distinction explains why the American Film Institute is not the American Movie Institute. And it explains why universities never offer movie courses or have movie departments; they offer film courses and have film departments.

But these categories are not rigid. Many motion pictures cross over from moviehood to filmhood. All that is required is a perceptive viewer to get beneath the surface of movies and take them seriously. For example, a pop movie like *The Mask* (1994)*, starring Jim Carrey, is the perfect showcase for Carrey's talents. It made a lot of money and deserved to. But for viewers who are able to think and laugh at the same time, *The Mask* is a movie with some seriousness about it. To them it's about a common human condition—maybe more a male thing than a female thing when a nerdy, held-back person who is really a super-dude needs help to let the inner person come out. Or maybe the truth of the matter is that the nerdy guy hopes he harbors a superdude inside, whether he does or not. Either way, a smart viewer senses that there is something real going on in a movie like this. *The Mask*, in fact, is part of a long line of films about the inner dude that includes *The Nutty Professor* (1996), *Superman* (1978), and

---

*Numbers in parentheses refer to the year the movie was released; in other words, *The Mask* (1994) means that *The Mask* was released in 1994.

The Mask. A film is born—in the imagination of the viewer. Photo by Darren Michaeles. New Line Cinema.

Rocky (1976). At any rate, the moment we start to think about movies seriously, even funny movies, we transform them into films. We also derive additional pleasure from viewing them.

But this isn't the only way films come into being. There have always been producers, writers, and directors associated with Hollywood or not associated with Hollywood who set out with the goal of making films, not movies, from the start. They don't wait for astute viewers, critics, or writers of books about film to confer the status of "film" on their work. Over his long career, the director Sidney Lumet has always made films rather than movies. Lumet has worked within the Hollywood for-profit system to put together such important films as *The Pawnbroker* (1965), *12 Angry Men* (1957), *Prince of the City* (1981), and *Q and A* (1990). Both *Prince of the City* and *Q and A* are cop films. What sets them apart from Hollywood cop movies are issues of character—the heroes of these films must struggle to know right from wrong and then must follow through and do the right thing. Lumet's cop films—he has done nine so far—never feature high-speed chases and prolonged shoot-outs. None has anything like a cackling psychopath who leads cops on wild goose chases. That's *movie* stuff. Instead, Lumet's cop films portray both cops and criminals as real human beings. (Lumet's cop films were doubtless major sources for the realistic TV cop series, *Homicide* and *NYPD Blue*.)

So filmness *may have two quite different origins that seem to be contradictory. Is a motion picture's "filmness" just in the head of the viewer? Or is there stuff going on in the actual motion picture to make it a "film"?*

I don't know. Maybe both. It doesn't matter. All I want to do in this book is stretch the way you relate to motion pictures more to the film side, whether you make movies into films in your own mind or follow the judgments of someone like me.

I describe several hundred movies and films in these pages, and I constantly urge you to go out, rent them, and watch them. You may rent most at a typically well-stocked video store. About a third you will find in the current releases section of the store, at least for a year or so after of the publication of this book. Another third can be found in the various movie sections rental stores set up—thriller, drama, comedy, classics, and so on.

As for the last third, these may be a little hard to find—films like *Ponette* (1996), the endearing French film about a girl of four adjusting to the death of her mother, or *The Grey Fox* (1982), the wonderful Canadian-made Western about a man who does a long stretch in prison, gets out, discovers that the stage coaches he used to rob have passed into history, and so takes to robbing trains. Films like these won't be stocked at your local Blockbuster. You'll need to phone around town to locate them. Virtually every city has one or two video stores that take pride in (though not much profit from) their collections of classic, independent, foreign, and art films. I hope you locate one in your town because I describe a lot of the kinds of alternative films they carry, and I hope you view them. Meanwhile, a place called Facets Multimedia in Chicago rents just about every damn video known to humankind. It's a national treasure. I suggest phoning Facets at 1-800-331-6197 to get their catalog and find out about renting from them by mail.

As for myself, I have taught something called "Introduction to Film" to adults of all levels of maturity for a couple of decades. I'm lucky enough to teach in an open-door college that admits all manner of humanity—kids as young as fifteen and seniors in their eighties, borderline morons and Stanford-bound geniuses, burger flippers, 7-Eleven clerks, housewives, felons, drug addicts, real-estate agents, suburbanites, inner-city people, an occasional homeless person—lots of just ordinary, everyday folk, and even a blind lady who turned out to be one of the best students I ever had. I run into these people all the time in the supermarkets of Fresno, and they tell me that I have spoiled simple kickback movie-watching for them. I thank them for the compliment.

I would like to hear from you about the book. Please feel free to e-mail me at *jkp21@csufresno.edu.*

Cinematics

This section aims to make you cinematically smart—in particular, wise to the ways of film photography, set dressing, sound, editing, and visual style. If the five chapters in this section work on you as I hope they do, you may never be the same. You'll have to start watching movies in two modes at the same time, the cinematic and the narrative. This is what I meant in the Introduction by "stretching."

chapter one

Shots

Recall the last time you read a novel. Think about that book not as a story or as a gallery of people working out problems, but as a string of sentences, one after the other, all marching down to the last page. Consider that what the author did was write the book one sentence at a time. Capital letter, string of words, period. Capital letter, string of words, period. Capital letter, string of words, period. Over and over again, from first page to last.

Of course, when you read that novel, the last thing on your mind was sentences. When you finished a chapter you didn't go, "Gee, what a lot of nice sentences." You didn't run off and grab your friend and tell him, "You gotta read this book. It has terrific sentences." Your friend would look at you funny. Or if you didn't like the book, you didn't say, "I just didn't care for the sentences." This is because you didn't really read a series of sentences. You read a novel.

Watching films for most people is a similar experience. Films are made up of hundreds of individual *shots*. A shot is a continuous running of film through the motion picture camera for the purpose of photographing some aspect of a movie story. Most shots seldom run over twenty or thirty seconds. After editing, the running time of the typical shot in a film is about six seconds. Any film you are likely to see is composed of hundreds of shots, just as any book has hundreds of sentences. Shots are to films what sentences are to books. And most viewers relate to them in the same way—which is to say they don't see shots at all. They didn't pay money to see a succession of shots; they paid to see a film.

And yet paying attention to shots is the first step in getting more out of a movie than simply experiencing a good story. Shots are the basic unit of film communication and the source of much of the medium's expressiveness. If one cares about the film medium at all, he must pay attention to shots. Five important aspects of film shots to keep in mind are *frames*, *angles*, *moves*, *optics*, and *composition*, plus a few more matters having to do with shots that run extra long and some meaningful properties of film stock itself. Ideally, you should keep track of all five of these techniques for every shot you see. So if a shot runs six seconds, you have just a little more than a second to think about each technique. Good luck!

Frames

There are five commonly used film *frames*. You probably already know the names of a few:

- extreme long shot
- long shot
- medium shot
- close-up
- extreme close-up

It's important to understand these frames and what they do. Let's run down their dramatic uses from wide (extreme long shot) to tight (extreme close-up).

Extreme Long Shots

Extreme long shots are used to show big, outdoor settings—the desert, the mountains, the ocean, row after row of tract houses shot from a helicopter, a cityscape, two armies in pitched battle in a desolate landscape. An extreme long shot shows a panorama of some sort. You can't do extreme long shots indoors because there isn't enough space.

In extreme long shots, people are less important than the settings they are in. Often people are mere specks in the frame, as the whole point of extreme long shots is to show people in their settings. In *The Edge* (1997), which stars Anthony Hopkins and Alec Baldwin, mountains are very important. They have a lot to do with the source of the conflict of the story. So we see the mountains a lot in extreme long shot, with and without Hopkins and Baldwin, as a constant reminder that the story is as much about mountains as about the egos of two men outside the boundaries of society. In fact, if it weren't for mountains, the egos of the two men would be safely suppressed. In this story, mountains unleash ego.

In the classic 1962 film *Lawrence of Arabia*, the desert is a formidable character which Lawrence, the charismatic English Army officer, nevertheless subdues. None of the Arab chieftains with whom Lawrence is allied believe that they can cross the vast desert to take the port of Aqaba from the Turks. (This takes place during World War I.) But Lawrence, played by Peter O'Toole, talks them into it. It's a long hot journey. The sun beats down on the contingent. Director David Lean

1.1. *Gone With the Wind.* This extreme long shot does more than establish setting. It suggests that the once-pampered Scarlett O'Hara (circled) is now superfluous—that is, beside the point. That's why she's so small in the frame and apparently in flight. For more about frame composition, see pages 20–23. See photo 8.10 for a look at Scarlett in better days. MGM.

uses many extreme long shots to show empty space, sky, sand, the burning sun, and the antlike procession of men on horses. These extreme long shots say, "These men may not make it. The desert may win." But the men do win, arriving at an oasis before the heat becomes deadly.

Long Shots

Long shots frame several people from head to foot and give them enough screen space to do a little moving around, like having a fistfight or stepping back from a charging watchdog. Also, long shots are wide enough to show some of the setting or to include big important props like lockers in a high school gymnasium where a couple of athletes snap their towels at each other.

Long shots establish settings—not panoramic settings like deserts and mountains, but people-scaled settings like a bedroom, backyard, or the inside of a bank.

1.2. *The Wizard of Oz*. Long shot. A clumsily composed long shot with everyone lined up on one side of the bed. Film directors today have more natural ways of arranging people. Warner Brothers/Turner Entertainment/Time Warner.

In *E.T.: The Extraterrestrial* (1982), the boy Elliott is in his bedroom when he first shows E.T. to his older brother Michael. The scene is filmed mainly in long shot. The camera is set up to show a window in the background, some bookshelves on the right, and the door to the room on the left. In the left background is a closet door. Elliott is in the foreground in the middle of the frame. Michael comes in the door and Elliott makes him close his eyes. Director Steven Spielberg has Michael face the camera so he can't see what is going on behind him. Then Elliott moves to the closet in the left background and leads E.T. out behind Michael's back. Michael turns, gets a load of the little guy, and, of course, freaks out. He backs up against the bookshelves and sends them crashing to the floor. The long shot is the perfect frame for this piece of business. We see everything in relation to everything else— the bedroom, Elliott and his move to the closet, Michael, E.T., Michael going *whoa!* and knocking the shelves off the wall. Used this way, long shots show where things and people are in relation to other things and people in the same space.

Medium Shots
Medium shots typically show two characters in the film frame from about the waist up, although there are many ways to arrange characters in medium shots. Not much of the setting is seen. Setting now recedes in importance; character becomes more important.

1.3. *Welcome to the Dollhouse*. Medium shot. Both of these kids live on the edge, she the constantly-picked on dork, he a near-delinquent. Given this information, what does the fence add? For more about fences, see pages 20–21. For more about the film, see pages 214–217. Photo by Jennifer Carchman. Sony Pictures Classics.

Film directors use medium shots for advancing a dialog between two people when neither has the dramatic upper hand. Medium shots are also the favored frame when the two characters have to physically interact in some dramatic or visually important way—one slips a knife into the belly of the other, a man and woman embrace.

One of the most famous medium shots in film history occurs in Elia Kazan's *On the Waterfront* (1954) when Terry (Marlon Brando) and Charlie, his brother (Rod Steiger), take a ride in a taxi. Though the scene consists of five shots in all (three medium shots and two close-ups), it is a frontal medium shot that dominates. This is the famous "I coulda been a contender" scene. The pair are seen sitting in the back seat of the cab. Charlie is trying to get Terry to go along with the mob and stop seeing Edie, the sister of the young man in whose death Terry is implicated. One can feel equality in this scene; that is, neither actor dominates.

Close-ups

Close-ups show only the faces or the heads and shoulders of film actors. The setting usually doesn't figure much because we already know where we are. A close-up is used by a film director largely to isolate a character from the setting and from all other characters so that you will pay attention only to that character, at least for

1.4. *Soldier.* Close-up. Movies have several ways to reveal character: words, movements, facial expressions. What does this face say? Before you decide, see pages 198–199. Photo by Ron Phillips. Warner Brothers.

a few seconds. Films with a lot of close-ups tend to feature characters who are lonely, cut off from each other, and isolated from society.

For example, in Mike Nichols's *The Graduate* (1967), the main character, Ben (played by Dustin Hoffman), is uneasy at his own graduation party, which is attended only by older people who are friends of his parents. In fact, Ben is uneasy about life in general. He has a college degree, but he doesn't know what the next step is. Usually in movies, parties are filmed in medium shot and long shot in order to show the party space and to show a lot of people and things going on. But Ben's party is rendered almost entirely in close-ups of just Ben. Thus very little of the setting (his parents' house) is seen, nor are guests seen. Instead the frame seems to enclose Ben's head oppressively, as if in a box. In this tight frame, he looks plainly worried, out of place, and isolated.

Extreme Close-ups

These show things like watch faces, suicide notes, eyeballs, or, in the case of *The Peacemaker* (1998), the digital counter connected to the atomic detonator, which is down to 00:01 when rocket scientist and terrorist expert Nicole Kidman finally disarms it. Movies can't do without extreme close-ups.

Angles

Nearly all photography worldwide is photographed at *eye level*—at the level of the eyes of the photographer. This is also true of movies, whether the motion picture camera is handheld or mounted on a tripod or dolly. Occasionally, however, a film director will want to place the camera below eye level—say, waist-high to the actor, or even lower. Or she* might elevate the camera and shoot down on the actor. These then are the three main options of angle: *low angle, eye level,* and *high angle.* Nearly every film employs all three angles, though eye-level shots always predominate.

Eye-level shots feel neutral. Because they approximate the way most of us see the world, there is no particular meaning associated with eye-level photography. That is the point, in fact—*not* to call attention to angle. But the other two angles feel different to us and do affect our feeling about action and characters.

Low-Angle Shots

Low-angle shots are always charged with meaning. They tend to render characters larger-than-life, intimidating, dominant, scary, confident, or in charge—depending on dramatic context. Low-angle shots are invariably employed in action-adventure films. For example, in *The Rock* (1996), a film loaded with heroics, every third shot of the twin heroes, Nicolas Cage and Sean Connery, is low angle. When Cage, driving a Ferrari, pursues Connery in a military Humvee in a harrowing chase through the hilly streets of San Francisco, the director Michael Bay had little cameras mounted on the floors of both cars to film Cage and Connery from extreme low angles. The technique makes them look like fearless drivers.

In the classic film *Citizen Kane* (1941), numerous low-angle shots of Kane punch up his character as a millionaire egoist. Later in the film, as Kane's egotism becomes hurtful to others, the low angles on him increase sharply.

High-Angle Shots

By contrast, actors filmed in high angle are "looked down on" and made to seem inferior, in trouble, put upon, or powerless. Victims are filmed in high angle; so are assorted wimps, losers, and weaklings. Children are sometimes filmed in high angle, sometimes not; it depends on the story. If the story is told primarily from adults' points of view, then the camera most likely points down at children so that audiences see them as adults do. However, if the story happens to be mainly about children, as is *E.T.: The Extraterrestrial*, then the camera is simply set lower to the height of the children's faces. This is what French director Jacques Doillon decided to do when he made *Ponette*, a film about a four-year-old girl (Victorie Thivisol) coping with the death of her mother. Nearly the entire film is photographed at a height of about three feet, or at the eye level of Ponette and other children in the story. We watch the film as adults on the children's level, the better to understand them.

Our first look at Rose in *Titanic* (1997) is from an extremely high angle—actually it's called an overhead shot. The shot has a twist. The scene is dockside as, hurly-burly, passengers board the ship in South Hampton. An expensive car drives

---

*To avoid the clumsiness of having to say "he or she" all the time, I have taken the liberty of making all indefinite directors, and all other indefinite film personnel, female—she, her, etc.

1.5. *Bonnie and Clyde*. High-angle shot. The blood on Warren Beatty's shirt doesn't seem like much today, but it was a big deal in 1967 when the film came out. You just didn't see much blood at the movies then. Warner Brothers and Orion.

up. The camera is positioned directly over a rear door, which opens. A woman emerges but at first we see only her fine, lavender broad-brimmed hat. Certainly this is a woman of high social order, we surmise, but why is she filmed this way, from overhead? Does this mean she is compromised or subjugated? Then the hat tilts and reveals Rose's face looking up. But this is not the face of a subjugated woman. She is looking up at the stupendous vessel and is not impressed. For her, size isn't everything.

Other Angles

Here are a few more angles commonly employed by directors who want just the right perspective on the scenes they are filming: side, front, rear, reverse, and over-the-shoulder. These angles introduce variety into filming. A director may order a side-by-side medium shot of two people, which, as I said, implies equality. Or she can call for an over-the-shoulder medium shot, which gives emphasis to the person facing the camera while naturally de-emphasizing the person who is seen only as a shoulder by viewers. Then the angle may be reversed so that the person who was facing the camera in the shot before is now seen as only a shoulder while the person seen before as a shoulder is now seen face on. The character emphasis switches, too.

Crazy Angles

Martin Scorsese used some crazy angles in his *Taxi Driver* (1976) when the main character, Travis (played by Robert De Niro), goes nuts and kills a creepy guy who is having sex with the teenage prostitute (Jodie Foster) whom Travis wants to rescue. It's a gory scene with lots of blood. This happens in a New York City hotel room, which Scorsese photographs from an overhead angle that goes on and on, as if the ceiling of the room has been removed so that Scorsese's camera floats above the room and views the carnage at right angles to the floor.

Scorsese's purpose for filming this way was probably to suggest the disturbed mind of Travis. Thus crazy man equals crazy angle. But Alfred Hitchcock did this first in *Psycho* (1960) when Norman Bates (Tony Perkins), dressed up like a woman (his mother), comes out of a room on the second-floor landing of his Victorian house and stabs the investigator (Martin Balsam) repeatedly with a long knife—all from a straight-down, overhead angle. The angle of the shot accomplishes two things. It hides the identity of the mother and it suggests psychopathology.

I once made a film with a crazy angle. It was about a guy in a pickup truck on a kind of haunted dirt road. The truck's radio kept going on and off, perversely so. The guy kept banging on the radio to make it work. I set up a shot that apparently was from *behind* the radio's display, as if from the point of view of the guts of the

1.6. Woody Allen lines up a shot. Film directors like Allen don't just direct performances; they also must be knowledgeable about all of the things this chapter discusses—frame, angle, movement, optics, and composition. Photo by Brian Hamill. Orion.

radio. I wanted to convey that the radio was somehow evil and out to get the driver. So I made a little transparent plastic sign with 102.3 turned backwards and got down on the floor of the front seat to shoot through the sign at the driver. Audiences laughed. That's all I wanted.

TRY THIS

See or rent a movie that promises to be visually interesting. Pay close attention to two things: frames and angles. Note the mix of frames. Try to get inside the mind of the director and determine why she chose a certain frame at such and such a moment in the drama. What did she gain? Do this for a half-dozen or more frames. Next, note the angles. Of course, most shots will be at eye level. But every now and then, a high- or low-angle shot will pop up. Also look for other unusual or uncommon angles. Stop the tape and try to determine what the director had in mind in using such an angle.

Moves

The camera and actors move in several ways: The camera moves in relation to stationary actors, actors move in relation to a stationary camera, or both camera and actors move. Each option has countless dramatic effects.

Camera Moves

Here are the *mechanical* ways that cameras move during the taking of shots:

- *Dolly shots.* The camera is mounted on a device that has wheels and moves on tracks. Just about every film made today uses dozens of dolly shots; they impart a smooth, liquid feeling to photography.
- *Handheld moves.* An experienced camera operator walks around with a lightweight camera. If smoothness is desired, the operator uses a device called a Steadicam, which incorporates a gyroscope so the operator can walk with the camera and get footage that looks as silky as dolly shots. Steadicam shots are employed when terrain or architecture does not allow for laying dolly tracks. Sometimes, though, smoothness is not desired, so the operator just hoists the camera onto her shoulder and shoots, maybe even jerking the camera a little.
- *Crane shots.* The camera is mounted on an actual crane or "cherry picker," as they used to be called. Crane shots are very dramatic. They might start at eye level, then sweep up over houses and trees. Films often begin or end with crane shots.
- *Pans and tilts.* The camera is mounted on a rigid device, such as a tripod, and the operator rotates the camera left to right or tilts it up and down.

- *Zoom shots.* When *zoom shots* are used, the feeling of movement is created optically, not mechanically, by gradually changing the focal length of the lens. In a *zoom-in* shot the subject appears to get gradually larger in the frame as the backdrop narrows; in a *zoom-out* shot, the subject appears to get gradually smaller as the backdrop widens.

Film directors always seek to move the camera in eye-pleasing or meaningful ways, some of which are covered below.

Dollying in for Gradual Awareness

Almost every movie made has this situation: A character becomes aware of something significant. Coinciding with the character's gradual awareness is a slow dolly in or zoom in on his face. Thus the frame changes gradually in midshot from, say, medium or long shot to close-up. This happens several times in Frank Capra's *It's a Wonderful Life* (1946) when George Bailey, played by James Stewart, realizes he can't get away from Bedford Falls and pursue his dream of becoming an engineer. He has to stay and run the family loan business. The dollying in of the camera on George's face is timed to George's gradually changing expression of disappointment. Dollying in is the spatial equivalent of leaning closer, paying more attention, getting inside a character. It's almost voyeuristic.

Not Your Typical Star Shot

In *The Fugitive* (1993), Harrison Ford's first appearance is during a complicated moving-camera shot. Usually a star as big as Ford gets a zinger of a first shot: He's likely to be framed all alone with glamorous lighting and a flattering angle. But the character of Dr. Richard Kimble, whom Ford plays, isn't even in the shot when it starts. Instead we see a gray-haired, paunchy detective in medium shot coming down a spiral staircase, looking grim. He moves left and the camera follows him, revealing an upscale condo. Finally the detective stops and looks down. The camera pulls back a little and tilts down to reveal Kimble sitting on a sofa in what looks like a state of shock—not a dazzling first shot by Hollywood standards. Soon we learn that Kimble's wife has been murdered.

Energizing Moving Camera

In *All the President's Men* (1976), a film about Watergate journalists Carl Bernstein and Bob Woodward (Dustin Hoffman and Robert Redford), there are two approaches to camera movement. When the reporters are stuck and can't get anybody to go on record about the nefarious political goings-on, director Alan J. Pakula keeps the camera still—no pans, tilts, tracks, or zooms. But when the reporters finally dig up some good stuff and make headway, the camera moves. For example, about halfway through the film, the reporters get their first big break on the phone to a witness. Suddenly everything becomes animated. Bernstein and

Woodward run across the spacious floor of the *Washington Post* newsroom to the office of their editor, and the camera races with them, matching visually the excitement of the reporters. From this point forward, the reporters gain confidence and poise and the camera work is correspondingly more fluid.

Circular Choreography

Woody Allen included an attention-getting moving-camera shot in his *Hannah and Her Sisters* (1986). The three sisters, Lee (Barbara Hershey), Hannah (Mia Farrow), and Holly (Diane Wiest), are seated around a table in a restaurant. It's an important scene that reveals much about the personalities of the three characters. Holly dominates. She doesn't know what to do with her life; she explains how she would like to try her hand at writing plays. The other two characters mainly react. Hannah is judgmental and discourages Holly, stating that Holly should pursue a more practical secretarial career. Lee is the quietest, but near the end of the scene she expresses the sentiment that Hannah should lay off Lee and give her encouragement. Allen filmed this dialog three times, the camera completely encircling the table for each take. Allen didn't just retain the best take; instead, he retained those portions of all three takes that best show the faces of the women. These takes were thoroughly rehearsed and choreographed to time camera moves to speakers either saying something important or reacting importantly. The camera shots were rehearsed so that each speaker was framed when she had something important to say, after which the camera moved on to frame a listener, registering her response.

Existential Pan to Black

In *The Net* (1998), Sandra Bullock can't figure out what is happening to her—or not exactly to her but to her credit standing. She's trying to get out of Mexico. She goes to an airport and tries to charge her airfare to California. But the ticket seller finds no evidence of Sandra having any kind of credit card at all. She's been expunged from all records. It dawns on her that without credit she has no identity. This is scary stuff, although on another level it's satiric, too. A close-up shows that Sandra is really spooked. Then the camera pans away from her to a black pillar that dominates the shot. Black equals nothingness, no existence, an unperson.

Actor Moves

Actors run, walk, crawl. But they also blink, tap their fingers on tables, shrug, etc. Every move by an actor is meant to be meaningful. Some typical actor moves are described below.

Shifting Eyes

These almost always mean someone is lying or culpable—the eyes move, the head remains stationary. In *The Juror* (1996), a mob guy is on trial for murder. Did he do it or not? Almost always, in movies, if mob guys are on trial, they did it. If you walked into *The Juror* a half hour late, you'd still know the mob guy, sitting next to his lawyer, did the hit or had it done, just by the shifty way his eyes move left and right. It's not so much that actors can do a lot of acting with their eyes (though some can). It's mainly a movie convention. Shifting eyes equal evasiveness.

In *Primal Fear* (1996), shy, stuttering Edward Norton has been accused of murdering a priest, but during the trial his eyes don't shift at all; in consequence you want to believe he is innocent. But after Norton is acquitted, it turns out that he really did kill the priest. Because his eyes didn't move shiftily before, we believed in Norton. We were set up.

Moving in Place Dynamically

In *Jerry Maguire* (1996), Tom Cruise moves in place a lot. He plays an inspired, born-again sports agent who wants to infuse the business world with a strong sense of ethics. He has the moves to go with such a personality. His hands, arms, torso, and legs are often emphatically in motion, punctuating his lines. The way Cruise's body moves puts the character across as much as the way he delivers his lines. Meanwhile, when he has to play humble, as he does from time to time with Renee Zellweger, Cruise knows how to hunch and slow his body down.

Moving in Place Nervously

Woody Allen expresses himself through movement, too. In his films when he stands and speaks to someone, he is constantly in motion, though not in the same way that Cruise acts when in motion. Allen shifts his weight, punches the air with his fingers, hangs his head, spreads his hands, shakes his head—all to convey his never-ending frustration with modern urban life.

Crosstown Running

In *Run Lola Run* (1999), Lola really does run, and she runs for over half of the movie. This is a German film directed by Tom Tykwer, and Lola is played by Franka Potente. In a nutshell, Lola has twenty minutes to deliver a lot of money to her boyfriend or he'll be seriously messed up by the German mob. Lola runs in long, clean strides, seemingly never tiring. But the film is not simply about her getting from point A to point B; Tykwer speculates about the significance of chance encounters and delays that might alter the ending. In fact, he provides three endings based on three plausible disruptions to Franka's sprinting. Truly, this film is Einsteinian in its playing with space and time.

When Camera and Actor Move Together

A lot of films oblige characters to run. So how does a big, heavy motion picture camera keep up? Early in *Forrest Gump* (1994), when Forrest has to run so much, the camera captures his running in these ways:

1.7. *Run Lola Run*. Frontal tracking shot. The camera crew had to pull the dolly fast to keep Lola the same size in the frame. With this option, the faces of the nuns are revealed one at a time instead of all at once. Photo by Bemd Spauke. Sony Pictures Classics.

- *Head-in.* Forrest runs toward a stationary camera and past it. We don't see his destination.
- *Tail-away.* Forrest runs away from a stationary camera. We see where he is headed.
- *Pan.* The camera is set back from the road Forrest runs on; he runs up to the camera and past it. The camera pans with him, and we can see where he's going.
- *Lateral tracking.* Forrest runs alongside the camera, which is mounted on a truck and captures him from a side angle. Truck and camera keep up with him. We can't see where he came from or where he is going; we just see the background swishing by.
- *Frontal tracking.* The camera is mounted on the bed of a truck and pointing at Forrest as he runs; truck and camera match his pace. Frames vary from long shot to close-up.
- *Rearward tracking.* This is just like frontal tracking except that the truck and camera are behind Forrest, again keeping up with him.

So director Robert Zemeckis had a lot of choices. Forrest runs about four times in the film, and each run is covered by three or four of these camera setups. Each setup renders the drama in its own way. Pans show the most. When they are used, we can see where Forrest comes from and where he is going. Lateral tracking shows least because the background is often blurred by the motion; however, this blurring has dramatic potential. Frontal tracking allows us to see Forrest's facial expression. Additionally, Zemeckis had the choice of framing only Forrest's legs or framing his face, frontally or in profile. Legs equal speed, power. Face equals determination. Tykwer had pretty much the same choices in *Run Lola Run* and used them. Film is a universal language.

Optics

Basically there are three kinds of camera lenses: *wide-angle, normal,* and *telephoto*. Wide angle lenses tend to keep everything from foreground to background in focus and exaggerate perspective (the viewer's sense of distance). Normal lenses render focus and perspective pretty much the way you and I see the world. Telephoto lenses keep only one plane in focus while objects nearer to or farther from the camera are blurred; also, perspective is foreshortened. Film directors who know optics use these lenses expressively.

Soft Focus

This technique is often used in romantic films. The telephoto lens blurs the background and renders it a lyrical wash of color so that only the lovers, in the foreground, are in focus. In *Elvira Madigan* (1967), Danish director Bo Widerberg kept many backdrops out of focus to suggest how the lovers, Pia Degermark and Thommy Berggren, have completely cut themselves off from the world. They are actually fugitives on the run in a largely rural setting. In many shots we view them in normal focus while the various wheat fields, forests, and hills they move across are blurred.

John Boorman used soft-focus photography for another purpose in *Deliverance* (1972), a story about four men who take a weekend white-water canoe trip in order to get back to nature. The trip turns into a nightmare when they are stalked by murderous mountain men, and soon the wilderness, which earlier had seemed so bracing, becomes sinister as the men fear their surroundings. To convey the rafters' dread, Boorman and his cinematographer Vilmos Zsigmond often used a telephoto lens that blurred the verdant background and made it seemed foreboding.

Deep Focus

The opposite of soft focus, deep focus renders everything knife-edged sharp and clear, whether near or far away. Some directors prefer this kind of clarity because it suits the story they are telling. Thus William Wyler's *Roman Holiday* (1953) was shot this way to make sure backdrops were always in focus. The story is about a pair of lovers, but there is a third character who is nearly as important as reporter Gregory Peck and princess Audrey Hepburn—beautiful, eternal Rome. Peck is handsome, Hepburn is beautiful, and Rome looks great, too—thanks to wide-angle photography.

1.8. *Picnic at Hanging Rock.* Soft focus. Loveliness isolated, thanks to the blurred background created with a telephoto lens. South Australian Film Corporation.

1.9. *Devil in a Blue Dress.* Deep focus. Central Avenue, heart of black Los Angeles, sharp foreground, sharp background, thanks to a wide-angle lens. Photo by D. Stevens. TriStar.

Citizen Kane, too, employed deep-focus photography. Although this film is nothing like *Roman Holiday*, Welles used wide-angle lenses for much the same reason that Wyler used them—to place a character (the millionaire Charles Foster Kane) in clearly seen backdrops that figure as much as any other aspect of the story. At the end of the film, Kane has holed up with his second wife Susan in an enormous castle he has built as a kind of monument to his colossal ego. Welles was careful to keep everything about the castle in sharp focus and to have Kane walk in front of clearly seen, ornate backdrops. He wanted you to see Kane (played by Welles himself) in all his bad-taste, nouveau richness. The rooms of the castle help define the man.

Perspective

Again, when a photographer wants to make things seem far away, she uses a wide-angle lens; to compress distance, she'll go telephoto. John Boorman had two good reasons for using a telephoto lens in *Deliverance*; it not only fuzzed out the wilderness backdrop but also made it seem to close in menacingly on the men. Welles used wide-angle lenses in *Citizen Kane* not only to keep the castle backdrop in focus, but to push out backdrops and render the castle vast. Big castle, big man—though ironically he turns out to be small of spirit.

The famous short film *An Occurrence at Owl Creek Bridge* (1962), adapted by Robert Enrico from the Ambrose Bierce story of the same title, uses all three lenses to alter focus, perspective—and reality. This film is about a Southerner who is hanged by Union soldiers for collaborating with the Confederate Army. In the split second it takes the man to fall thirty feet from the bridge with a rope around his neck, he has an extended fantasy. He imagines that the rope breaks and he successfully escapes, first by swimming downstream, then by running. He runs and runs. (Enrico uses just about all the camera options Tykwer and Zemeckis used.) He stops, can't believe he is still alive, shouts with joy, then keeps on running toward home and his beautiful, supportive wife. As he runs, he is not filmed with a normal lens. He is filmed running in telephoto against a blurred, unreal background, and he is filmed running in wide angle, which makes his lope impossibly swift. Astute viewers know something is wrong; the optics tell them that. Finally, the man reaches the gate of his country estate. He continues to run, now in telephoto, but as he runs toward the camera, he doesn't seem to make much progress. He seems to be running in place, a dramatic effect of filming in telephoto. Then it happens: As he slows to embrace his wife, who has run out of the house to meet him, the perspective suddenly changes to normal. Trees, hedges, walls—everything now seems real. Then the man suddenly stops as his head is jerked violently backwards. We hear the snap of a rope. In the next shot we see the man back at the bridge, hanging. Normal optics have brought us back to reality.

Start paying attention to optics in the movies you see. Note the camera's focus—when it is shallow, when it is deep. Also note perspective—when things seem optically distorted—that is, too close or too far. Try to get the hang of wide-angle, normal, and telephoto photography. Finally, connect the various optics to something meaningful about the film.

Composition

This has to do with the way elements of a shot are placed in the film frame. It matters mightily whether a certain prop is placed high or low, left or right, foreground or background. At the most elemental level, good composition is important to clear communication; it moves the story along and helps viewers understand basic matters. On a deeper level, good composition has potential for conveying important meaning.

Directors strive to get as much into a shot as they can. If they have a lot of props and people to fit into the frame, they have to be careful about where everything goes. Thus in one shot in *E.T.: The Extraterrestrial,* Steven Spielberg finds he has to use a lot of stuff: a globe, a world atlas, the children, E.T., and a bit of special effects to convey crucial information. In the shot, Elliott, on the right, turns a globe and points to various continents in an attempt to get E.T. to identify his homeland (the children don't yet know that E.T. is from outer space). The other children are in the middle of the shot, a little farther back. Meanwhile, in the same frame, to the left, E.T. does not respond to Elliott's globe-pointing. Instead, he turns the pages of the atlas, presumably hoping to find some sort of representation of his home. He finds nothing, and Elliott starts to despair. The other children lose interest. Then E.T. runs across a representation of the solar system with planets seen circling the sun. He makes happy little noises of discovery. The children lean closer and see the picture of the solar system. Finally, E.T. performs a little magic by causing some little balls that happen to be at hand to rise into the air and start revolving around a larger ball representing the sun. The children are very impressed. Without thoughtful composition, Spielberg could not have packed all this into one frame.

Often directors will compose a scene with actors and common articles or props in order to depict something meaningful. Take fences, for example. Fences are a staple in movies and often communicate the separation of human beings from each other. For example:

- In John Ford's *Stagecoach* (1939), at a kind of rest stop, an ex-prostitute named Dallas (Claire Trevor) and Ringo (John Wayne), a broad-minded man who has been taken into custody, take a little walk away from the other stagecoach travelers. This should be a romantic getting-to-know-you-scene and it is, but it can only go so far because Dallas can't tell Ringo what she used to be. Thus psychological distance is felt, and, to underscore this mood visually, Ford has the couple walk on opposite sides of a low fence.

- In *On the Waterfront*, the dramatic situation is very similar to that of *Stagecoach*. One person has a dark secret he can't bring himself to reveal, and it's holding up the romance. Marlon Brando can't tell Eva Marie Saint that he had something to do with the murder of her brother. Elia Kazan probably told his art director, Richard Day, to locate lots of fences for shooting the various waterfront settings of the film. Kazan uses these fences, which are mostly hard ugly things with spearlike tops, to compose shots that suggest the distance between Brando and Saint.

- In *The Pawnbroker*, Rod Steiger is a bitter, repressed Holocaust survivor who will not open up to the world of Brooklyn of the 1960s. Director Sidney Lumet filled Steiger's pawn shop with heavy, floor-to-ceiling chain-link fences, and Steiger is often filmed through them to suggest his separation from humanity. Lumet could have had his art director design a pawn shop without fences—although I've been told that pawn shops often do have such fences—but he knew that with the fences he could communicate much, visually, about the lost soul of the man.

1.10. *The Pawnbroker.* Heavy fencing, heavy psychology. Also see photos 1.3 and 2.4. The Landau Company.

1.11. *Deliverance.* Artistic composition. You don't often see film frames so formally composed and carefully lit, especially in such an otherwise raw film. For a discussion of lighting, see pages 30–36. Warner Brothers.

The trick is to employ composition *naturally*, without artistic pretension. For example, in Arthur Penn's *Bonnie and Clyde* (1967), an early shot of Bonnie (played by Faye Dunaway) finds her in bed pouting. She is bored living the life of a nobody waitress. Penn photographs Bonnie through the iron bars at the foot of the bed to suggest that she exists in a kind of prison of working-class tedium. The bars seem natural, maybe even more natural than the fence that separates Ringo and Dallas.

Composition starts to get a little arty-looking in a few places in *Toy Story 2* (1999), but we are okay with that, since it's such a terrific movie. Buzz and his chums have broken into Al's toy store. Alone, Buzz walks down an aisle with dozens and dozens of Buzz Lightyears just like him on shelves. The composition is geometric, with many shelves parallel to the top and bottom of the frame and the boxes of Buzzes arranged in neat columns. Buzz himself is composed very small in the very bottom of the frame. He looks up at all the dozens of copies of himself towering over him. Being reminded of his utter lack of uniqueness in the world, his insignificance, could plunge him into despair. But we recall that in the first *Toy Story* (1995), Buzz learned to accept himself for what he really is, just a toy. So he doesn't brood for long. He just keeps walking, bent on finding Woody.

Composition is also employed *formally* to create pleasing shapes, lines, and geometric forms. For example, in *Lawrence of Arabia* the circularity of the sun and the horizontality of the empty desert landscape is innately pleasing—breathtaking,

1.12. *Saving Private Ryan.* Tasteful composition. The men have arrived to inform the woman that one of her sons has been killed in combat. In a brilliant piece of directorial understatement, Steven Spielberg has the woman collapse with her back to the camera and at a tasteful distance, instead of shoving a camera in her face to capture her desolation. DreamWorks Pictures.

in fact. In the Japanese masterpiece *The Seven Samurai* (1954), director Akira Kurosawa uses many diagonal lines to tell the story of a handful of professional warriors who train villagers to defend themselves against marauding bandits. The film contains numerous shots of swords and spears composed diagonally to the borders of the film frame; that is, the props form lines running from upper left to lower right or the other way. There is strength in these diagonals.

TRY THIS

The next time you see a movie that seems to be thoughtfully photographed, watch it for meaningful and artistic composition. Not every shot will be a masterpiece in this way, but every now and then you'll be likely to notice a shot that looks like some care went into the arrangement of elements, or you'll see that the props communicate beyond words. Give these some thought.

The Long Take: High Art or Playfulness?

There is a kind of game being played by some Hollywood directors that the public in general knows nothing about. It's called the "long take." This is a shot that goes

1.13. *American Beauty.* Satiric composition. How do you suggest visually that this is not a close family? Get a long table and set the camera back. Make sure the daughter is in the middle; i.e., close to neither parent. Also see pages 212–214 and photo 10.9. DreamWorks.

on much longer than the usual take—minutes, in fact, instead of seconds. The director, her cast, and cinematographer figure out a way to capture a very long piece of action without stopping the camera. During the several minutes of the take, the camera moves almost constantly—from room to room or from outdoor to indoor or vice versa. During the take, various actors swim in and out of the frame, which can vary from close-up to long shot. I say that all this is a game because directors seem to strive to outdo each other to produce the longest, busiest, most complicated take. It's all good fun.

All of this probably started when Orson Welles pulled off the famous long take that opens his classic *Touch of Evil* (1958). The shot starts with a close-up of a man's hands—we don't see his face—setting the timer on a bomb and then running to a nearby car (a convertible) and placing the bomb in the trunk. The bomber runs off as the camera cranes up to show a seedy part of a Mexican border town in extreme long shot. It's nearly night. We see dirty streets, parked cars, storefronts. Then a gangsterish guy floats into the frame with a floozy girlfriend. They get into the convertible and drive off, the camera following from a great height. After this—this is all one take, don't forget, no cuts—after this, the camera descends to follow Charlton Heston and Janet Leigh walking along a sidewalk. They cross in front of the convertible, which is stopped at an intersection. Now the camera is close enough to frame Heston and Leigh in medium shot. From their talk we discern that the pair are newly married. Ahead of Heston and Leigh is a border crossing. The couple stop, and a guard steps up to ask Heston a few questions. By now about a minute and a half have elapsed without a single cut. Meanwhile, the Henry Mancini music seems to be building to some sort of climax. In fact, the ticking of the bomb is built right into the rhythm of the music. Before Heston and Leigh move on, the convertible, bearing the mob guy and the floozy, drives up to the border gate. Heston and Leigh move off to the background, in search of ice cream. The girl in the convertible complains about a ticking sound. The convertible is waved through the gate. The camera sweeps across the street to find Heston and Leigh again. Then it happens: Ahead, on the U.S. side of the border, the bomb explodes off-camera. We hear the explosion and see its flash on Heston's and Leigh's faces. Finally, the film cuts to the car in mid-explosion. That first take lasted three and one-half minutes.

Why would Welles want to open the film and record the action in this way? The recently restored version of *Touch of Evil* is much more laden with fancy film techniques than is the mindlessly recut original released by Universal. Some viewers feel that the film, seen in its entirety, reveals itself to be Welles's self-parody of his own highly innovative visual style. Other viewers still prefer to take the film straight. Another famous long take occurs in the Martin Scorsese film *Goodfellas* (1990), which is about a couple of non-Italian, small-time, wanna-be mobsters. One of them, played by Ray Liotta, wants to impress his date (Lorraine Bracco), so he takes her to a classy nightclub where everyone knows his name. They enter the club through the back door and go through the kitchen where the chefs chime, "How ya doing, Henry?" This is all one take that lasts about a minute and a half—from the alley, through the back door, into the kitchen, and out onto the floor of the club where the manager snaps his fingers, getting a couple of waiters to set up a table for the couple right next to the stage. They're just in time to hear comedian Henny Youngman give his classic one-liner, "Take my wife—please."

By the 1990s, the long take had become a kind of inside joke or challenge to Hollywood filmmakers. Who could do the longest, the trickiest? Robert Altman opens his satiric *The Player* (1992) with a long take that is every bit as complicated, though maybe not as graceful, as Welles's opening long take in *Touch of Evil*. A crane takes the camera up and down, someone steps off the crane with the camera mounted on a Steadicam, and actors float in and out of changing frames. The setting is the parking lot of a contemporary movie studio. Many kinds of people cross paths in the shot, and there is a great deal of outrageous movie talk going on. *The Player*, in fact, is Altman's send-up of movie business, so maybe such a shot is justified; outrageous talk equals outrageous take. The shot starts with a clapper to note scene and take, and, about halfway through, actor Fred Ward has some lines to deliver about Welles's long take in *Touch of Evil*, unaware (as a character in the movie) that he is a participant in one of the longest takes in movie history—over six minutes!

Since then, Brian De Palma opened his *Snake Eyes* (1998) with a take that is even longer than the one in *The Player*, as Nicolas Cage, going from room to room in an Atlantic City casino, tries to get information about a murder. Not to be outdone, in *Boogie Nights* (1997), Paul Thomas Anderson also employed a long take to get his film going—from a street in Reseda, California, to a disco nightclub, to all the main characters of the film inside the club, and finally to Mark Wahlberg, the main character of the movie who is a mere busboy.

Film Stock

The phrase "film stock" refers to the raw, unexposed film on which a movie is photographed. The look of a movie starts with stock. Here are several perspectives on the connections between film stock, on how people feel about stock, and on what the various stocks are supposed to impart.

Black-and-White Stock

It's too bad about black-and-white film. It's gotten a bum rap over the last fifty years. Younger viewers simply don't like it. They think color is better. Media magnate Ted Turner bought the rights to a library of black-and-white movies and had them colorized by a computer on the premise that TV audiences like color better. Cinematic purists protested. Woody Allen commented that colorizing black-and-white movies is like painting Michelangelo's *David* a flesh color. Turner finally stopped it.

Well, color isn't better; it's just different. It took over Hollywood in the sixties for the same reason color TV took over in the same period—it was more commercial and more superficially appealing, and it helped to rescue the film industry from oblivion when box office receipts took a nosedive. But color did a disservice to the many fine black-and-white films that the industry had produced until that time. The fact is, monochromatic photography was (and still is) a highly evolved and sophisticated branch of photography. All you have to do to confirm this contention is to spend an hour or so at an exhibition of Ansel Adams's black-and-white photographs of Yosemite Valley and the Sierra Nevada, or thumb through a big book of his work. I doubt that you'll walk out on the exhibition because *Half Dome* isn't in color. The photographs are simply breathtaking in their tonal range and use of light. Like all black-and-white photography, they abstract their subjects by removing the color factor. The viewer is then more free to contemplate form and subject. Beyond this advantage, the actual abstraction becomes a subject of contemplation in its own right. Viewers ponder, for example, the photographer's use of gray, black, and white, although such rendering may not seem as "real" as color photos. Real isn't the point.

 TRY THIS

Recently, I have seen in theaters restored versions of Satyajit Ray's great Bengali film *Pather Panchali* (1955) in Berkeley, California; Federico Fellini's deeply moving *Nights of Cabiria* (1957) in San Francisco; and Orson Welles's weird *Touch of Evil* in San Luis Obispo, California—all in black and white. It's a good bet that a restored black-and-white film masterpiece will soon play at a theater—a *real* theater—near you. See it. Or see any respectable black-and-white film in a movie theater. You just can't get a feel for the subtleties of monochrome from home video.

Some Uses of Black-and-White Stock

Having said all this, I must now mention some films shot in black and white for reasons other than the creation of abstract beauty. Peter Bogdanovich shot *The Last Picture Show* in black and white in 1971, long after it was routine to make films in color, and he did it to make the little dead-end Texas town where the story is set look drab, thereby confirming Philistine expectations. Mel Brooks shot *Young Frankenstein* in black and white in 1974 to evoke the look of Frankenstein movies of the black-and-white era. (There were about a dozen, by my count.) This may be a better reason for shooting in black and white. *Schindler's List* (1993), by Steven Spielberg, was photographed in black and white for the purpose of evoking World War II newsreel footage, which was always in black and white. Later Spielberg directed *Saving Private Ryan* (1998), also about World War II, but shot it in color. Why the switch?

Often independent filmmakers on shoestring budgets shoot in black and white to save money, as 16 mm black-and-white stock is cheaper than color stock. Their productions may or may not benefit from the monochromatic look. Would Kevin Smith's *Clerks* (1994) be any less or more meaningful in color?

Manipulating Color Stock

Not all color films look the same. You have to wear sunglasses to see Vincente Minnelli's *Meet Me In St. Louis* (1944), so bright and saturated is the color. Judy Garland's red, red lipstick alone knocks you out of your seat. Since those days, color cinematography has been toned down. Some color films are very drab, for example. Rumor has it that Hal Ashby wanted to shoot *Bound for Glory* (1976) in black-and-white stock, but his studio (United Artists) wouldn't let him. The film is about the life of folk song composer-singer Woody Guthrie and the 1930s Dust Bowl conditions that formed the backdrop of his life and music. Ashby's cinematographer Haskell Wexler shot much of the film through panty hose to diffuse the color and affect a dusty look and had everyone wear drab, brownish costumes. He also manipulated the stock in the lab to tone down the color values. I believe this is a better approach to creating a drab look.

It is commonplace today to shoot downbeat films in downbeat colors such as blues, greens, and grays. Mel Gibson's gloomy *Payback* (1999) is shot this way, and so is the downer *The End of the Affair* (1999). Meanwhile, a warm film like Pedro Almodovar's *All About My Mother* (1999) is shot warm; Almodovar created its warm feel by dressing sets in yellows, browns, and reds and by selecting a color stock with a warm bias and tinting the film a little at the lab. The magnificent Chinese epic film *The Emperor and the Assassin* (1999), directed by Chen Kaige, is suffused with a yellow tint for most of its nearly three-hour running time, probably because the color yellow has special significance for Chinese audiences.

Photographer Newton Thomas Sigel, who shot *Three Kings* (1999) for David O. Russell, broke Hollywood's addiction to Eastman Kodak professional motion picture stock and went with Japanese Fuji color stock, which he then "fogged" (pre-exposed) in order to achieve a completely original look for the desert sequences of the film. The story is a sidebar to the Persian Gulf War; in Sigel's capable hands, the desert looks both washed out and full of contrasts, a kind of visual equivalent of the initial cynicism of the principal characters. I ought to report here that Spielberg did something similar for the opening invasion scene of *Saving Private Ryan;* namely, he had the color washed out of the Eastman Kodak stock and decreased the tonal range to impart a harsh, newsreel-like feel to the scenes.

 TRY THIS

Just keep track of the color values in films you see in theaters. The movies will not all look the same. Some will seem cool, some warm, some saturated, some subdued. Why?

chapter two

Scenes

The title of this chapter is taken from the French term *mise-en-scène,* which has to do with the look of a film scene, especially its theatricality. Art directors, set designers, and their crews are highly paid professionals who put in a lot of time to make movie sets look just right for the kinds of films they are working on. Sad to say, most audiences rarely tune in to such diligence. They seldom look behind the story to appreciate the choice of illumination, textures, colors, props, and space that add so much to movie storytelling. But you can. You can go to a party after having seen a movie with strong visuals, such as *The Sixth Sense* (1999), and intone, "Well, I thought the story was kind of messed up, but I really liked the mise-en-scène." People will just nod and look at the punch bowl.

The fact is that in many films the interiors have nearly as much to do with overall meaning as anything else. For example, when Michael Mann made his acclaimed film *The Insider* (1999), he worked with cinematographer Dante Spinotti to produce scenes containing elements of dark and light. Dark dominates; even scenes that realistically ought to be brightly lit—a high school chemistry lab, a coffee shop—are dark. But every scene also has a sizable patch of bright white, such as a fully illuminated face, a sun-drenched window, or the gleaming surface of a white table. So the scenes are not all dark; there is always light.

What was Mann's reason for making his scenes look this way? Here's a guess: The subject matter of *The Insider* is very dark. The film is about corporate irresponsibility at its worst—namely, how cigarette manufactures actually engineer addiction into their products and the news media suppress reporting of this manipulation. The darkness of the scenes is thus metaphorical; it stands for the shady dealings of corporations. But there is hope in the figures of Jeffrey Wigand, a chemist (played by

Russell Crowe) who blows the whistle on the cigarette industry, and of Lowell Bergman (Al Pacino), a *60 Minutes* producer who successfully fights his fraidy-cat bosses to get the story aired. Crowe and Pacino, then, are the hope, the light.*

Lighting

Thus, keeping track of how a movie is lit can be very edifying. Even if the film doesn't particularly work on the story level, you might at least appreciate its lighting and thus salvage something. An improbable movie story like that of *End of Days* (1999) is still worth seeing for the ingenuity of its lighting.

Professional cinematographers will wince at the following informal scheme for classifying movie lighting styles, but I did it this way to avoid becoming too technical.

Practical Lighting

Call this suitable lighting, adequate lighting, even demure lighting—it's lighting that does not call attention to itself, and it's associated with probably 85 percent of the movies you see. *Runaway Bride* (1999), the Julia Roberts vehicle directed by Garry Marshall, was shot with practical lighting. It's a competent romantic comedy with a few laughs having to do with a woman's fear of marriage. She gets to the altar; she runs away.

2.1. *Fatal Attraction.* Practical lighting. Just the way you'd expect the interior of a house to look. Photo by Andy Schwartz. Paramount.

---

*The trouble is, videotape distributors of *The Insider* have lightened up many scenes so that much of the effect I describe is lost. The same problem afflicts *Se7en* (1995), masterfully dark on the screen but conventionally brightened up on your TV. DVD versions of both films may be more faithful to the celluloid originals.

None of this is particularly fanciful or stylized. Everything about the film is cal-culated to throw all the attention to the leads, Roberts and Richard Gere, the pair who struck gold before in Marshall's *Pretty Woman* (1990). The photography is serviceable and never "artistic," and so is the lighting. Rooms are supposed to look the way they look in real life, as long as they make the leads look good. Each scene is lit just the way we would expect. Thus if characters in a hardware store stand close to the window, the light comes from the window. Sides of faces turned to the window are more brightly lit than the other sides.

Titanic is presumably a more serious film than *Runaway Bride*, but it too has practical lighting. Spaces on the great vessel are lit as we might expect. The grand dining room where Jack joins Rose and her group sparkles with light, as well it should. The third-class accommodations where Jack takes Rose for partying and dancing isn't a gloomy place at all, as other films about the *Titanic* have depicted steerage. Since the goings-on are joyous, the room too is joyously lit—not sparkling, as the dining room is, but suitably cheerful.

Don't think for a moment that practical lighting is unsophisticated, unprofes-sional, or slapdash. Lighting crews spend just as much time, employ just as much equipment, and bring just as much expertise to bear on practical lighting as do light-ing crews who do more obviously artistic or eye-catching set illumination. In a way, these crews are unsung heroes, working very hard to light scenes in ways almost nobody notices. But that is the point: to make the lighting unobtrusive.

Dark Lighting

If a movie isn't shot with practical lighting, it's almost always shot with what I call "dark lighting," a catchall category embracing many styles of lighting. Here are two: *low-key lighting* and *subdued lighting*. "Low-key" is a well-known film term; "subdued" is my term.

Low-key lighting is all about contrast. The film scene is mainly black, or at least very dark. Only a character or two or some important prop is highlighted, and only part of the subject, such as a face or a profile. Everything else in the scene is kept low-key. Hollywood moviemakers borrowed low-key lighting techniques from directors in Europe, where the style flourished in the 1920s and 1930s. Orson Welles used it in many of his famous films, including *Citizen Kane*, *Lady from Shanghai* (1948), and *Touch of Evil*. People in these films are always either emerging from darkness into light or disappearing from light into darkness.

Low-key lighting is also associated with a *genre* (or type) of film known as *film noir*, derived from the French phrase literally meaning "black film." Noir is the-matically dark. It's about entrapment and hopelessness. Noir characters, nearly always men, are desperate, on the run, doomed. Darkish lighting is perfectly appro-priate. Classic noir films, like *Lost Weekend* (1945), *Raw Deal* (1948), and *Sunset Boulevard* (1950) exhibit low-key lighting.

In *Raw Deal*, Dennis O'Keefe has escaped from prison and is on the lam. He

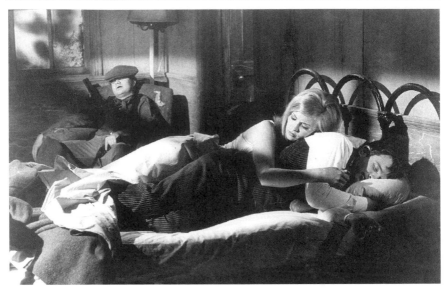

2.2. *Bonnie and Clyde.* Noir lighting. Details are seen in the dark areas, however, making the *mise-en-scène* less sinister than serene. (The bank robbers really needed some serenity after a day of running from the law.) Warner Brothers/Seven Arts.

2.3. *Titanic.* High-key lighting. Rose, now an old woman, inspects a mirror brought up from the wreckage. As the main subject of the frame, she gets the key light. Photo by Merie W. Wallace. Twentieth Century Fox/Paramount.

sneaks through the open window of his ex-girlfriend's apartment—this was during a time when single women felt okay sleeping next to open windows. He wakes her up and explains how he needs her help. The lighting of the room is a study in contrasts: Backgrounds are dark, but the woman's face is brightly lit; bright bands of light flank the bed. When O'Keefe leans to kiss her, his profile is artfully silhouetted against a bright headboard.

Francis Ford Coppola lit Marlon Brando low key in two films that are considered modern classics. The famous opening scene of Coppola's *The Godfather* (1972) is stygian dark. This is the scene where Marlon Brando, as godfather, takes care of some nefarious business before going out to his daughter's wedding reception, which is taking place on the lawn of the family compound. He okays the beating up of a punk who raped a friend's daughter. Brando's face is bright enough, and so is a cat in his lap, and you can see the face of the friend well enough, but everything else about the scene is nearly lost in blackness. The point of course is this: Dark room equals dark dealings. In a few minutes, the story moves outside to the happy, brightly lit wedding party—though when son Michael (Al Pacino) tells the famous story about the time his father told a guy he'd have either his brains or his signature on a contract, he sits (meaningfully) in the shade with fiancée Kay (Diane Keaton).

2.4. *Close Encounters of the Third Kind.* Backlighting creates mystery. Why the fence? Spielberg could just as easily have filmed without it. See also photo 1.3 and pages 20–21.

Coppola also lit Brando low key in a few of the closing scenes of *Apocalypse Now* (1979), but even more so. The contrast between light and dark is extreme. Brando fronts the camera in tight close-up, half of his face in total darkness, the other highlighted, and murmurs, "The horror, the horror"—whatever that means. It's the film's logo shot.

Subdued lighting is simply dark lighting that is not especially contrastive. Some subjects get more light than others, but the range from light to dark in the scene is not as extreme as in low-key lighting. David Fincher lights his films this way. In his *Se7en* (1995), detectives Brad Pitt and Morgan Freeman poke around dark rooms after corpses that have been variously mutilated by a brilliant-but-mad serial killer. When Pitt and Freeman show up at the crime scene, it's usually night so they turn on the lights. But the scene remains disturbingly dark. Even though the lamps and lighting fixtures in the scene have been flicked on, darkness persists. Luckily, the detectives think to pack flashlights.

Fincher's *Fight Club* (1999) is not as dark-looking as *Se7en* but it's pretty dark all the same. The basements where the men gather to engage in enraptured fisticuffs are dimly lit, though faces get a little more light than backdrops. A muted greenish hue suffuses these scenes.

The British film director Ridley Scott is a master of creating subdued lighting. His films feature dim rooms, though these are more meditatively dim than scary dim. For example, the interiors of Scott's *Blade Runner* (1982), a sci-fi film about the morality of killing humanlike androids, are darker than you or I would tolerate, but we appreciate looking at them all the same. In an apartment inhabited by Deckard (the detective figure played by Harrison Ford), light streams in, dusky and diffuse, through a louvered window that looks out on an orange-tinged world.

Dark lighting is seldom realistic lighting; practical lighting turns out to be much more realistic. Nobody lives in houses as dark as the abandoned house where Edward Norton and Brad Pitt of *Fight Club* are encamped—you could not see to make coffee in there. No detectives have to conduct investigations in the kind of gloom that Freeman and Pitt work in. And a lot of people wouldn't be able to read their mail in a dim apartment like the one Harrison Ford keeps in *Blade Runner*. In the real world, various murders and atrocities probably take place as often in broad daylight as on dark and stormy nights. But none of this matters. These places aren't for real people; they're for movie people, and they exist in half-darkness for our viewing pleasure.

Flat Lighting

Flat lighting has no shadows. It's bright everywhere but dull, too, the kind of efficient lighting you find in libraries and hospital rooms. Directors, cinematographers, and art directors use it sparingly, for a variety of reasons: to suggest a kind of leaching of spirit, to make it impossible for anything to hide, or to emulate institutional lighting. Two examples:

George Lucas's first film, *THX 1138* (1971), is about a soulless futuristic society that lives underground, I guess because atomic radiation lingers on the surface. Somehow art director Michael Haller and director of photography David Myers figured out a way to construct totally white sets with no seams—no corners, no lines where floors meet walls or where walls meet ceilings. In fact, the backdrop, the *mise-en-scène*, is nonexistent. Also, there are no shadows at all in these interiors. The lighting is completely flat. It doesn't take much mental effort to figure out why Lucas wanted this look: Flat lighting equals flat lives.

Flat light is used differently in *All the President's Men*, which is about Watergate journalism. In this film, reporters Redford and Hoffman visit a near-interminable succession of apartments and offices trying to track down people who will go on record about who abused whom in the Washington power game. These scenes, as you might suspect, are shot in subdued light. But when the scene shifts to the offices of the *Washington Post*, the lighting is bright and somehow pure looking. The truth will out, is what the light says; there are no shadows in which deception or ignorance might hide. The cut from dark apartment to bright newsroom is often shocking.

Classy Lighting

What I call classy lighting is elaborate and finessed lighting. It's never as mundane as practical lighting, nor is it as murky as dark lighting. In fact, everything is clearly seen in a kind of midrange of illumination. Scenes are rendered in gentle pools, arcs, bands, and mottles of light and dark, yet nothing calls attention to itself, so subtle is the execution. You have to look twice to realize how artful and intricate the lighting is. Faces are softly illuminated on one side, delicately shadowed on the other. Extremes are avoided. Characters are often "rim-lit," which means the principle source of light comes from behind the actors and from an angle so that they seem to be rimmed on one side with light. Additional light is thrown frontally onto subjects' faces so that they don't go completely dark. In effect, subjects' faces and bodies are carefully sculpted with light, and the result is nearly always flattering.

Backgrounds, too, are carefully lit. Shadows are soft edged and colors are usually muted. If the film is photographed in black and white, grays, not black or white, will predominate. If windows are seen, they are employed to justify increasing illumination in some places while letting space farther away go darker. If the windows happen to have venetian blinds, lighting cameramen can't seem to resist creating parallel bands of light and dark that fill rooms diagonally and play across faces.

Classy lighting is associated with the most prestigious Hollywood films—in fact, with any kind of film that purports to present a subtle and tasteful front to the world. The directors of many historical films—*Elizabeth* (1998), *Sense and Sensibility* (1995), *Little Women* (1994)—use classy lighting for their scenes. The films of Anthony Minghella—*The English Patient* (1996), *The Talented Mr. Ripley* (1999)—are classy and exotic. Minghella lights them with finesse. Many of the old

Hollywood classics about prestige and pretension—*A Letter to Three Wives* (1949), *The Heiress* (1949), *All About Eve* (1950)—exhibit classy lighting.

Set Design

Beyond lighting, there is much that movie people can do to affect *mise-en-scène*. When art directors design sets, they work mainly with space, color, texture, decor, and props. What follows is a miscellany of movie interiors that employ these elements of *mise-en-scène*.

Spoofy Factory

In 1936 Charlie Chaplin made the largely silent *Modern Times*, a left-leaning spoof of industrialism and assorted social ills of the period. The set of the factory Charlie works in for a time is like something out of a cartoon. Machines have big levers and massive interlocking gears, and production lines speed along absurdly fast. There are lots of laughs, none based on spoken words; instead, they are derived from this abstracted factory setting. Chaplin gets caught in the gears of a preposterous machine that then moves him along until he is disgorged at the far end. But he isn't really hurt—he's just dazed for a few minutes. This is not a vicious indictment of capitalism but only a satiric jab. The particular take on the factory setting is the perfect visual equivalent for the *tone* of the film. Credit Charles D. Hall with designing this factory.

Scary Living Room

Director David Lynch's *Blue Velvet* (1986) puts out an entirely different tone, that of perversion. Much of the story takes place in the apartment of a nightclub singer played by Isabella Rossellini. The walls of the living room are painted deep maroon and the place is practically devoid of lamps or light fixtures. Windows too are nonexistent or unseen. There is a single abhorrent plant with thick dark leaves that looks capable of entrapping small animals. The furniture is heavy and dark, the overall effect airless and oppressive. You want out of that room. No actual human being would want to live in it. But this is a movie, and Rossellini has to be there so that Dennis Hopper can drop by now and then to do weird sex to her, and the way the room looks is just fine for this. The thankless job of putting this room together fell to Patricia Norris.

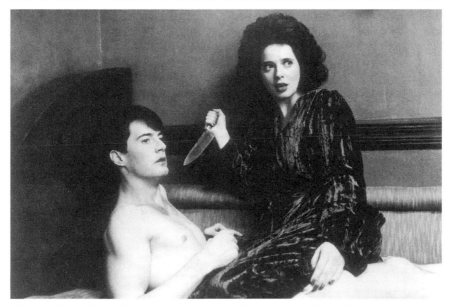

2.5. *Blue Velvet*. Set design (scary living room). Knock, knock: Dennis Hopper pays a visit. De Laurentiis Entertainment Group.

Kitschy Living Room

The Mafia depicted in Jonathan Demme's *Married to the Mob* (1988) is apparently undergoing a profound change. Some families are moving out to the suburbs, just like the rest of us. Demme must believe that deep down the Mafia members have bad taste, which maybe didn't show up in their walled compounds back in New York. His production designer Kristi Zea put together New Jersey living rooms with kitschy stuff all over the place—lamps made out of busts of Venuses de Milo, velvet wall hangings of slinky cats, clocks stuffed inside model World War II airplanes. There is a lot of clutter and bric-a-brac, and the colors of the walls, drapes, and furniture are abominably mixed. The foreground story is funny; so is the background set dressing.

Soulless Police Station

Warren Beatty's *Dick Tracy* (1990) is different from other movies inspired by famous comic strips. Its *mise-en-scène* is the most faithful to the source strip. The Superman movies don't try very hard to capture the comic-book look of Metropolis or the lairs of the likes of arch-nemesis Lex Luthor. The Batman movies come closer. Their sets are dark and hard, as are those of the original strip. But *Dick Tracy* goes farthest. Production designer Richard Sylbert made the sets of the film actually look like comic strips by annihilating depth and painting everything with cartoonish primary colors. The costumes of the players are fashioned from basic greens, blues, and reds, and so are the walls of the police station. The sets want you to think you are in a cartoon, but the faces of people like Beatty, Dustin Hoffman, Al Pacino, and Madonna keep reminding you that you are in a live-action movie.

There's a point to all this set crafting. *Dick Tracy* is a movie about identity. It wants to know: Is it possible for comic-strip characters to have depth or soul? Is it possible for them to live down their label of flat "comic-strip characters" and become "round"? Sylbert's sets constantly remind us of this theme of human dimensionality.

Absurdly Small New York Apartment

Most characters in films who live in New York City rent places they could never afford in real life. The apartments are just too vast and nice for the money the characters make. In *Election* (1999), directed by Alexander Payne, a visual joke is made by going the other way; that is, by making a New York City apartment absurdly small in keeping with the small income of the tenant, Mathew Broderick, a museum guide. Broderick lives in what must surely be filmdom's tiniest apartment. It's about six feet square and has a midget kitchen along one wall, a small sofa crammed onto the back wall, and a bathtub on a third wall. (We don't see the fourth wall.) Jane Ann Stewart supervised the design of this set, and she must have had fun doing it.

Tricolored *Mise-en-Scène*

The Wachowski brothers' *Bound* (1996) is a revisionist film noir. Instead of the usual, hounded male leads, the main characters are female lovers played by Jennifer Tilly and Gina Gershon, only they aren't defeated in the end as are most noir men. They knock off some mob guys and get away with a lot of money. This is a tough-ass film in which three colors hold sway: black, white, and red. If the Wachowskis had a choice, they went with one of these colors or a combination of them as much as they could. Thus Gershon wears a couple of red shirts, Tilly is turned out in black, and the mob guys pretty much dress in black. The women drive a red truck; the mob, a black sedan. Walls are often red or black, and more often white. There is a brutal murder over a toilet; blood splashes onto white porcelain.

This is not a cartoon like *Dick Tracy*. The coloration is so subtle you could miss it. Other colors sneak in, but the Wachowskis keep them muted and dark. What were the brothers thinking? Let's guess. Black-and-white equals homage to the classic, black-and-white noirs. Black is always a good color for gutsy, cool people. I'm not sure what white means, but red—that's obvious.

Ready-Made *Mise-en-Scène*

I've made a couple of short films that depended heavily on being shot in the right interiors. Because of my low budgets, I couldn't do much to alter or add to these interiors. But I didn't really have to; they worked for me fine, I thought, just the way they were.

One of my films like this is about the end of a relationship between a young woman, a college student, and a young man, a dropout. The only thing binding the couple together is addictive sex that lingers like a bad cold. The story is simple: What the woman really wants is to finally break off the sex and return to her studies and disciplined life, but the young man just keeps hitting on her and hitting on her. He keeps following her around the library, pressuring her in whispers to stop studying and go off with him. She finally gives in.

I set this film in a library, where I had the complete run of the place on Sundays, allowing me to bring in extras, a sound recordist, and a person to set lights. I could have shot the film almost anywhere, but the screenplay really did not come together for me until I had the library setting. It occurred to me that I could play the formality and coldness of the library, where reason prevailed, against the strong passions of the couple. I called the film *The Age of Reason* (1986). I wanted to make the library a kind of character in its own right, a censoring agent. Fortunately, the library was designed and built in the 1930s, when libraries looked like libraries, so it offered the perfect *mise-en-scène* with its vaulted ceilings, stained-glass windows, busts of dead scholars, and hard, echoing rooms. Passion was not welcome there.

The Same, Only Different

You can learn a lot about *mise-en-scène* by comparing the sets of films that are dramatically similar but physically different, as follows:

Women in Jeopardy: *The Texas Chainsaw Massacre* (1974) and *Psycho*

It's instructive to compare the set of *The Texas Chainsaw Massacre* with the famous shower scene of Alfred Hitchcock's *Psycho*. The former film, directed by Tobe Hooper, is one of the most dread-full films ever made. Many people can't watch it. It's about five young people traveling across rural Texas who one by one get buzzed up by a madman with a chainsaw. Finally it's up to a young women, played by Marilyn Burns, to find out what's going on. She ventures into an out-of-the-way farmhouse, which serves as a good example of low-cost but effective lighting and set decoration. Sure it's dark, but when you do glimpse things, they are ritualistically frightening. There are complete skeletons hanging from walls, there are piles of bones heaped on tables and large body parts hanging from ropes. The old farmhouse is crudely furnished. Tables and chairs are ancient and battered and probably never were in fashion. Burns goes into the dark, dark basement—as women in horror films tend to do—to find one of her companions hanging from a wall like a side of beef, and cut up like one, too, though butchers have more respect for meat. Then a group of men, all apparently related, descends upon her. They love tying women up and terrorizing them, and this is what they do to Burns. It's really awful to watch.

Burns finally escapes. She's more resourceful than is Janet Leigh in *Psycho*. As you probably know, Leigh gets slashed to death in the shower of her motel room.

2.6. *The Texas Chainsaw Massacre.* Set design (women in jeopardy). Is there a connection between the type of person who cuts up women and bad house-keeping? Read about slasher films on pages 195–96. Vortex.

But what makes Hitchcock's motel room and bathroom so different from Hooper's farmhouse are the high levels of light. There are a few shadows in the motel room, but generally the room is well lit; in fact it probably has more light than even present-day motel rooms. The bathroom, however, is *really* lit up in a bright, bright, flat white. The walls are white and the tiles of the shower space are white. It's the kind of shower that's above a tub, and there's a white shower curtain with rings that slide on a chromium pipe. In the crucial shot, Hitchcock films Leigh from the back wall of the shower so that the plastic curtain is visible behind her. (He had a shower with breakaway walls built on the studio soundstage.) As for the curtain, it's opaque; all we can see is a blurred suggestion of the bathroom door opening and a figure approaching the curtain. But it is all out of focus and completely terrifying because it's out of focus, the opaqueness working for Hitchcock as few natural qualities of props have worked for film directors. If the curtain had been a colored print or transparent, the horrific effect would have been lost.

Anyway, the figure pulls the curtain open and starts slashing Leigh with a long knife. And since the curtain has been pulled back, we should be able to see the assassin, right? Wrong—in spite of the tons of light, *we don't see the face of the attacker because it is backlit and rendered a silhouette.* This is the only thing that is dark in the entire scene, and of course it's completely unrealistic. What justifies the strong backlight and the plunging of the pervert's face into darkness? Absolutely nothing. But I have never heard anyone complain about this departure from reality, or even mention it.

It is shocking and extremely sad to see Janet Leigh's life slip away in such unrelenting illumination. It is as if Hitchcock had no respect for her death. We are ashamed of ourselves for gawking at her death throes in such bright light. Hitchcock probably intended this.

Sucky Workplaces: *The Apartment* (1960), *Office Space* (1999), and *Being John Malkovich* (1999)

Rarely is a workplace in a movie neutral. Instead, art directors and set designers love to create workplaces that *signify*. The way the space looks says a lot about how the employees feel about their jobs and about themselves.

Jack Lemmon in Billy Wilder's *The Apartment* starts off as a pretty naïve guy. In narration, he explains the monster insurance company he works for in a brisk, hopeful tone of voice. He's confident of moving up. For the time being, though, he's just a number: ". . . work station 440 on floor 16." As Lemmon narrates, we see where he works. It's a room about the size of four basketball courts with banks of parallel light fixtures pouring flat light over hundreds of desks all arranged in neat rows. The composition and the lighting of the *mise-en-scène* say it all—you work here, you lose your soul to the corporation. But it takes Jack most of the film to learn this.

2.7. *Office Space.* Set design (oppressive workplace). Director Ron Livingston matured substantially with this film. His first effort was *Beavis and Butthead Do America*, which is about vague, pointless skateboard-culture rebellion. Here the object of rebellion, the oppressive work place, clicks in sharp and clear. Photo by Van Redin. Twentieth Century Fox.

By contrast, not only does Ron Livingston in Mike Judge's *Office Space* dislike his job from the start, but his workplace is also very different from Lemmon's. Livingston is a computer programmer. The people who run his company have sliced and diced the work area with those thin plastic room dividers you see in offices. The result is a grid of cubicles that define individual work spaces. The privacy they are supposed to impart is fraudulent because nobody really has any privacy. The cubicles lack doors, and since they are only about five feet high, just about anybody can look over the tops of the dividers to see what is going on inside. You can tell from the bored, trapped look on Livingston's face that he is miles ahead of the chipper Jack Lemmon—he already knows the score.

One of the most ingenious workplaces of recent cinema was conceived by screenwriter Charlie Kaufman and actualized by art director Peter Andrus in *Being John Malkovich*. It's an office located on floor seven and a half of a New York City office building. Seven and a half means it got wedged between floors seven and eight. Andrus actually had the set built so that the office is only about four-and-a-half or five feet high, floor to ceiling—okay for sitting and working at a desk, but not okay for walking around. You have to stoop. The idea here isn't so much that the workplace is oppressive, though you can't help thinking that; it's more that the office is hidden, clandestinely tucked between two floors. Strangely, none of the workers seems negatively affected by this physical state of affairs. They just go on working and stooping. The low workplace is more in keeping with the zany, surreal premise of the whole film, which is that you can go through an Alice-in-Wonderland-like low door and slide—literally—into the mind of John Malkovich, the actor. Nutty.

Rich Digs: *Scarface* (1983), *The Glenn Miller Story* (1954), and *Juliet of the Spirits* (1965)

There are a lot of rich people in movies, but they don't all live the same. Their surroundings reflect who they are and how they have made their money.

In *Scarface*—the 1983 version directed by Brian De Palma—Tony Montana (Al Pacino) has come up from poverty to be a drug lord in the Miami area. He's made a lot of money, and he's spent a lot of it, too. He lives in a big, marbled castle or mansion where he is never quite comfortable because drug lords have a way of getting bumped off, just as he has had to bump off a few himself to get to where he is. So the mansion has tall fences, watchdogs, guards, and an elaborate surveillance system—all part of the *mise-en-scène*.

The architecture and decor of the mansion run from tacky to tasteless. There are a lot of phony classic-type statues—women-without-arms kind of thing—standing around. There are great columns of marble rising to lofty ceilings. There are cascading drapes. When Tony does business, he sits in a chair with a back about seven feet tall and a crest that says "TM" embossed on it. He wants to be King.

In one scene, Tony takes a bath in a bathtub about the size of a tennis court in a bathroom about the size of a baseball diamond. He's pissed over something—he growls at his longtime buddy (Steven Bauer) and disses his icy wife (Michelle Pfeiffer). The color of the scene, golden, is a reminder of how he got to be this way. Everything about the bathroom shimmers golden—walls, columns, furniture, even the little ceramic seraphim holding the light fixtures. Gold equals money, which equals corruption, which equals the losing of one's soul. Tony Montana is not a nice person, and De Palma's art director gave him what he deserved.

A real-life good guy, orchestra leader Glenn Miller, also made a lot of money as one of the leading swing music bandleaders in the 1930s and 1940s. But when movie good-guy James Stewart plays Miller in *The Glenn Miller Story*, you don't see the money. You don't even feel it. The houses that he and wife June Allison live in get progressively nicer and bigger, but they are never too big. They are tasteful and well-appointed, and their colors are muted. Nothing about these sets suggests big ego. By the time Miller gets killed at the end of the movie—his plane goes down in the Atlantic on his way to entertain the troops during World War II—June mourns in refined digs with lots of classy wood paneling, cozy books, and a bracing fire in the fireplace. This is because there is a rule in Hollywood that if nice people happen to make money, they do not flash it around. They somehow learn good taste in a hurry. They do not go crazy. If they did, audiences wouldn't like them.

The great Italian filmmaker Federico Fellini created some of the most fantastic interiors of all filmdom, most of which were meant more to convey mental states than to capture reality. In his *Juliet of the Spirits*, for example, a shy, held-in middle-aged woman played by Giulietta Masina considers indulging her senses. She visits a neighbor, one Susy, an incredibly voluptuous and uninhibited woman (Sandra Milo) who surrounds herself with sexy young men, soothsayers, dancers, poets, and sugar daddies, half naked or dressed in all manner of flowing, colorful garments. Susy's residence is a temple to sensuality. Spatially it's indefinite. It has no walls and no windows, suggesting infinite possibilities. The lighting is incredibly complex: it comes from above, from below, and from the side. Dark areas alternate with bright pools of light. The decor is a swirl of diaphanous curtains, lush vines, enormous vases of yellow flowers, and pearly screens. The camera sweeps past all of this, following Susy up an enormous staircase and into a limitless bedroom where, after making love, she slides down a tunnel into a vast marble pool.

What is to be said of such a *mise-en-scène*? It's all in Juliet's mind, of course, though Fellini never does anything so crude as to, say, zoom in to Juliet's closed eyes as she smiles to transporting harp music. The transition from real to fanciful is so subtle that you almost believe Susy's digs are real. And you love the film for this.

Warm Brothels: *Pretty Baby* (1978) and *Taxi Driver*
A surprising number of movie brothels do not seem dehumanizing or exploitative, as we might expect. In fact, they are not particularly bad places to be in. You can

sense this in *mise-en-scène*. For example, Louis Malle's *Pretty Baby* is about growing up in a brothel in New Orleans just before World War I. The brothel is a large,
comfortable house in a not-so-bad neighborhood. It's bathed in soft light, wrapped
in warm colors, turned out in soft textures, and decorated with an abundance of
hairbrushes, hand mirrors, and vanities for pampering the ladies. Correspondingly,
the ladies, always dressed in loose, flowing clothing, do not seem to have been in
any way brutalized. The worst that can be said about them is that they are bored.
Each awaits the one special man who will fall in love with her and take her away.
The story centers on twelve-year-old Brooke Shields, the daughter of a prostitute
played by Susan Sarandon. In all, the brothel, as Malle presents it, seems a good
place to grow up in. Brooke, carrying a baby brother, flits from room to room, chat-
ting with customers and prostitutes, teasing the grandfatherly piano tuner, flirting
with a younger boy who lives around the corner—normal stuff. She is surrounded
by a lot of caring aunt stand-ins and jovial male visitors. She could have done far
worse. Later she is auctioned off as a virgin, but it is not the end of the world for
her.

You would think that the room where Jodie Foster, playing a child prostitute
in *Taxi Driver*, receives her customers would be dirty, dark, and sordid, so awful is
the situation. But instead, Jodie's room is incredibly neat and well lit. Again, warm
colors prevail. It's a large room. A couple of dozen lit candles adorn the back wall.
The bed is neatly made and the floor is picked up. In fact, director Martin Scorsese
shot much of the scene between her and taxi driver Robert De Niro in long shot so
you can see how kept-up, even *middle-class*, the room is. Why would Scorsese order
such a *mise-en-scène*? I frankly don't know. The moment De Niro steps out of the
room and into a hallway—he never does have sex with Jodie—everything gets
seedy, as we might expect. A naked bulb spews garish light. The dirty orange walls
are besmirched with graffiti. The hotel man who takes money for the use of his
room is fat and disgusting.

I might guess that Scorsese was trying to convey Jodie's immaturity or denial
or mental isolation by depicting her room as so neat and clean. The room is like
her state of mind; she doesn't feel corrupted, as she is supposed to. She doesn't act
corrupted either.

Spaceships, Mythic and Real: *Star Wars* (1977) and *2001: A Space Odyssey* (1968)

All deep-space sci-fi movies feature spacecraft of one kind or another, glimpsed
now and then from the outside floating past the stars, but mainly seen from the
inside. Art directors probably relish designing these interiors—all those flashing
lights, levers, and buttons! But the actual look of the inside of a movie spacecraft
depends very much on the kind of movie it is.

The *Millennium Falcon*, Han Solo's spacecraft in George Lucas's *Star Wars*, is
a blend of hot-rod and World War II fighter aircraft, because the movie as a whole

plays off familiar cultural myths that audiences bring to the theater with them. Myths in this sense are not falsehoods; they embody truths through the telling of resonant tales and the use of meaningful imagery, instead of depicting reality as audiences expect it. Lucas is interested in myths of good and evil, father-son relationships, spiritual ascendancy, and the transcendence of youth. Solo's *Falcon* evokes its own set of myths. First, Solo does combat with various Empire fighters, roaring and zooming and rat-a-tatting like a World War II fighter pilot. Second, when he brags about how he can outrun the Empire's best fighters, he has reverted to the role of the hot-rodding Bob Falfa he played in Lucas's *American Graffiti* (1973). World War II dogfighting, drag racing on Main Street—these are the mythic experiences Lucas grew up absorbing and later imparted to his galactic epic.

Luke, Princess Leia, and all the rest walk around in the *Falcon* as if they were in a Winnebago with normal Earth-style gravity; of course, there is no gravity in deep space. They ought to be floating around and bumping into each other, like the black-and-white videos of real astronauts we see on the news. As they are pursued by Empire spacecraft, Solo presses the pedal to the metal, mythically, and the Falcon bumps and pitches ahead as if buffeted by winds or speeding down a rough country road—but there are no winds or potholes in space. Nor is there any air to lend sound to the many explosions in the film. But I hardly need to say that if you fault the Star Wars movies for these lapses of reality, you really miss the entire point of the series. Myth, not realism, is the point.

Meanwhile, consider the spacecraft in Stanley Kubrick's masterpiece, *2001: A Space Odyssey*. It has no natural gravity—flight attendants, yes, but no natural

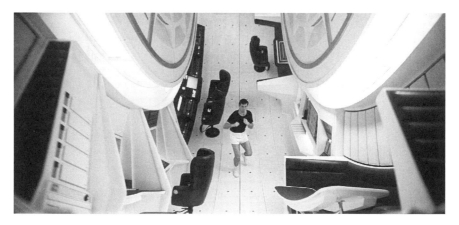

2.8. *2001: A Space Odyssey.* Spacecraft. When this film came out in 1968, the press had a lot to say about Kubrick's research into the way spacecraft might look and operate in the year 2001. You saw the film as much to settle into the strange, disjointed "story"—it's less a story than a psychedelic essay—as to note what space travel would be like in the near future. MGM.

gravity. Moon-bound PanAm flight attendants walk down aisles in shoes with Velcro soles that go *rip, rip, rip* with each deliberate step. A sleeping passenger lets a fountain pen slip from his fingers. It floats magically in the air—no, not magically; you've seen stuff like this before floating in real orbiting satellites with zero gravity. Flight attendants, PanAm, floating pens—we are a long way from *Star Wars.*

When the scene shifts to the deep-space story, called "The Jupiter Mission," the two men who watch over the craft live under conditions of gravity, but it's an artificial gravity created by centrifugal force. Everything loose is made to hug the inside walls of the huge rotating sphere of the living quarters. Kubrick makes a big deal of this. One of the most self-congratulatory shots in the history of deep-space movies shows one of the space travelers, Frank, played by Gary Lockwood, jogging laterally around the inside of the sphere—by laterally I mean his body is shown left to right, not up and down. Another shot picks up Frank's jogging from behind. We clearly see the curvature of the floor as Frank makes a complete lap around the "track." To achieve this affect, Kubrick built the enormous spherical set on an axis and made it turn like a Ferris wheel while Frank actually ran in place like a hamster on a treadmill.

TRY THIS

Rent a film. Note the *mise-en-scènes.* Note lighting, set decoration, colors, space. Determine an overall style or look for each interior. Then figure out what these interiors mean. Also figure out what the interiors mean in relation to the film as a whole. Here are five films with compelling *mise-en-scènes* you might consider renting:

- *1984* (1984). George Orwell's fascistic futuristic novel brought to the screen. Directed by Peter Hyams (United Kingdom).
- *After Hours* (1985). A kind of down-the-rabbit-hole, incredible night journey through the SoHo district of New York City. Directed by Martin Scorsese.
- *Barton Fink* (1991). New York playwright gets caught up in high-octane Hollywood screenwriting scene. Directed by Joel Coen.
- *Hardcore* (1979). Conservative Michigan man traces his runaway daughter to the fleshpots of Los Angeles. Directed by Paul Shrader.
- *The Talented Mr. Ripley.* Young man is sent to Europe to see what has happened to rich man's son. Directed by Anthony Minghella.

Sounds

We talk about *seeing* a film but never about hearing it, even though the experience is as much aural as visual. No one says, "Gee I heard a great movie last night." No one leaves the theater exclaiming, "Wow. Terrific sound track!" Still, sound counts in at least four ways—dialog, narration, music, and effects—which we'll take up in this chapter. We'll also consider how these sounds are mixed and paired with images.

Dialog

Here are three ways to think about movie dialog.

Short and Long Dialog

Some film purists never got over the passing of the silent era, which happened with the advent of synchronized sound tracks in the late 1920s. These nostalgists believe that film is first and foremost a visual experience. They hold that spoken words ought to be kept to an absolute minimum, that film writers and directors should communicate through moving pictures as much as possible.

There is much truth to these sentiments. We do tend to fall for films that reduce talking to a minimum and show us lovely pictures instead. There is very little talking in *The Black Stallion* (1979), the great boy-and-horse film directed by Carroll Ballard, yet the film never fails to communicate. Gary Cooper doesn't have a whole lot to say in Fred Zinnemann's *High Noon* (1952), yet he gets the job done; mainly, he kills off the bad guys. In *Heartland* (1979), a realistic Western about a woman who moves West with her daughter and marries a rancher, there is elegant

3.1. *The Black Stallion.* Lovely pictures that say it all. This film is like a fairy tale, a story with a lesson so embedded that children can't articulate it, which is the way it should be. For more on films about kids and their relationships with fairy tales, see page 198. United Artists.

scene after elegant scene, each getting along nicely with five or six words. In Jane Campion's *The Piano* (1993), a fine film about life in nineteenth-century rural New Zealand, the main character (played by Holly Hunter) doesn't speak at all. Instead, she plays her piano *at* people to express herself.

At the same time, when words are witty or profound, we ought to pay attention. Moviegoers (and now tape renters) have always admired the sparkling dialog in the talky *All About Eve,* a 1950 film about sophisticated theater people starring Bette Davis, Ann Baxter, and George Sanders. The whole reason for seeing *Get Shorty* (1995) is to hear John Travolta do his macho-confident lines. With the terse "Look at me," Travolta works his will among assorted small-time thugs and marginal movie producers.

In 1981 the respected French director Louis Malle did an English-language film called *My Dinner with Andre.* This film is 99.9 percent talk. The principals, Wallace Shawn and Andre Gregory, pretty much play themselves—one is an avant-garde playwright, the other a professional seeker of truth. The whole film takes place during a single dinner. They talk, talk, talk. Fortunately, the talk is interesting for appreciative audiences. In fact, the talk is more than just interesting—in time it becomes mesmerizing, like its own music, its own art form.

Admittedly, Malle took enormous risks with *My Dinner with Andre.* Other directors who have their characters talk a lot are not so lucky. The estimable American director Spike Lee, in such films as *Mo' Better Blues* (1990), *Malcolm X* (1992), and *Summer of Sam* (1999), lets his characters talk too much. The talk is good but wearying; with tighter writing and editing, it might have felt better to viewers. Nor was Martin Brest tough enough with his screenwriters when he made *Meet Joe Black* in 1999. The story is dumb enough as it is: Death walks around in the body of Brad Pitt, who, inexplicably, needs a hair cut. Claire Forlani—unconvincing as a pediatrician—falls in love with Pitt, a stick of a man who is supposed to be profound because he uses words like "splendid." But worst of all is the dialog, which goes on and on and on in every scene and stretches the film to nearly three hours.

Stylized Dialog

A handful of film directors are less interested in making dialog sound real than in manipulating some of its elements, just as film editors manipulate time and space. From the viewer's point of view, this may take some getting used to. If you object on the grounds that such dialog sounds stilted or weird, you could just cheat yourself of an important dimension of film viewing.

The American playwright and filmmaker David Mamet writes dialog in which the characters give their lines in a flat monotone and often repeat words—their own words and words of other speakers. In his *House of Games* (1987), a famous psychologist played by Lindsay Crouse has been humiliated by Joe Mantegna, a confidence man. She tries to con him back, but he catches on. The following scene takes place in a deserted baggage area of an airport. Note especially the repetition; read the dialog as though it were music:

> CROUSE: It was fate I found you.
> MANTEGNA: Yes, it was.
> CROUSE: Because together we can–
> MANTEGNA: Yes, we can.
> CROUSE: And when I saw, when I saw that they came after me—
> MANTEGNA: It's all right now. You're safe.
> CROUSE: No, I knew, I knew that I was being punished.
> MANTEGNA: No, it was an accident.
> CROUSE: No, I knew—that I was bad.
> MANTEGNA: No—
> CROUSE: No, I knew that I was bad. You know why? You know when I knew?
>   Because I took your knife. That's when I knew.
> MANTEGNA: What knife?
> CROUSE: Your knife from the hotel room. And I said that's why it happened. Yes,
>   because I'm bad. Because I stole.

Much of the high style of the great Stanley Kubrick derives from a kind of formality he imparts to his dialog, not only by the nature of the words themselves, but

3.2. *House of Games.* Stylized dialog. The scam goes down, the woman is the mark. So far she's in the dark, like the background. Orion.

by having his actors pause on the long side when the speaker changes. You can learn a lot about his characters by studying their faces during these pauses. Here is piece of dialog from a dueling scene in Kubrick's *Barry Lyndon* (1975), which is set in eighteenth-century England. Ryan O'Neal is Lyndon, whose stepson Bullington (Leon Vitali) hates his guts. A gentlemanly referee, Lord Richard, is present. Imagine long pauses between lines each time there is a change in speaker.

> *Bullington fires his pistol accidentally.*
> RICHARD: That counts as your shot, Lord Bullington.
> *Bullington can't believe he messed up. He's scared to death.*
> RICHARD: Mr. Lyndon, are the rules of firing clear to you?
> LYNDON: Yes.
> RICHARD: (to Bullington): Are you ready to receive Mr. Lyndon's fire?
> BULLINGTON: Yes.
> RICHARD: Very well, then. Mr. Lyndon, cock your pistol and prepare to fire.
> *Bullington runs to the wall and vomits. In time, he gains control and returns to his position.*
> RICHARD: Are you ready, Lord Bullington?
> BULLINGTON: Yes.
> RICHARD: Is your pistol cocked, Mr. Lyndon?
> LYNDON: Yes.
> RICHARD: Then prepare to fire. One, two—
> *Lyndon fires into the ground.*

RICHARD: Lord Bullington, in view of Mr. Lyndon having fired into the ground, do you now consider that you have received satisfaction?

BULLINGTON: I have not received satisfaction.

Thirteen exchanges. Can you guess how long all this took? Three and a half minutes.

TRY THIS

If you believe that films ought to be visual and not verbal, then give yourself a treat and see a few silent films. Here are five great ones:

- *The Birth of a Nation* (1915). This three-hour Civil War epic practically invented the concept of the feature film. Directed by D. W. Griffith and starring Lillian Gish.
- *Sherlock, Jr.* (1924). Sad-sack projectionist walks into the movie he is projecting, becomes a part of the story, and solves a crime. Directed by and starring Buster Keaton.
- *The Gold Rush* (1925). The Little Tramp turns up in the north country in search of gold and ends up falling for a dance-hall hooker. Directed by and starring Charlie Chaplin.
- *Sparrows* (1926). All-out melodrama in which girl protects orphans against bad guy. Directed by William Beaudine and starring Mary Pickford.
- *Sunrise* (1927). Gripping, humane, realistic. Farmer plans to murder his wife so that he can be with another woman. Directed by F. W. Murnau and starring George O'Brien and Janet Gaynor.

Also start paying attention to dialog in the other films you see, especially offbeat films that seem to break some rules. Don't be so quick to condemn quirky dialog; give the screenwriter the benefit of the doubt for a while. Here are a few Mamet films you might check out:

- *Things Change* (1988). Elderly shoe repairman agrees to serve a short prison term for a mobster.
- *Oleanna* (1994). College teacher is accused of making sexual advances on a student.
- *Glengarry Glenn Ross* (1992). A look at the brutal dog-eat-dog world of real-estate sales.

And watch these by Kubrick:

- *2001: A Space Odyssey.* Fast forward to "The Jupiter Mission" segment for some really long pauses between lines by an astronaut and his perverse computer.
- *The Shining* (1980). Writer-caretaker goes murderous in a mountain hotel shut down for winter.

- *Full Metal Jacket* (1987). A two-part tale of harrowing basic training experiences and somewhat less harrowing combat in Vietnam.

Narration

Narration is off-camera storytelling by a character in the film. Employed with intelligence, narration can move a story along swiftly and make it unnecessary to dramatize or show stuff that just isn't important.

Director Martin Scorsese uses narration to speed up his often dense stories. *Goodfellas*, for instance, is a rich film with lots of scenes, lots of characters, lots of things going on. Scorsese succeeded in packing so much into the film because he used narration deftly to explain background, to bridge scenes, and to speed matters up. The narrating is done by Ray Liotta, who plays the small-time hood Henry Hill. Hill finally rats on everyone and goes into the witness protection program.

Halfway through the film, when pressure on Hill starts to mount, we follow him through a particularly hectic Sunday. We see him stuffing three or four guns into a paper bag, then dropping the bag into the trunk of his car. He drives off, then notices a helicopter overhead. He seems worried about the helicopter.

What are these largely noncommittal visuals meant to convey? We wouldn't have a clue without Hill's narration:

> I was going to be busy all day. I had to drop off some guns at Jimmy's to match some silencers he had gotten. I had to pick up my brother at the hospital and drive him back to the house for dinner that night. Then I had to pick up some new Pittsburgh stuff [cocaine] for Lois [Hill's wife] to fly down to some new customers I had near Atlanta.

We hear this as we see Henry driving and looking worriedly up at the helicopter. Then he's at Jimmy's, but Jimmy (Robert De Niro) doesn't like the guns. In dialog we learn from an angry Jimmy that his silencers don't match the guns. Henry narrates:

> Right away I knew he didn't want them. I knew I was going to get stuck for the money. I only bought the damn guns because he wanted them, and now he didn't want them.

Some of this we don't need to hear because we can see that Jimmy is pissed when he looks at the guns and tries to match the silencers. But what we can't see is how Henry had bought the guns as a kind of favor to his friend. To film that particular plot wrinkle would have taken time and money for writing, setting up, rehearsing, lighting, filming, and recording dialog. Henry implies as much in ten words at almost zero cost.

Later we see Henry in the hospital picking up his brother, then at the hotel room of the Pittsburgh guys who gladly buy the guns, then at home fixing dinner. Without the narrative setup, these scenes would have seemed disjointed and confusing. Near the end of the day, dialog finally makes the presence of the helicopter clear. Henry thinks the feds are tailing him. Dramatize, narrate, dramatize, narrate—back and forth. Scorsese knows how to apply the right mix.

Music

Movie music—it's a kind of con game or bully. In general, films have too much of it. Insecure directors, or their producers, feel that scenes need punching up, so they have composers pour on music that obliges you to feel this way or that way, whether you want to or not. Directors fear playing scenes without music; they're afraid you will miss the emotional point. The following admittedly personal classification of film music invites you to think about the music you hear in movies and, I hope, develop a taste either for less of it or for more subtle music than what Hollywood usually slathers over its products.

Big, Loud, Movie Music You Can't Ignore

Generally, the more people a film is trying to reach—that is, to lure into theaters— the bigger, louder, and more intrusive its music. Steven Spielberg likes this kind of music, and apparently his viewers do, too, because his films sell a lot of tickets. It's a shame that such a consummate film artist either has such bad taste in music or distrusts his audiences so much. For example, there are few film sights as awesome as that of the huge, shimmering mother ship hovering above the remote Wyoming landscape in Spielberg's *Close Encounters of the Third Kind* (1977). The problem is that we can't just take in the ship and feel our own natural awe; we are instead bludgeoned into being overawed by the big, loud, impossible-to-ignore John Williams score. Maybe we'd like to form our own judgments about the ship. Some viewers, for example, think that it looks more like an oversized Christmas tree ornament than like something from outer space. But Spielberg and Williams won't let you have another thought or feeling. They strap you into your seat like a doomed criminal in an electric chair, and throw the switch. Overstated, bogus-spiritual music courses through your body. You had better believe.

To his credit, Spielberg ratchets the music down in his more serious films, namely in *Schindler's List* and in *Saving Private Ryan*. In the former, he sat on Williams (who again did the score) and muffled the music. And guess what? Williams got an Academy Award for that score.

Sentimental Movie Music

The music in sentimental movies is sweet—cloyingly so. If you are diabetic and see a movie with too much sentimental music, they may have to carry you off on a stretcher. In recent years, Robin Williams seems to turn up in films with a lot of sentimental music. Maybe he has the power to demand it. *Patch Adams* (1998), *What Dreams May Come* (1998), *Millennium Man* (1999)—these movies have music that really pours it on thick. You come out of the theater and have to go home and take a shower, you are so sticky.

Sentimental movies go after the heart in a big way. For instance, *Mr. Holland's Opus* (1995) is a sentimental story about a high school teacher played by Richard Dreyfus. He has spent most of his adult life working on a single symphony. Also, he has a son who is deaf. Also, after a lifetime of teacherly dedication, he loses his job. All this is calculated to summon tears. In the final scene of the film, Holland is lured into the school auditorium for a surprise farewell tribute. The school orchestra alumni, whom he has so conscientiously honed for years, are hidden behind a curtain on the stage, all ready to play. Sob, sob. And guess what they play? Mr. Holland's opus, his symphony. We've waited through the whole film to hear it, and what do we get? Might it be dissonant? Dark? Daring? Punkish? No way. It's predictably, conveniently, appropriately sweet. It's sentimental, uplifting, inspiring, and positive. Sob, sob. It's the perfect music to roll end credits to and send audiences away happy.

Condescending Movie Music

Music that condescends is music that fits in. It's always out to please the largest number of people, who then will like the movie (often without knowing why) and recommend it to friends. It's never too down and dirty or too high class. It goes right down the middle. It spells apple pie or touchdown in the hearts of Mr. and Mrs. U.S.A.; it's the kind of music that pours out of the ceiling at Burger King. In other words, a commercial film such as Garry Marshall's *Runaway Bride* has middle-brow, romantic-comedy music to match the kind of story it is—music which, in the case of Marshall's film, is crafted to make Julia Roberts and Richard Gere seem like really, really nice people.

Movie Music You Barely Hear

Now and then, however, a movie will come out with music that has some integrity; it isn't on the make. The composer of such music would like you to listen to it and appreciate it as you watch the film and take in the story itself. This kind of music has an artistic life of its own, which also enhances the movie.

James Cameron has made some of the most dramatic films to come out of Hollywood. He could have followed the tendency of most thrillers to use a lot of crash-bang music; instead, he has had the good sense to keep the music subtle and actually in the dramatic background. In both *Aliens* (1986) and *The Abyss* (1989), both of which he directed, most of the music is so low key that you scarcely hear it. Both films employ heavy metal—lots of big hardware and chunky technology that clangs, beeps, hisses, and whooshes. In places the music is nearly indistinguishable from these sounds. For *The Abyss* composer Alan Silvestri uses drums, strings, and brass—very subdued—to enhance the story of an ocean oil-rig crew that dives deep to salvage a nuclear sub.

The musical score for *Aliens*, another thriller, feels a lot like the score for *The Abyss*, though it was composed not by Silvestri but by James Horner, who received an Oscar nomination for his work. Horner keeps his score low key during the low drama scenes. Again, the music is often hard to separate from the many techy sounds of the film. Is the sound of the freight elevator really the sound of the freight elevator, or has Horner enhanced it with woodwinds? Is the clanging on the metal hull of the space colony habitat really something clanging on the hull, or did Horner tweak the sound with tympani? You should see this film and *The Abyss* at least twice—the first time for the story, the second time for the artistry of the music.

Among four Academy Awards garnered by *The English Patient* was one for Best Musical Score. The story was written and directed by Anthony Minghella and has to do with an English map maker out in the Sahara Desert who gets involved with some World War I stuff, crashes his airplane, gets burned all over, and is finally tended by a caring nurse. It's a classy film in the old-Hollywood, big-picture tradition. Maybe one reason this film seems so classy is that the music is very subdued and in very good taste. Gabriel Yared traffics mainly in minor-key strings and woodwinds kept so low they are scarcely heard at all. You can almost feel the dry desert wind coming from the screen.

Movie Music a Bit Louder, and Deservedly So

Don't object to music that's cranked up a little if it's worth listening to. Some films with listenable, engaging music include *Driving Miss Daisy* (1989), *Il Postino* (1994), and *The Decalogue* (1988).

Bruce Beresford's *Driving Miss Daisy* is about an older, set-in-her-ways Southern lady (Jessica Tandy) and her black chauffeur, Hoke (Morgan Freeman). The time that Miss Daisy spends with Hoke humanizes her, and they become good friends. This is a warm film that avoids sentimentality, thanks in large part to the score provided by Hans Zimmer, which keeps things bouncy and light rather than syrupy. The main musical theme is toe-tapping and happy, with a touch of the blues.

The Italian film *Il Postino*, or *The Postman*, is an absolutely original story about the great Chilean poet Pablo Neruda and the unlettered yet deeply feeling man, Mario, who brings him his mail. Without meaning to, Neruda teaches Mario a couple of things about the essence of poetry, not just its rhythm but also its soul. Mario learns enough to utter a few words of genuine poetry to the woman he loves, with positive results. Luis Enrique Bacalov received an Academy Award for his score, which is sentimental but done with a light touch, too. We hear strings and some woodwinds, and now and then a guitar. An accordion comes in frequently to suggest a kind of provinciality. And best of all is the inclusion of a gentle celeste (chimes), which gives the story a nice tinkly quality. This is a terrific marriage of story and music.

The Decalogue is a series of ten short films, none running as long as an hour, that Krzysztof Kieslowski made for Polish television. Each film explores one or more of the ten commandments, though some are hard to pin down to this or that commandment. At any rate, these are truly little films made on impossibly small budgets. The approach too is little—understated, minimal. The music is also sparse. The first film of the series, about a scientist whose faith in statistics leads to the death of his son, uses a little dissonant violin music at the start and a little dissonant violin music at the end. For the rest, you rely simply on the drama for emotion—with no problem.

Found Movie Music

"Found music" is my term for music composed long before the film was made, by a composer who had nothing to do with the film. One of the first films to do this was *Elvira Madigan*, which lifted an *andante* from Mozart's Seventeenth Piano Concerto to be played during some love scenes between an AWOL soldier and a circus girl. The Mozart is lovely and delicate and creates the perfect mood. No one could have written better love-making music. In the years following the movie's debut, some music people have come to call this concerto the "Elvira Madigan."

Then, a few years later, the Australian Peter Weir borrowed the slow move-

3.3. *Picnic at Hanging Rock.* This image is so instructive it deserves a second appearance. Beethoven would approve. South Australian Film Corporation.

ment from Beethoven's Fifth Piano Concerto, also magical, to lend Botticellian loveliness of a young woman in *Picnic at Hanging Rock* (1975). The girl mysteriously disappears during an outing in the countryside. This film has often been called a masterpiece of atmosphere, though few people think to credit Beethoven. Thanks, Ludwig.

At about the same time, the renegade independent director Terrence Malick made *Badlands* (1973), a film that has also been called a masterpiece of sorts. It's about a young man and woman on the lam for killing a couple of people. Instead of using the usual hyped-up, on-the-run music, Malick employed the modern European, post-Viennese music of Carl Orff and Eric Satie. Orff specializes in percussive music backed up by choirs. It's driving, repetitive, and hypnotic, casting a spell of primitivism over the runaways, played by Martin Sheen and Sissy Spacek, as they build a tree house in a remote forest. Meanwhile the Satie piano pieces, which are meditative and elusive, ask you not to judge the couple too harshly. This is an utterly brilliant use of found music.

Nowadays it is common for all manner of movies to use found classical music, modern music, jazz, ragtime, pop, rock, rap, and folk songs behind the action. It's hard to find a Martin Scorsese film that does not employ some kind of contemporanous pop music. The score for *The Big Chill* (1983) is wall-to-wall pop, as is the music for *Forrest Gump*. What would *The Sting* (1973) be without the Scott Joplin rags dogging the characters? *Se7en* uses Gregorian chants and assorted church music to create an apocalyptic mood, as do numerous other religious-themed horror films, from *The Omen* (1976) to *Devil's Advocate* (1997). Woody Allen loves to sprinkle his films with old standards. Much of the appeal of *When Harry Met Sally* (1989) is derived from Rob Reiner's good taste in selecting such oldies as "It Had to Be You," "Our Love Is Here to Stay," and "I Could Write a Book" to play ever-so-softly behind the gradual surrenders of Billy Crystal and Meg Ryan to each other.

Practical Music

This is music produced by musicians, singers, or stereos that are actually present in scenes. The rest of the film may or may not have any separately scored music at all—usually it does. An example is Peter Bogdanovich's *The Last Picture Show*, an astonishing piece of American heartland realism. This is a film about trying to find your identity when you are young, unremarkable, and unable to bust out of the small town you were born in. So insistent was Bogdanovich on keeping the tone realistic that the film has no proper score at all—because life, after all, does not come with music playing off camera. Yet there is still music in the film. It emanates from jukeboxes and radios present in scenes. Bogdanovich made sure the mood of the music matched the mood of the moment. If a scene is jubilant, we hear toe-tapping Flatt and Scruggs—all the music is country—from a radio. If a character is down in the dumps, we get Hank Williams heartbreak seeping from a car radio.

3.4. *The Last Picture Show.*
There are two kinds of small
towns in American films. Towns
like Brainard, Minnesota, in
Fargo are cozy, friendly, and supportive, and you would never
want to leave them. Towns like
Anarene, Texas, where this film
is set, are bleak and dead-ended,
and you can't wait to get out.
Jeff Bridges (right) gets out;
Timothy Bottoms doesn't.
Columbia.

The Belgian Dardenne brothers, Luc and Jean-Pierre, do award-winning, realistic films that forego musical scores altogether. Their acclaimed *La Promesse*
(1996), which is about an adolescent trying to do the right thing when his father
pressures him to cover up a death, lacks a score and has only one scene of practical music that takes place in a night spot. The Dardenne brothers—and the handful of other directors around the world who are not addicted to musical scores—are
brave indeed. They have enough confidence in their work to believe that the writing, the directing, and the acting are sufficient in themselves to communicate and
engender feeling. Audiences for these scoreless films, if they have kicked the music-
score habit, are freer to supply their own interpretations without the tyranny of
music. This is democratic filmmaking and film viewing.

Computer-Generated Music

Vangelis used an electronic score for *Chariots of Fire* (1981), a story about a pair
of British runners who took gold at the 1924 Olympics in Paris. The score is the
damnedest thing: It just doesn't seem to have much to do with the film. It feels contemporary (for 1981) and computerish, whereas the story has to do with quaint,
pre–World War I values. But the Vangelis score was hugely popular; its sound track
was a big seller.

At any rate, computer-generated music has taken off and is here to stay and
has put a lot of musicians out of work. One person working alone with a computer

can create complex music that sounds like a full orchestra. Plus, the music doesn't sound like computer music any more. Thanks to sampling technology, we hear real strings, real brass, real woodwinds. Although the composer manipulates sounds via a computer, the source of the instrumentation is authentic.

People who create scores on computers also tend to have cutting-edge tastes in music. Their compositions are likely to be subtle, slightly dissonant, and often washed over with the most current pop musical trends. The scores for *The Matrix* (1999) and *Fight Club* are like this; their scores stand alone. You buy the CD and enjoy it for what it is, alone, and not necessarily for how it goes with the film.

 TRY THIS

It's really hopeless to try to discuss movie music in book form. The thing for you to do is to rent some of the films I've mentioned and hear them as you watch them. Listen to the music and try to determine what it has to do with the movie as a whole and with the particular scene it accompanies. Think taste. You don't have to like the music. On the other hand, if you hear some really good music, savor it as you watch the film. You don't have to agree with me on particular scores. Mainly, I hope to raise issues for you to think about.

Sound Effects

Here are three sound effects for you to consider: the plinking of bullets on metal in *Saving Private Ryan*, rain falling on puddles in the same film, and the ship breaking up in *Titanic*.

At the start of *Saving Private Ryan*, when the invading Americans are trying to gain a toehold on Normandy's Omaha Beach, they hide behind big cast-iron objects that look like giant spiders or jacks that kids used to scoop up after bouncing a rubber ball. These objects really don't provide much cover, but the invaders have no choice—there is nowhere else to hide. There is, of course, a lot of firing and yelling and confusion, but through it all you hear the distinct plinking of bullets hitting the spidery things. You can't see whizzing bullets, of course, nor would you be able to hear them hitting water or sand, but you *can* hear them striking the cast-iron objects. Their plinking is an aural reminder of how exposed the invaders are. You can just imagine Spielberg's smile when he learned about these obstacles on Omaha Beach.

Later in the film, there is an interlude between skirmishes when it starts to rain. The drops start slowly, making a muted popping sound as they fall on puddles. But the raindrop pops gradually segue into the pop-popping of gunfire, meaning— what? That nature weeps for Captain Miller's (Tom Hanks's) factious band?

In *Titanic*, you will recall, the big ship nearly breaks in two before finally sinking, its two halves held together by a bent keel. It's a highly dramatic and stupendously visual moment when the hull of the ship breaks. It should be accompanied with equally arresting sound, and it is. Sound designer Christopher Boyes concocted a sound that is part metallic and part animal-like roar. It's the crack of doom for the gilded age. The sound is loud, reverberant, and sustained, and it's like nothing else you have heard in a movie. It could reach all the way to New York or back to Europe, and it did. It's part of the reason the film took an Oscar for best sound.

I mention these three sounds because they are good examples of meaningful yet subtle aural concoctions most viewers don't even hear. Sound designers seldom get enough recognition.

Oscars for best sound effects tend to go to high-tech action movies with complicated sound tracks, movies in which a lot is going on. These movies may not be narrative gems. *Speed* (1994), for example, does not as a story engender literary critics' admiration, but it took two Academy Awards, one for Best Achievement in Sound (credit Greg Landaker and three colleagues) and another for Best Achievement in Sound Effects (created by Stephen Hunter Flick). See it again just for the sound.

TRY THIS

Rent a big, noisy film with lots of action and special effects. Try *Jurassic Park* (1993), *Lost World* (1997), *End of Days*, *True Lies* (1994), *Terminator* (1984), and *Terminator 2* (1992), and listen. Isolate individual sounds and appreciate their clarity. They may not be totally realistic. They may be enhanced, processed, hyped up, as was the sound of the Titanic breaking up. Usually that's good. Try to figure out why a particular sound sounds the way it does. Relate the quality of the sound to the meaning of the scene or to the meaning of the film as a whole; for example, the momentous sound of the *Titanic* breaking up equals the momentous sinking of the Euro-American leisure class.

However, don't do this with just your nineteen-inch Magnavox and its three-inch speaker. You will miss half of the sound and all of its subtlety. Instead, go out and buy a big Dolby Digital Surround sound system to go with your TV, or see the movie with a friend who does have a big video sound system.

Sound Mix

Often only one sound, usually dialog, is recorded when a film scene is photographed; other sounds needed for the scene are mixed in during post-production. Sound mixers are artists in their own right, and a good thing it is that there are Oscars for their work. Here is a miscellany of film scenes with noteworthy sound mixes.

Clarity of Sound: *Rocky*

This 1976 boxing film ends with a lot of sound, and director John Avildsen's sound mixer wanted you to hear all of them. Rocky (Sylvester Stallone) and the champ (Carl Weathers) duke it out. Sound mixer B. Eugene Ashbrook pretty much gives equal volume to the stirring Bill Conti music, the thud of boxing gloves on flesh, the roar of the crowd, and the yelled encouragements of girlfriend Adrian and trainer Mickey, as well as assorted bells, grunts, referee admonitions, and popping flash bulbs. Miraculously, every sound is clearly heard, but to savor them you have to train your ears on them one at a time, a good reason for running the last ten minutes of the film over and over.

Thuds and Opera: *Raging Bull* (1980)

Martin Scorsese, in his masterly *Raging Bull* (1980), another boxing movie, meant to turn his depiction of the prize fight into a kind of art form in which the aural component is nearly equal to the visual. When the Jake La Motta character played by Robert De Niro goes against Sugar Ray Robinson (Johnny Barnes), Scorsese breaks away from a realistic portrayal of the match and stylizes it through slow motion and an incredible rendering of sweat splattering from punches. Sound makes a big contribution, too. Scorsese had his sound mixer drop the level of the

3.5. *Raging Bull.* Robert De Niro (left) is unquestionably America's most versatile actor. He does it all—drives cabs (*Taxi Driver*), hears confessions (*True Confessions*) rubs out mob guys (*GoodFellas*), fucks up (*Mean Streets*), hunts deer really good (*The Deer Hunter*), crashes talk shows (*The King of Comedy*), and awakens from thirty-year comas (*Awakenings*). United Artists.

crowd noises to zero, bring up the level of the punches (processing them to make them sound especially punishing), then mix in an intermezzo from the Italian opera *Cavalleria Rusticana*. The effect is a kind of mythologizing or sanctifying of the boxing. Actually, the meaning is more profound: It isn't just boxing that's being glorified, it's the whole male thing for violence. Or is it all meant to be satiric? Wonderful to contemplate.

Napalm and Wagner: *Apocalypse Now*

In Francis Ford Coppola's *Apocalypse Now*, Robert Duvall leads a helicopter assault on a Vietnamese village suspected of being an enemy stronghold. It's an amazing scene. We hear helicopters, rockets, screaming villagers, Duvall on the radio barking orders to his pilots and gunners, chopper pilots answering back, and Richard Wagner's demonic "Ride of the Valkyries" over it all. The music is not an overlaid score but rather is in-scene (practical) music ordered up by the fanatic Duvall. It blasts out of speakers mounted on the choppers. In all, it's one of the most thrilling—and disturbing—mixes in all filmdom, and it won sound editor-mixer Walter Murch an Oscar.

A Quiet Mix: *The Limey* (1999)

In addition to applauding the big-sound scenes, the real attention-getters, we should give credit to little films with subtle, artistic mixes that the Academy Awards peo-

3.6. *Boys Don't Cry.* Usually, when a scene like this is shot, only dialog is recorded. Additional sounds—a band, a juke box, background conversation, the clink of glassware—are mixed in during post-production. Killer Films-Fox Searchlight.

ple usually overlook. *The Limey* is a little film, an art film, really, made interesting mainly through its editing, which fragments time the way a cubist painting rearranges space. You have to really like the film medium as such to get with this film because it's not such an original story. An older man, known as the limey (a Britisher) and played by Terence Stamp, gets out of prison and embarks on a single-minded mission. Never mind the details. It's the editing and the sound mix you might enjoy over the story. Sound mixer James E. Webb keeps everything low-key and dreamlike. For example, the sounds of a party in the Hollywood Hills are mixed on the muted side: People arrive in cars with silent engines, the closing of doors is muffled, conversation is subdued. One woman dresses in near silence. And washed over all this is a most intriguing musical score by Cliff Martinez. It's quiet and minimal and dissonant. You have to listen for it, and when you do, you appreciate how it complements the other low-key sounds of the party, and how the whole mix casts an unreal spell over the party. A pistol shot rings out, loudly, and breaks the spell, but editing tells us that the firing of the gun took place only in the Brit's mind. It's hard to tell what is real from what isn't—on purpose.

Sound to Picture

When editing sound, the obvious thing to do is pair a sound with its source—the bang and the pistol—in the same shot. But sound becomes much more interesting when it is paired not with obvious sources but with something else in the same shot.

Cutaways: *On the Waterfront*

In *On the Waterfront*, Elia Kazan's famous film about a crooked teamster union local, a priest (Karl Malden) gives a speech to stevedores in the hold of a ship. One of the workers has just been "accidentally" killed because he was about to go to the authorities about another mob-connected death. Malden's speech is about standing up to union officers and doing the right thing. A lot of people are present: workers, top mob guys, mob punks, and Marlon Brando, who is trying to make up his mind about testifying before a Senate investigating committee. Only about half of Malden's speech is on camera. For the other half, editor Gene Milford showed people in cutaways listening and reacting. The mob guys aren't too happy. The workers are discouraged and ashamed of themselves. Brando seems undecided. If the camera had shown only the priest giving his speech, many opportunities to show the effect of his speech would have been lost.

Melancholy Strings: *Titanic*

In *Titanic*, a strangely dedicated string quartet keeps playing on the slanting deck of the ship while people all around them lose their heads. Director Cameron has the quartet play a poignant air. Then he cuts away from the quartet to show the dumbfounded captain, played by Bernard Hill, alone in the ship's pilot room, water sloshing around his ankles. He is profoundly sad in long shot. At the cut Cameron drops all other sounds from the track except the quartet's music, which realistically could not be heard from the pilot room. The score isn't practical now; it's laid-on score. No water sounds, no sounds of panicking passengers—only the string quartet. The effect is to set aside the immediate drama to invite viewers to contemplate the many meanings of the sinking, as doubtless the captain does.

Doleful Silence: *Fargo* (1996)

This film is about a dumb-shit car salesman who makes a deal with a couple of punks to have his wife kidnapped for a big ransom that he is sure his rich father-in-law will pay. The salesman, played by William Macy, plans to split the ransom money with the punks. The punks enter the house, run down the wife, haul her off. Later the car salesman gets home and calls out something like, "Honey, I'm home," knowing full well the wife is not there. The plan is for him to call the police and comfort his son, all the while acting appropriately distraught. But for a few seconds, when he first comes through the front door of his house and sees the signs of struggle strewn across the living room carpet, he is sad, afraid, remorseful—all of these at once. My God, what have I done? says the look on his face. Director Joel Coen places Macy in long shot in the living room to achieve this effect (akin to Cameron's placing the captain in long shot in the pilot room to produce a similar effect), and plays the scene in silence. The silence gives viewers emotional space to consider, as Macy does, what a terrible thing has happened. Sometimes the best mix is no mix— in other words, silence.

Popping the Cork: *The Right Stuff* (1983)

This film is about the U.S. Mercury space program of the 1960s. The goal of the program was to put a man in orbit to restore the program to a position of prestige, as the Soviets at that time were outrocketing the Americans. At first the Mercury program was a technological embarrassment. The Americans couldn't even get a rocket off the ground. In a series of shots meant to span months, rocket after rocket either topples from its gantry, explodes on the launch pad, or goes haywire in the air and has to be aborted. All these shots use realistic sounds. However, the last shot of this sequence uses a bit of expressionistic sound to make a cruel comment. First an engineer presses the Go button; then the camera cuts to the rocket on the pad. Nothing happens. Cut to worried engineer. Cut back to rocket. Finally the payload, a cone sitting atop the rocket, pops off—to the sound of a champagne cork popping.

Wind in Trees: *Blowup* (1965)

In this metaphysical mystery put together by the great Italian director Michelangelo Antonioni, a professional photographer (David Hemmings) may have unwittingly photographed a murder in a park. He went there to take a break from his hectic life of photographing fashion models and just pointed his camera here and there,

3.7. *Fargo*. Marge, the pregnant Police Chief of Brainard, Minnesota, and her husband Norm. When these characters go "Ya" and "You betcha!" we are set up. We fear that people who talk like this can't stand up to punks. We are wrong. Photo by Michael Tackett. Polygram.

snapping this and that, trying to get back to something basic and renewing. But when he develops the film, he keeps seeing something funny in the prints—suggestions of a face, an outline of a prone body barely seen in the bushes, a hint of a pistol. He thinks he can get to the reality of the moment by successively blowing up the negatives, and as he does this, the sound track features not darkroom sounds or suspenseful music—as lesser directors might have opted for—but the low, sharp, nearly imperceptible sound of wind in leaves—a sound which of course wouldn't be heard in the darkroom. I don't believe we can fully appreciate how difficult it was to achieve this sound effect clearly with 1960s sound-mixing technology. Later when the photographer goes back to the park to experience reality directly, we hear the same wind-in-leaves sound. Entirely original and positively metaphysical.

TRY THIS

Just start listening to the sounds of movies and think about how they are put together. For example, rent *The Talented Mr. Ripley*, a film with a sound track just as subtle and complex as the lives of the characters it follows. Note how sound designer Ivan Sharrock plays with music—now you hear Chet Baker jazz, now you hear the subdued score of Academy Award winner Gabriel Yared, now the sound of a piano across a Venice canal—all mixed and slid backwards and forwards with

3.8. *Blowup.* Click, click. But these clicks have been punched up by the sound mixer to be loud and harsh, intensifying the photographic rape. Bridge Films/ MGM.

the edited picture track, the music segueing against dissolves of picture. Experience the sound as you see the images and follow the story. Don't shove sound to the background of your consciousness. Instead, bring it up front and note how it pairs with images.

Also, consider seeing these films, which won Academy Awards for Best Sound, Best Sound Effects Editing, or Best Music (Original Score). Listen as much as you look.

- *The Last of the Mohicans* (1992). Revolutionary era. French soldiers, British soldiers, and a fearless Indian scout. Directed by Michael Mann, starring Daniel Day Lewis and Madeleine Stowe.
- *Bram Stoker's Dracula* (1992). No more visual accounting of the Dracula legend has been produced. Directed by Francis Ford Coppola, starring Gary Oldman and Winona Ryder.
- *Dances with Wolves* (1990). AWOL Civil War officer makes contact with Sioux Indian tribe and is transformed. Directed by Kevin Costner, starring Costner, Graham Greene, and Mary McDonnell.

✷

chapter four

Cuts

The film that comes out of a motion picture camera has a long way to go before it is useful for telling any kind of coherent story. It's the job of the film editor to trim these shots and then splice them into meaningful sequences. Actually, the film editor is an artist in her own right. She's an artist of *form*. This means that she contributes nothing material to the film. Instead, she takes other people's handiwork—long ribbons of light-exposed celluloid—and cuts them up, thereby producing "cuts." Actually, there isn't much scissors-snipping in the world of professional film editing these days. Nearly all film editing is now done on computers. Thus the computer mouse is to the film editor what the pen is to the poet, what the brush is to the artist, and what the hammer and chisel are to the sculptor.

The film editor is a collaborative artist. Before she makes that first cut, she must read the screenplay and know it well, and she must consult with the film's screenwriter and director. She has to know the characters in the film like she knows her own children, and she has to be completely familiar with nuances of meaning embedded in both the words of the script and aspects of the photography. Always the film editor works with the director of the film to settle on an editing strategy or style. She can't save a bad film by her efforts, as the popular mythology goes, but she enjoys great freedom and power to enhance the vision of the screenwriter and the intentions of the director.

Basics

Here are some basic procedures having to do with film editing.

Many Takes, Few Usable Shots

What was called a "shot" in chapter 1 is actually the product of many "takes" that the director ordered during principal photography—Take One, Take Two, Take Six, and so on. The director has her cinematographer photograph a particular scene many times until the actors give their lines to perfection and move exactly right. When the director finally does get the perfect take, she hollers, "Print it," which means that she wants this take to be turned into a viewable "positive" by the film lab. It's a keeper. Or the director may print several takes because she's not sure which one she likes. She may feel that it's better to print all of the halfway good takes and decide later how they might be used. At some point the director and the editor have to go over all these good or semi-good takes and decide which will actually be used in the finished film. It's the film editor's job to assemble these snippets just so.

One Take, Many Shots

Often one keeper take will produce many shots in the finished film. The editor will cut them into several pieces and stick them in at several points. Chapter 1 mentioned that the typical shot in a finished movie runs about six seconds. The original take from which the shot is pared may have run for twenty or thirty seconds. The editor might, for example, use five seconds of it here, ten seconds of it there, and maybe two seconds of it somewhere else.

Rough Cut, Fine Cut

The first job of the film editor is to assemble a *rough cut*. This is simply a very crude, overly long version of the entire film with all of the keeper takes (and even a few questionable but promising takes) spliced in the right order, from the start of the story to the end. After the editor finishes this cut, she views it with the film's director, who says things like, "No, that shot comes too early. Put it in after the crash, not before." Or: "Reverse those two shots." Or: "Wow, I hadn't thought about using that shot *that* way. Good going!"

The editor keeps hacking away—or mouse-clicking away—at the rough cut, taking out footage, resequencing shots, trimming and trimming, tightening, retaining only the choice moments of a take. She may even go back to her bin or hard drive full of outtakes and find snippets of film to connect two scenes that didn't blend well before. In short, she works toward a *fine cut*, which starts to look like the finished film you will see in the theater. She keeps meeting with the director, they keep looking at scenes, and then she follows the director's suggestions, or she comes up with solutions to particular storytelling problems herself. The director stays in close contact with her, as the director knows that the film will succeed or fail based on the skill and art of the editor.

Grammar

All contemporary films exhibit the following types of cuts in great abundance. These comprise the *grammar* of film editing.

Match Cuts

Matching the action of two cuts is indispensable for smooth continuity. The action is smooth and continuous across the cut. For example: Someone throws a punch in close-up. Cut to the punchee in long shot taking the punch and reeling back. Also, in the second shot, the puncher is seen following through, his arm swinging forward, his body lurching. The editor had a good reason for showing this piece of action in two shots instead of one. The close-up shows the puncher's angry face, and his punch in such a tight frame seems explosive, in your face. Meanwhile, the long shot provides the wider frame needed to show the punchee falling back.

During filming, the director made sure that the punches were duplicated or at least overlapped for the two takes. In the close-up, the puncher threw the punch and followed through, even though he lunged out of frame. In the long shot, the punchee took the punch again, then fell back. Thus, during filming, the punchee got punched twice. Maybe retakes were required. (Who says film acting is easy?) To make the match cut, the editor simply deletes the overlapping action. But she has

4.1. Film editing. *High Noon.* Everyone works harder when a scene involves action. Directors have to take more shots—long shots, close-ups, cutaways—that create much footage for editors to cull, sequence, and trim. United Artists.

some choice in the matter. She can cut early, before the punch, she can cut at the very moment of impact, or she can cut a few moments after impact, though this last choice seems unlikely. Cutting at the moment of impact would probably be the most dramatic alternative.

Other kinds of match cuts are less dramatic. We see a guy in two shots in sequence: If he is smiling in one shot, he ought to be smiling in the next. We see a woman smoking: If she takes a drag in one shot, she should be at the exact same stage of inhaling or exhaling in the next shot. We see a ballet dancer executing a pirouette: Wherever she is in her spin in one shot, she should be at the exact same place in the spin in the next shot. Keep in mind that these requirements apply only to two shots in sequence of the same action in real time.

Jump Cuts

Two shots that are supposed to match but don't are said to make a *jump cut*. The shots don't match in space and time. There is a dislocation, a disunity. Generally, jump cuts are considered mistakes, the result of sloppy workmanship. Jump cuts seldom occur in professionally produced movies. Directors, actors, and editors are assumed to be competent enough to avoid them. Directors will think to have the action in successive shots overlap. An actor is supposed to know that if she lifts a wine glass on a certain word in the long shot, she had better remember to lift the glass on the same word in close-up. Editors have a whole store of tricks to avoid jump cuts. One is explained a little later during the discussion of cutaways. Jump cuts are occasionally used on purpose in comedies as a kind of visual joke. One second a subject is in one position, the next he's in another, as in a bad home movie.

Cutaways

Cutaways are brief cuts to some secondary subject on the fringe of the main dialog or action; they are the spice of film. They flavor the main thing going on. For example, in *The Buddy Holly Story* (1978), a movie about the birth of rock 'n' roll music in the fifties, Holly and his Crickets are playing obligatory, drag-ass, "respectable" pop music at a small-town roller rink. Everyone is bored—the kids, Holly, his band. Then Holly gets the idea to play his kind of music, namely, nascent rock 'n' roll. He nods to the Crickets—and they go into the rock classic "Peggy Sue." It's get-down, sexy, heavily rhythmic. How does this new music go over? Cutaways tell us. The rink manager likes it, though he knows the owner hates it. The kids love it, too. They stop skating and dig the music. They move toward the stage, clapping and jiving.

Cut-Ins

Film directors and editors could not get along without cut-ins any more than writers could get along without verbs. Cut-ins are usually extreme close-ups of small objects. The shots may have been taken by a second unit crew at a time and place

4.2. Cutaway. *The Buddy Holly Story.* Holly's band plays their "new sound," fifties-era rock 'n' roll. The girl in the box might get her own cutaway showing her appreciation for the music. Columbia.

entirely different from that of the principal photography. For example, in *High Noon*, the classic adult Western of the fifties, the passing of time is extremely important. Local marshall Will Kane, played by Gary Cooper, has to confront a trio of ex-cons arriving on the noon train in about two hours, bent on revenge. Director Fred Zinnemann had Cooper take out his pocket watch several times and look at it to check the time. He also had Cooper look at various wall clocks in saloons, post offices, and the like. A second unit crew usually films subjects like these—a hand holding a pocket watch, a wall clock. They could do this while the main cast is having lunch. Afterwards, editors Elmo Williams and Harry Gerstad spliced this secondary material into the main story.

Crosscutting
Just as all movies routinely include dozens of match cuts, cutaways, and cut-ins, they also can't really get by without frequent use of an editing technique known as crosscutting. This amounts to taking two or more long takes—twenty seconds or so—and checkerboarding pieces of them in the pattern of ABABAB or ABCAB-CABC. In *Home Alone* (1990), the abandoned kid played by Macaulay Culkin is on one side of the door of his house while the would-be burglar played by Joe Pesci is on the other, trying to sweet-talk his way into the house. The pair talk to each other. This takes a minute or so. During photography, director Chris Columbus had

Culkin give all his lines in one rather long, uninterrupted take, all at the same time. Then he set up the camera on the other side of the door and had Pesci give all *his* lines in one longish take. Afterward, editor Raja Gosness alternated pieces of the Culkin shot with pieces of the Pesci shot.

Crosscutting allows the viewer to be in two places at the same time, or if not exactly the same time, then rapidly in the first place and then in the second place. The two places could be mere feet apart, as in the *Home Alone* scene. Or they could be miles apart, as in *E.T.* when editor Carol Littleton crosscuts from E.T. drinking beer at Elliott's house to Elliott at school feeling very tipsy and engaging in some very unstudentlike behavior. It's the crosscutting, in fact, that explains what is happening to Elliott. It also establishes an important theme of the film, namely, that children are better tuned to the particular sensibilities of alien creatures than are adults.

POV Shots

POV stands for "point of view." Point-of-view shots occur no less frequently in finished films than do match cuts, cutaways, cut-ins, and sequences of crosscutting. In a typical POV edited sequence, a character appears to look at something, usu-

4.3. *Taxi Driver.* The passenger (who, by the way, is the film's director, Martin Scorsese), says he's gonna kill his girlfriend for cheating on him. Hate, rage, pathology, scumbaggery—all in a day's work for driver Robert De Niro. Following this wide shot, Scorsese took a close-up of himself, a close-up of De Niro, an extreme close-up of De Niro's eyes, and a shot of the rear view mirror framing Scorsese. Then editor Marcia Lucas cut all of these shots together. Columbia.

ally in close-up. Cut to what the characters sees. Then cut back to the character reacting. In *E.T.*, little Gertie (Drew Barrymore) gets her first look at E.T. Cut to E.T., then cut back to Gertie screaming.

Certain horror and science fiction films use lots of POV shots and reaction shots. Characters in these films see things that humans have never seen before. Then we see what they see. Understandably their reactions are extreme—they scream, register awe and wonderment, approach, run away. If you have seen Spielberg's *Close Encounters of the Third Kind*, recall all the shots of Richard Dreyfus and Melinda Dillon gazing transfixed at the hovering mother ship. There is something like blessedness in their faces.

There is also a connection between POV shots and character development. When in a film we see what a character sees, and we see her looking and reacting several times, we tend to know that character better. We know how that character is in the world. For example, in Martin Scorsese's masterpiece *Taxi Driver*, Travis notices everything in the streets of New York City where he drives his cab. He notices hookers, he notices respectable women he can't have, and he notices crazed men shouting at nothing at all. And always we see his reaction to each of these varied goings-on. We also hear his thoughts, which boil down to how the city is totally decadent and beyond hope.

TRY THIS

Watch any good movie. Find instances of basic-grammar editing. Cry, "There's a match cut!" Holler out, "Aha! That was crosscutting." Exclaim, "Look at all those POV shots!" Or murmur, "That cutaway had a very definite dramatic purpose." (Don't do this in a theater.)

Time

The film editor is partly but importantly responsible for the viewer's sense of passing time in a movie. The editor has three choices. She can render a scene, even an entire movie, in what is called "real time," she can compress time, or she can expand time. One of the pleasures of watching a well-put-together movie is paying attention to the various ways the editor has improved the telling of the story by just the right manipulation of time.

Films in Real Time

This means that events in the movie take place in about the same length of time as they would in real life. It isn't often that an entire movie unfolds in real time. One that does is *High Noon*, which is only eighty-four minutes long. The story starts at about twenty after eleven in the morning. Then the noon train arrives with the bad guys. It takes Gary about forty minutes to put them away.

Compressing Time

Generally though, editors have to compress time more than they have to stay in real time or stretch time out. The trial that opens *The Fugitive*, when Harrison Ford is found guilty of murdering his wife, takes place in about three minutes of movie time, which is far shorter than most movie trials. The reason director Andrew Davis and his editor Dennis Virkler (plus five assistants) made the trial so short is that it's not the main thing of the movie. The film-long chase—Tommy Lee Jones after Ford—is the dramatic center of the story. So why stretch out the trial?

The trial is short but perfectly understandable. This is because Davis filmed only its highlights—the prosecution's opening statement, the presentation of key evidence, the verdict, the sentence. He may actually have filmed more, but Virkler pruned the trial down to its essentials in breathless succession. The defense didn't get much time. Quick cutaways to a worried Ford and his frustrated lawyer stand in for lengthy scenes of defense and rebuttal. Too bad for Ford but good for the movie.

Expanding Time

Now and then, however, it's up to the film editor to stretch time out. The director might accomplish this by ordering a shot in slow motion. The editor has different techniques. She might overlap action from several shots, she might let heads and tails of shots run longer, or she might cut in to sequences that need stretching and insert other shots. All these techniques would tend to stretch out movie time and slow pacing. In Oliver Stone's *Any Given Sunday* (1999), a film about pro football, crucial plays are stretched out in two ways: by filming them in slow motion and by elaborate overlapping of shots by editor Stuart Levy. What in real life would just take a few seconds—the throwing of a touchdown pass, for example—is three or four times as long in the movie, to heighten the drama.

Returning to *The Fugitive*, we notice that the climactic scene in the laundry room of the hotel where Jones, Ford, and bad-guy Jeroen Krabbe are brought together s–l–o–w–s t–i–m–e d–o–w–n. Jones is trying to communicate to Ford that he knows he is innocent. Krabbe is trying to kill Jones. Ford is trying to lead Jones to evidence that proves he is innocent. The setting has lots of chains, tracks, heavy metal things, hanging laundry, carts, posts—good stuff for hiding behind and creeping around. Director Davis took lots of shots, long-running shots, to cover this scene. Editor Virkler also let these shots run long. The whole scene is slowed down and stretched out so that viewers can feel the tension.

Both in One Scene!

D. W. Griffith both compressed time and expanded it *in the same scene* in *Orphans of the Storm*, his underrated silent-era melodrama of 1922. The story is about two sisters caught up in the bloody aftermath of the French Revolution. One sister, Henriette, played by Lillian Gish, is falsely convicted of counterrevolutionary activity and is about to be beheaded before a blood-thirsty crowd. Meanwhile her benefactor, the eloquent Danton, played by Monte Blue, gives a moving speech to the Revolutionary Council and secures Gish's release. The question is, can he get the paperwork to the site of the execution in time to save Henriette? Two lines of action then develop: Henriette being prepared for her execution and Danton on his horse, reprieve in hand, galloping to the execution site. Griffith cleverly cross-cut the two so that at first it seems that Danton cannot possibly reach the scaf-folding in time. Henriette is led up the steps. Cut to Danton just mounting his steed. Cut to Henriette as the black-hooded executioner ties her hands behind her back. Cut to another execution guy standing around on the scaffolding, looking official. Cut to Danton and his horse, galloping like mad. Cut to Henriette being lowered to the chopping block. Her head is secured by a wooden thing. Cut to Danton having to slow his horse when he runs into a bunch of carts and children in the street. Cut to a close-up of the hand of the executioner grasping the lever that will release the guillotine. Cut to Danton, free of the traffic, his horse in full gallop again. Cut to the scaffolding—ah, but the executioner is slow to pull the lever. His hand still rests on it. Quick cut to Henriette's face: She's about to pass out. Cut to executioner turning his hooded face to one of the execution officials. Cut to official, nodding. Cut back to Danton and by some miracle he has finally reached the scaffolding, which in the previous shot of him was nowhere in sight. Brandishing the stay of execution, Danton pushes his way through the crowd, mounts the steps, and flings the document into the face of the main official. The official understands and immediately jerks Henriette away from the chopping block a nanosecond before the executioner finally pulls the lever and sends the blade crashing down. Henriette, though in a swoon, is fine. Griffith's crosscutting saved the day.

But Griffith cheated. He brought off Henriette's rescue by fiddling with time. He expanded time in the Henriette-execution line of action, and he compressed time in the Danton-galloping line of action. Audiences, then as now, love this kind of cinematic slight of hand.

Space

Editors are also critical to the presentation of space in film. Of course, directors and their cinematographers have to keep track of space during scenes where space is important. After all, if viewers are confused about where things are happening, the movie isn't going to make much sense.

Here are some ways editors help orient viewers in space.

Establishing Shots

These are always long shots or extreme long shots that establish a particular place or setting for a scene to take place—a small town, a park, the exterior of an office building. Just think of how many films you have seen that are set in New York City.

They always, always open with shots of the city's skyline. Consider how many films set in Los Angeles open with shots of the L.A. freeway tangle.

The Classic Sequence

There was a time when practically every movie had a sequence like this: first a long shot that established setting, then a medium shot of two or more people in dialog, then alternating close-ups of the speakers, then, later on, another long shot of the actors that was meant to reestablish setting for viewers who had forgotten where they were. There was dramatic logic to this, going from wide to tight, then back to wide. In such an approach the long shot actually has two jobs—to establish setting and to launch the dialog. Since it is a long shot, viewers initially feel relatively detached from the drama. Then, after setting has been established, the editor moves in closer, and as she does, the drama intensifies. The concluding close-ups are, of course, the most intense shots of all. People raise their voices, plead, lie, clam up—in close-up. Then, after the drama of the scene has played out, the editor finishes the scene with the long shot, which is just a piece of the introductory long shot, to give viewers some space to think about what they have seen. Of course, the editor can't do any of this if the director has not thought beforehand to cover the scene with all these shots.

This business of going from wide to tight and then wide again is called "the classic sequence." You don't see it as much in contemporary movies, as directors have found other ways of accomplishing the same thing, namely by moving the camera in closer during a take. However, the technique is alive and well in TV drama.

Space and Drama

In Alfred Hitchcock's masterpiece *Rear Window* (1954), space is the whole thing. All the suspense is driven by space. James Stewart plays a photographer, Jeff Jeffries, who is laid up with a broken leg. His living room window happens to look out on a courtyard surrounded by apartments whose tenants don't close their curtains very often. Jeffries is something of a voyeur; he likes spying on his neighbors through a telephoto lens. Soon he discovers that a woman in an apartment on the other side of the courtyard has been murdered by her husband, played by Raymond Burr, and soon the murderer realizes that Jeffries is spying on him.

But Hitchcock never moves his camera into the apartment of the killer. He keeps it on Jeffries's side of the courtyard, and we see everything from his vantage point. Jeffries has his woman friend Lisa (Grace Kelly) enter the murderer's apartment and poke around for evidence. This turns out to be a dangerous thing to do. Drama builds. Jeffries can see through his camera lens that Lisa is in trouble, but Lisa doesn't know this, and Jeffries can't communicate with her. Lisa gets out of this one, but later the murderer comes after Jeffries. Much of the suspense then is based on the presentation of space, which Hitchcock had to make very clear in his filming. Then editor George Tomasini had to cut these scenes just so, to make matters of

4.4. *Citizen Kane.* Director Orson Welles believed that scenes should be minimally edited. He preferred to let the camera run (see pages 24–25) in order to "cut within the shot" by moving people in and out of the frame. Thus the man at the far left walks into the frame from the room after the dialog starts, creating a new dynamic. That's Welles himself second from right, playing Kane. RKO/Turner Entertainment.

space clear while also intensifying the drama. He alternates deftly among shots of Jeffries peering through his camera, point-of-view shots of what Jeffries sees, unmagnified shots of the garden and the windows of the killer's apartment across the way, magnified shots of garden and window (as seen through Jeffries's telephoto lens), and Jeffries reacting to what he sees.

The drama of many war films depends on the editing of shots that reveal and define space. The editing may reveal space realistically, or it may make spatial matters purposely confusing for the purpose of intensifying drama. Much of the horror of the initial beach invasion scene of Spielberg's *Saving Private Ryan* is based on a kind of fudging of space. The way this scene has been photographed and edited, it seems impossible that the Allied invading force will gain any kind of toehold on the beach, much less survive. The camera is kept low and pointed toward the sea as the landing barges hit the sand and disgorge troops. Then the camera angle is reversed to show the terrain behind the beach where German gun emplacements cut down the invaders, nearly to a man. The Germans seem to have the total spatial advantage, located as they are on a slight rise and close to the beach. The way editor Michael Kahn presents space in the opening minutes of the invasion, the invaders have no hope at all. Captain Miller (Tom Hanks) looks very worried indeed. The invasion is not working. The Germans are not giving up precious space—that's what Kahn conveys through his cutting.

Then the presentation of space seems to change. The advantage swings to the Allies. From hundreds of feet of footage Kahn had to sort through, he uses fewer shots of falling American soldiers, more shots of unscathed Americans advancing. Now the view of the German gun emplacements goes through a distinct change: They are not so close to the beach now, and they are not so high. Also, the terrain takes on little hillocks and depressions, places for the invaders to move up to and take cover behind. We didn't see these geographical features before when all seemed lost. Shots that show the invaders in spatial relation to the German defenders convey the sense that the invaders are making progress and will eventually gain the upper hand.

Is this believable? I have never heard anyone complain about this change of space in the film, just as no one back in the 1920s objected to Griffith's fooling with time to effect Henriette's rescue in *Orphans of the Storm*. Spielberg simply wanted to put you through hell-in-space for a time before he eased up, changed space, and let the good guys prevail.

TRY THIS

Rent a respectable film and view it with a partner. Try to find instances in which the film editor plied her craft either to manipulate time in some important way or to control space for a good reason. When you discover one or the other, pause the tape and explain to your partner what is going on. Maybe after a while your partner will catch on and the two of you can play this game.

Art

As I said at the outset of this chapter, the film editor is not just a technician who culls bad takes and dutifully assembles footage in predictable ways from the film director's instructions. Editors are also artists in their own right. Here is a miscellany of creative cuttings that, in their own way, take their rightful place alongside the art of the screenwriter, the director, and the photographer.

Meaningful Match Cuts

Occasionally film editors use match cuts in especially telling ways, and not just to effect smooth continuity. Such match cuts occur in Stanley Kubrick's *2001: A Space Odyssey*, in Mike Nichols's *The Graduate*, and in Karel Reitz's *The French Lieutenant's Woman* (1981).

In *2001*, a proud ape man throws a large leg bone triumphantly into the air. It rotates in slow motion. Match cut to an elongated spacecraft, moon-bound. The cut is startling and makes viewers think. Both the bone and the spacecraft are tools, or if you like, expressions of technology, one for killing, the other for transportation. The ape man had just discovered the power the bone-weapon lent him, or the power that technology imparted to him. He was ecstatic, celebratory at the discovery. The spacecraft represents the most complex and sophisticated expression of technology, yet ironically, everyone on board is indifferent, even bored, with technology. They've lost the ape man's exuberance.

In *The Graduate*, the young college graduate's life has become a blur of having unfeeling sex with an older woman and lounging by the pool of his parents' house. At one point in this sequence—sex, pool, sex, pool—the young man slides onto a raft in the pool. Match cut to his body sliding onto the body of the woman in bed. The point of the match cut is to suggest, entirely visually, that Hoffman doesn't find the sex any more important than his life by the pool, or the pool life any more important than the sex. They blend. There may be other meanings in this match cut, too.

Because of its complexity, the novel *The French Lieutenant's Woman* by John Fowles was long thought to be impossible to adapt to film. Then British playwright Harold Pinter came up with a solution. He wrote two stories in one, the first set in Victorian England, the second in contemporary England. In the second story, a film is being made about the earlier story. In the present-tense story, Meryl Streep and Jeremy Irons rehearse. The script she consults calls for her to stumble; match cut to the earlier story as Irons catches her. What could have been a jarring cut, from a contemporary London apartment where the pair rehearses to a nineteenth-century rural footpath where the heroine stumbles, comes off super smooth, thanks to the match cut.

Let's give credit to these three resourceful editors: Ray Lovejoy for *2001*, Sam O'Steen for *The Graduate*, and John Bloom for *The French Lieutenant's Woman*.

Shot Length and Memory

One of the most frequently used film editing techniques is the flashback. You've seen dozens of them. The editor rearranges time by cutting into the main story and dropping in a story or part of a story that happened before the main story. Often the flashback is used when a character is harboring a secret about the past that has to come out sooner or later in order to make the main story clear. The screenwriter and, later, the director have a choice of simply allowing the character to explain the past or actually dramatizing the past through filming and editing in flashbacks.

In *The Pawnbroker*, director Sidney Lumet slips in a few flashbacks to explain why Rod Steiger, a New York City pawnbroker, is so repressed and bitter. He's a Holocaust survivor. He underwent terrible things that he struggles mightily not to think about. But the past won't stay in the black box of his mind. It keeps getting out, at first in little flashes of memory, then in longer and longer recollections, and finally in sustained, full-blown remembrances. Editor Ralph Rosenblum communicates Steiger's mental struggle through shot length and effective crosscutting. At first, the concentration camp shots are so short as to be unintelligible to viewers.

They are probably only one twenty-fourth or one-twelfth of a second in running time. The viewer just cannot make any sense of these subthreshold shots cut in. But then neither can the pawnbroker. His memories come back in barely perceptible flashes. The length of these flashback shots, then, corresponds to the way Steiger's mind works in the story.

By making the flashbacks longer and longer, Rosenblum is communicating that Steiger is at last allowing the past entry into his consciousness, which he has to do before he can regain his mental health. Events in the present trigger recollections of the past. Thus when a prostitute bares her breasts to Steiger, he looks away. Cut to the concentration camp when the Nazi guard forced Steiger to look at his bare-breasted wife, who had been repeatedly raped by guards. All this, then, is editing with great psychological meaning.

Cutting on Similar Objects and Shapes

This artful cutting technique is similar to the linking device of breasts in *The Pawnbroker*. Often editors will find similar shapes or objects to link successive scenes, frequently very dissimilar scenes. In *Forrest Gump*, Forrest as an adult shuts his eyes tight in close-up; cut to a child in close-up who also has his eyes shut tight. We know from the similarity of eyes that we are flashing back to when Forrest was a child.

In the epic *El Norte* (1983), about the migration of desperate people from Central America to the United States, director Gregory Nava and his editor Betsy Blankett frequently use circular forms as a transitional device to cut from Los Angles to Guatemala and vice versa. Thus the image of the circular rotating hopper of a cement mixer in Los Angeles dissolves into a poetic full moon in Guatemala in the past. Life is hard in Los Angeles. The cement mixer is associated with long hours and backbreaking work that the main character, Enrique, has to endure; the moon beckons the disillusioned Enrique to remember a sweeter life in Guatemala.

A + B = C

Occasionally film editors have opportunities to create symbols by splicing two shots together. The cumulative effect of the two shots produces a third thing, some idea or abstraction that lifts the film story beyond mere event for a few seconds. In *The Graduate*, the young Ben (Dustin Hoffman) is trying to regain Elaine's affection after she has learned that he slept with her mother. She can't stop him from following her to the San Francisco zoo. What Ben doesn't know is that Elaine, played by Katharine Ross, is meeting a fraternity man there. When Ben finally learns this, he is dispirited. He slumps against the monkey cage. Editor Sam O'Steen then cuts to a very despondent-looking orangutan in the cage. He holds the shot for two or three seconds. The two-shot combination of Ben looking downhearted and the monkey also apparently down in the dumps insinuates that the fraternity guy has made a monkey of Ben. Audiences laugh when they see the monkey. It's a complex laugh that straight storytelling alone could not evoke, a special laugh conjured by the art of editing.

Cutting and Meaning

I once made a short dramatic film and accidentally discovered how two simple shots could be cut together in many ways, each affecting the scene's meaning. Here is the story: A straight woman has run off with a hippie young man—if "hippie" is the right word: He's bohemian, artistic, happy-go-lucky, irresponsible, longhaired—stuff like that—and appealing to the woman because of these very qualities. The couple are in love, but after a time the woman doubts that she should cast her lot with the man. They ride around in a VW bus, smoke pot, go to an outdoor concert, have an idyllic picnic, make love. Finally the woman asks the man to take her to a bus station. She wants to go home. So they go to the bus station and she buys a ticket. I had them sit on a bench so I could take a close-up of each. You don't see the guy in the girl's shot and you don't see the girl in the guy's shot. They are pensive, quiet, distant. First I took the close-up of the young woman: She looks straight ahead, then she looks at the young man, and then she looks away. Then I took a close-up of the young man doing the same thing. Later, when I was editing this scene, I discovered that I could spin the meaning of the end of the film in one of several directions, *and actually change the whole meaning of the film*, depending entirely on how I cut these two shots, as follows:

- *First spin:* She ceases to love him, but he still loves her. *Shot 1:* He looks at her. *Shot 2:* She is looking away.
- *Second spin:* He no longer loves her, but she still loves him. *Shot 1:* She looks at him. *Shot 2:* He is looking away.
- *Third spin:* Each has lost interest in the other. *Shot 1:* She is looking away. *Shot 2:* He is looking away.
- *Fourth spin:* They are still in love and she will stay with him. *Shot 1:* She looks at him. *Shot 2:* He looks at her.
- *Fifth spin:* Both are confused, out of sync. *Shot 1:* She looks at him. *Shot 2:* He is looking straight ahead, then he looks at her. *Shot 3:* She is looking away, then she looks at him. *Shot 4:* He is looking straight ahead. *Shot 5:* She stops looking at him and looks ahead. *Shot 6:* He looks at her.

TRY THIS

The sequences I describe in the films below are considered masterpieces of film editing. Rent the films, watch them all the way through, then afterwards run the edited sequences I mention a few times to discover why they work so well. Collectively they comprise a textbook on the editing of violence.

- The Odessa steps sequence in *Potemkin* (1925), also called *The Battleship Potemkin*. This is a Russian film directed and edited by Sergei Eisenstein, who brought a lot of intelligent theory to the art of film editing. (It was Eisenstein who first proposed the $A + B = C$ theory that I explained earlier.) In the Odessa steps sequence, Czarist Cossacks shoot down peasants on the wide civic steps of Odessa. It occurs near the end of the film.

- The climactic battle scene of *The Seven Samurai*, the 1954 masterpiece by Akira Kurosawa, which showed the world how to edit sword-and-arrow warfare. This sequence is probably unequaled in the annals of combat editing.
- The final shoot-out of *The Wild Bunch* (1969), a Western by Sam Peckinpah. This is violence transformed into high art. It doesn't even seem violent. It seems aesthetic.
- The gunning down of Bonnie and Clyde in the 1967 version directed by Arthur Penn, which is as terrible and beautiful as Peckinpah's art. They fall out of their car and fall out of their car and fall out of their car. This happens at the very end of the film.
- The baptism and gunning-down scenes of *The Godfather*, which also occur at the end of the film; they exemplify a triumph of crosscutting and of lifting sound from the baptism scenes and laying them over the scenes of violence.

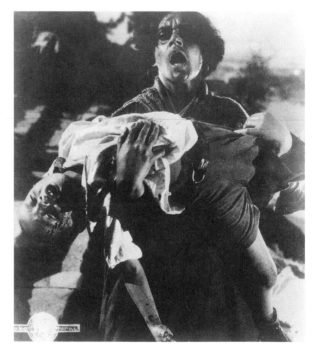

4.5. *Potemkin.* Though this scene about the massacre of innocent peasants prior to the Russian Revolution is famous for its editing, it also contains powerful individual shots. Goskino-Amkino Corporation.

chapter five

Styles

This chapter sums up the four that came before by describing how photography, *mise-en-scène* (scene-making), sound, and editing often combine to create distinctive styles in filmmaking. It's just as pleasurable to watch a movie to detect style as it is for anything else. Even if you don't like the story much, you can always sit back and enjoy the ride.

The Great Divide: Realism versus Formalism

About a hundred years ago, three French filmmakers created what I call the great divide in filmmaking, with *realism* on one side and *formalism* on the other. The Lumière brothers, Louis and Auguste, were present at the dawn of moviemaking. In 1895, they commenced a career of making short *actualités*, or documentaries, featuring such stupendous subjects as workers entering a factory, a train arriving at a station, and waves lapping at a beach. They took their subjects as they found them—no lighting other than what the sun provided, no camera moves, no embellishment or manipulation of any kind. Thus they trafficked strictly in realism. They made films about things that moved, including people, the way the things really were, and they were proud to record the world of movement this way. With such plain fare the Lumières went into business, setting up a string of theaters in Europe and making a lot of money, mainly because people had not seen any kind of moving pictures before this and were fascinated by ninety seconds of anything that moved on a twenty-foot screen.

Meanwhile, the third Frenchman, Georges Méliès, felt that the Lumières had it all wrong. Realism was fine, as far as it went, which for him was a decade or so, but he surmised that in the long run the big money was in movie magic. He made longer films with lots of special effects and elaborate *mise-en-scènes*. He is best remembered for *A Trip to the Moon* (1902), a sixteen-minute film featuring a whimsical moon rocket, a futuristic (for the time) launch site, astronauts costumed like they belonged in a children's play, and a cartoonish man in the moon who looks chagrined when the rocket lands in his eye. As you might expect, Méliès is called the father of a style of filmmaking that is the opposite of realism. For a variety of reasons, film people today call this style "formalism."

Today both impulses are felt in commercial moviemaking. Audiences expect the stories they see to be realistic in the sense that cows don't fly and rockets don't hit a moon-face in the eye. They expect tough guys to talk like tough guys and cops to talk like cops, and so on.

At the same time, formalism is definitely in ascendancy these days, thanks to the rise of the art of special effects and computer-generated imaging in the last twenty years. Moviegoers want to see something new, and Hollywood is willing to spend millions of dollars to oblige them. Stark realism is hard pressed to compete for audience affection with the likes of Godzilla, E.T., and the errant asteroid that threatens Earth in *Armageddon* (1998). Realism today is associated with low-budget, limited-circulation independent or foreign films—*Laws of Gravity* (1991) or *The Dream Life of Angels* (1999), for example. It's formalism that hogs the box office.

Elements of Style

Here is a rundown of the main differences between the realist style and the formalist style.

Photography

Realist photography at its purest is unadorned and self-effacing. The camera acts like it is ashamed to be around at all. There are no fancy zooms or elaborate moving-camera shots in realist films. Long takes are preferred, but not the kind of pretentious long-running takes described in chapter 1. Often the camera is handheld. Normal lenses predominate so that perspective is not distorted. The shakiness you note is intentional and is intended to give the production a documentary feel. Instead of being prisoners of the film frame, actors are free to move as they might in real life; it's up to the camera to keep up with them. On the other hand, formalist camera work may often employ wide-angle or telephoto lenses to produce distortions of perspective and focus. The camera usually moves a lot, whimsically as often as purposely. The moves of actors in formalist films are carefully blocked to stay within the frame of the camera. Camera work calls attention to itself; in fact, in many formalist films it's more important than the acting.

Mise-en-Scène

Realist films tend to be shot on location, making use of real apartments, pool halls, and factories. There seems to be very little set dressing, though you can't be sure. A classroom looks like a classroom in a realist film, but we don't know how hard the production designer had to work to make it look like a real classroom. Maybe she showed up at a real classroom to find it had a lot of atypical stuff that would distract from the film. So she had to decorate the classroom to look like a real classroom. Realism, as a style or an outcome, may have been on the producer's mind far less than simply saving money: The more a set has to be manipulated, the more money it costs.

Formalist filmmakers love to tinker with *mise-en-scène*. Walls can't just be your standard white or beige. They have to be painted red or gold. Lighting is elaborate. Certainly no chemistry lab or board room has such artful shadows, such gradations from light to dark. Often studios are willing to spend millions of dollars to make formalist interiors look weird, out of this world, dreamlike, or otherwise distinctive.

Sound

Realist films employ minimal musical scores; some have no scores at all. After all, life is not scored. Formalist films come with big scores that you often cannot ignore. Also, everyday sounds that realists would simply leave alone are enhanced and processed to sound like nothing of this world. A door closes—*thoom*, big booming bass sound.

Editing

Realist films tend to be plainly edited—no complicated sequences of crosscutting. Instead of cutting from character to character in a dramatic scene, the camera pans from character to character as in a one-camera documentary film. The editing is not supposed to intrude. Formalist films, on the other hand, may be complicated in their editing. Many shots run just a fraction of a second. Fast cutting comes with fast music. Formalist editors want their craft up front and noticeable.

Makeup and Costuming

These are plain for realist films and elaborate and showy for formalist works. Tom Joad (Henry Fonda) in the realist *Grapes of Wrath* (1940) dresses down in drab clothing, whereas Batman (Michael Keaton), in the 1989 formalist drama of the same name, is a comic-strip fop in his crenellated cape and bat-eared headpiece.

Story and Characters

Realist style calls for certain kinds of stories and methods of storytelling; so do formalist films. Realist films tend to tell episodic—not intricately plotted—stories of everyday life. Characters are "real" people, neither all good nor all bad. The challenges they face are not so different from the challenges you and I face—getting a girl, holding a job, making a marriage work. Many realist films end unhappily, because realist filmmakers often see life as tough and unforgiving. Realism is sometimes associated with the political left; if people are eventually devastated, it's the fault of the uncaring capitalist system. A branch of realism called naturalism, derived from Darwinian views of existence, is even bleaker. Naturalists see human beings as leaves before the wind, helpless and doomed. The youthful Hughes brothers, who wrote and directed the estimable ghetto tragedy *Menace II Society* (1993), have a fine sense of the forces arrayed against their teenage protagonist Caine. He's too young, too embittered, too enmeshed in the life of the hood to escape it.

Formalist films are the ones with courageous heroes and beautiful women—or handsome men and courageous women. These stories often take place in exotic settings and often end happily. Melodrama prevails over tragedy—see chapter 6 for more about this. The dominant tone or mood of formalist stories is that all's well that ends well. The characters may be put through hell, but in the end, they are much more likely to be given a happy ending than are the characters in a realist film. At the same time, loads of formalist films don't end happily. For example, Ken Russell, the lovable British formalist, made many down-toned films, including *The Devils* (1969), *Women in Love* (1971), and *Tommy* (1975). The highly respected *Titus* (1999) is probably the most formalistic, and the bloodiest, adaptation of a Shakespeare tragedy.

Four Films

Marty (1955) is the ultimate realist film. Directed by Delbert Mann, it tells the story of a shy, unattractive man (Ernest Borgnine) who is groping to have a relationship with shy, unattractive Clara (Betsy Blair). Marty is a butcher, Clara a school teacher. Love triumphs—the exception to pure realist narrative—after Marty discovers it's okay to love a woman even though his hypocritical and loveless peers disapprove of her. The nation loved this break from so much star-saturated, luster-lipped Hollywood fare. Marty won four Academy Awards.

A more recent realist film of note is *Boys Don't Cry* (1999) directed by Kimberly Peirce. This story takes place in Nebraska and has to do with a young woman (Hillary Swank) who yearns to be a man. She's that "man trapped in a woman's body" you've heard of. Finally she can stand being a woman no longer, so she cuts her hair, buys men's clothes, and moves to a small town where nobody knows her. Soon she has made friends, male and female. In fact, one of the working-class young women of the town actually falls in love with her. But the men are macho shit-kickers, rowdy and violent and definitely not sympathetic to people with sexual identity crises. You fear for Hillary should they eventually find out about her. They do.

You've Got Mail (1998) is a pretty typical piece of Hollywood formalism. There are more fanciful films, to be sure, but this one picks up a lot of the features of formalism—namely, the look of the characters and the *mise-en-scènes*. This too is a

5.1. *Boys Don't Cry.* The guy on the right is really a woman, headed for big trouble in the unenlightened heartland. See pages 108–10 for more about tragedy. Photo by Bill Matlock. Fox Searchlight.

love story, but instead of a pair of plain-looking lovers, we are served pretty, pert Meg Ryan and cuddly Tom Hanks, just about the most winning pair in Hollywood. The plot has to do with businessman Tom putting in one of his chain bookstores up the street from Meg's quaint, little, one-of-a-kind bookstore; he pretty much puts her out of business. This is in the middle of Manhattan where rents are high. Meg's bookstore looks like a million dollars and ought to rent for nearly as much. It's tastefully decorated and attractively lit, as is Meg's spacious, airy apartment.

Tom and Meg finally kiss and make up and fall in love—just how, I won't go into. The point here is that it isn't so much the love-conquers-all story that makes this a formalist film. It's the clean, well-lit tastefulness of the *mise-en-scènes*.

On a scale of one to ten, where one is pure realism and ten pure formalism, *You've Got Mail* would come in at about five or six. *Edward Scissorhands* (1990), directed by Tim Burton, is more like a nine. What makes it so formalistic is the character of Edward (Johnny Depp) who does not have normal hands. Instead, he has giant scissors for hands because his inventor (Vincent Price) died before he could give him real hands. He's just a kid. He lives alone in a spooky old mansion until a suburban housewife (Diane Wiest) discovers him and brings him back to her tract house. Her tract-house daughter (Winona Ryder) can't deal with Edward's scissorhands, nor can she muster any kind of feeling for Edward's plight. The tract-house neighborhood looks like something out of a cartoon. All of this is metaphor and satire and wonderfully expressive.

Ones, Twos, and Threes

Below are brief descriptions of six realist films, each given a rank of one, two, or three in terms of its realism. Keep in mind that a one isn't better than a three; it's just more realistic, stylistically speaking.

Greed (1925)

Director: Eric von Stroheim. Rank: one. Unadulterated realism, largely because of the clear, unsentimental photography, von Stroheim's obsessive attention to detail, and the naturalistic tale in which a man is driven to death by his lust for money. He ends up in Death Valley handcuffed to the man he has killed and is doomed because of it. The original version of this silent film ran eight hours. Self-indulgent von Stroheim never got away with that. What you get now is a version that runs a little over two hours.

The Crowd (1928)

Director: King Vidor. Rank: two. The anti-dream, social pessimism. A young man thinks he is special, wants to succeed, and lays plans to make something of himself. But Vidor shows all the societal and commercial forces arrayed against this dream.

5.2. *The Bicycle Thief.* Realism is often about everyday hard times. If the man can't find his bicycle, he can't work. If he can't work, his family won't eat. Desperate to find the bicycle, the father had deserted the boy for a time. The boy feels taken for granted. Realism is like this. Characters have flaws and behave badly at times, yet they aren't villains or bad guys to us. We know that real life is more complicated than that.

In the end the man becomes just one of the crowd. Vidor shot this film in many real locations and among real crowds who did not know they were being photographed, giving the film a documentary quality and adding to its realism. Warning: This film too is silent. Like *Greed*, it employs titles to communicate what people say to each other.

The Bicycle Thief (1949)

Director: Vittorio Di Sica. Rank: one. Italian film made during the post–World War II period, when Italy was prostrate with defeat. After decades of enduring fluff from their peers, certain leftist Italian filmmakers wanted to get back to something real and show the poverty in which most Italians lived. Their movement was called "neorealism." This film was shot on location in Rome and employed natural lighting, amateur actors, straightforward photography, and functional editing. It tells a little story made big because of its humanity.

Pather Panchali

Director: Satyajit Ray. Rank: one. Another masterpiece of realism about a Bengali family struggling to keep body and soul together in the face of widespread poverty, natural disasters, and human failings. Simply yet elegantly photographed and edited, and produced on location. None of the usual film trickery is used to move you. Instead, it's pure setting, acting, story, and revelation that get to you. Valuable too as celluloid anthropology—as is *The Bicycle Thief*, for that matter.

La Promesse

Directors: Jean-Pierre and Luc Dardenne. Rank: one. Plain and simple (yet not so simple) film about growing up in industrial Belgium. After a decade of overproduced Hollywood buff and fantasy films, this little film surfaces to reaffirm the realist style. I've written about it in previous chapters—the handheld camera, available lighting, long takes, minimal editing, and lack of music. It's about a boy of fifteen who has trouble doing the right thing. Sounds banal maybe, but the Dardennes make it high drama.

Saving Private Ryan

Director: Steven Spielberg. Rank: three. Many viewers and reviewers of this compelling film were struck by the realism of the first twenty minutes, when Allied forces storm the Normandy beaches during World War II. Never had combat been so vividly portrayed; eye-level, handheld cameras suggest documentary footage of bodies tumbling, blood flowing, limbs hurtling, mouths screaming. And yet artifice is at work, too—especially in the editing, which, as I suggested in chapter 4, was carefully calculated to produce confusion and dread.

Eights, Nines, and Tens

Now for some films positioned at the far right end of the stylistic continuum. Again, a ten isn't better than an eight, nor does it's being on the "right" make it conservative; it's just more formalistic in terms of style.

Triumph of the Will (1935)

Director: Leni Riefenstahl. Rank: ten. One of the most aesthetic propaganda films of all time, and a great editing achievement. In fact, much of the effect, which is to idolize Hitler and transform into deities the athletes at the 1934 Olympic games in Germany, is achieved through the kind of formal editing—that is, cutting on objects of similar form, as I discussed in chapter 4. Riefenstahl had unlimited resources available to her as her many camera crews captured Hitler and the athletes from every possible frame and angle.

The Wizard of Oz (1939)

Director: Victor Fleming. Rank: nine. Basically, it's Kansas realistic, Oz formalistic. And Oz is just a dream. For a long time, Hollywood felt it had to justify the formalistic style by making it (the story) all a dream.

Star Wars

Director: George Lucas. Rank: nine. Unapologetic fantasy. Luke Skywalker doesn't wake up in Malibu to find that it was all a dream. Lucas is one in a long line of special-effects filmmakers, but this film caught on as none before had and encouraged a whole generation of filmmakers to go fantasy, producing films such as *Raiders of the Lost Ark* (1981), *Jurassic Park*, etc.

5.3. *The Empire Strikes Back.* With his low-slung pistol and loner personality, Han Solo (Harrison Ford) evokes the Western hero. There is a lot of the Western in deep-space epics like Star Wars: both genres are saturated with myth, quest, mission, and derring-do. See pages 207–208. Twentieth Century Fox.

Legend (1985)

Director: Ridley Scott. Rank: ten. This little-known movie ought to be better known, not for its story, which is something of a mess, but for the magic fairy-tale settings, complete with perpetually falling petals, purple haze, unicorns, and an evil prince named Darkness. Tom Cruise is Jack, and his job is to save a fair maiden from Darkness.

Batman

Director: Tim Burton. Rank: ten. Dark, dark, as Batman himself always has been when compared to, say, Superman. It's comic-strip film noir, a world of capes and masks and exotic vehicles. Batman is always swinging into the action from ropes, and the Joker is forever cackling and going around in a painted face.

The Matrix

Directors: Andy and Larry Wachowski. Rank: eight. This film is like *The Wizard of Oz* in that there are two worlds, the real world and the computer world. Or is it the computer world that's the real world? I get that mixed up. What is remarkably formalistic about this film is the cool ways people move. Slow motion has never looked better—neither has costuming, nor have not-so-speeding bullets.

Any Given Sunday

Director: Oliver Stone. Rank: eight. A similar split. Stone intends for the football story to feel really real. And it is. Cynical orthopedic doctors managing pain, loss-

5.4. *Batman.* Retro cool. Formalist production designers have so much fun.

engendered tensions, male ego, pride, more pain, more male ego, jealousy, racism. But the visuals are like nothing you ever saw in *North Dallas Forty* (1979), the commendable football film starring Nick Nolte. In *Any Given Sunday*, director of photography Salvitore Totino got down in the trenches with his beefy, Sunday-ugly actors and filmed plays so close-in that they become formalistic blurs, violence abstracted, at once punishing (for viewers) and beautiful. Play-action images dissolve to black-and-white–filmed NFL games of yore, Vince Lombardi, mythic sweep, epic grandeur. A nonstop score combines just about every kind of music you can think of: hip hop, jazz, blues, Mormon Tabernacle, Gregorian, atonal. But you will be disappointed if you buy the CD of the film's soundtrack and expect to hear such variety. Instead, all the music of the film has been rendered as hip hop. It's very boring after three tracks. (The same thing happened to *Gone in Sixty Seconds* (2000), a film with an engagingly varied musical score. You buy the CD, and you are cheated. It's all been turned into rap—I guess because it's more commercial to do so.)

The Rise of the Stylistic Middle
But it is in the middle—that is, four, five, and six on my realist-to-formalist continuum—that studios prefer to position their product, and it is in the middle where most Hollywood movies cluster. The middle feels safe, accessible, commercial.

5.5. *On Any Given Sunday.* Formalist directors love to backlight falling rain. Photo by Robert Zuckerman. Warner Brothers.

Most of the directors noted above made or continue to make films in the stylistic midrange, including King Vidor, Steven Spielberg, Ridley Scott, and Oliver Stone. In fact, *most* of the films from these directors fall into the middle.

Classic Hollywood Style

Over the decades a consistent style of filmmaking has been developed by centrist film directors. It's commonly called "classic Hollywood style" or just "classic style." Classic style provides filmmakers the clarity and fluidity they need to tell stories, reveal character, and crank up the drama. Classic Hollywood style is so fundamental that it is nearly impossible to imagine films without it. The early innovator D. W. Griffith probably was the father of the style. Later it suffused the filmmaking practices of virtually every filmmaker worldwide. How fundamental is classic style? As fundamental as rhyme and meter are to poetry, as theme and variation are to jazz and classical music, and as perspective is to art. Here are two main features of the style:

Varied Coverage

Classic style is based on the practice of obtaining *varied coverage*. This means that in photographing a film scene the director calls for a number of different shots of essentially the same dialog or action. The director doesn't retake just because someone flubbed a line. She orders retakes from a variety of frames and angles. As we have seen in chapter 1, as frame varies, so does the cinematic feel, the interpretation. The same is true for angle and movement. Varying the coverage thus releases the power of cinematics for fuller expression.

Later all these varied takes are turned over to the editor so that she can pare the footage down to something that is clear and swiftly moving. Working from the basic grammar of editing explained in chapter 4—that is, cutaways, cut-ins, POV sequences, and crosscutting—plus countless other choices having to do with trimming and sequencing shots, the editor can tweak scenes this way or that way to create subtle effects beyond mere photography.

Invisible Technique

The second characteristic of classic Hollywood style is the *invisibility* of all these techniques. This means that all personnel strive to make their handiwork seem effortless and unobtrusive. Viewers should be aware only of the unfolding of the film story and not, for example, of the interplay of long shots, medium shots, and close-ups or the insertion of cutaways or POV shots. As the style originally developed, directors, editors, and movie photographers of the 1930s, 1940s, and 1950s took great pride in keeping their various crafts in the narrative background.

Much of the invisibility of technique is due to audiences' simply growing to accept whatever style or technique Hollywood hands out. Hollywood has taught viewers the language of cinema. And just as you and I are unaware of speaking nouns and verbs or of constructing sentences with dependent clauses—though we do it effortlessly and unconsciously hundreds of times a day—movie audiences are not instinctively aware of the techniques used in filmmaking. We see just movies— not crosscutting, classic sequences, pans, or dollying. In other words, we make technique invisible by our own uncritical acceptance of it.

Classic style is alive and well. Even Oliver Stone, though he obviously wanted to bring new techniques to making a football film, had to resort to classic style to make things clear. Quarterback Jamie Fox gets sacked; cut away to coach Al Pacino, who is disappointed—that's pure classic style. You can just feel Stone and his editor, Stuart Levy, chafing against classic style, trying to find new ways to tell their story, but eventually reverting to the tried and true.

Five Practitioners of Classic Style

The films of the five directors I discuss below were extremely different from each other, yet there was a commonality of style among them. All employed classic style without realizing it or calling it anything. If you had asked them how they liked working in classic Hollywood style, they would have had you forcibly removed from the set.

John Ford (1895–1973)

Ford was a triumphant, controlled sentimentalist. He made films which Americans took to their hearts. He especially excelled at Westerns such as *Stagecoach*, *She Wore a Yellow Ribbon* (1949), *The Searchers* (1956), and *The Man Who Shot Liberty Valence* (1962). In Ford's hands, films like these were not just about a bunch of good guys riding hard after a bunch of bad guys. They were written in mythic script that captured the essence of America: family, individualism, heroism, and the building of a nation.

Ford's frames are often symmetrical and elegant. Seldom are backgrounds out of focus. For the most part, his scenes are brightly lit, his colors warm. Bracing, quasi-patriotic or poignant folksy music overwashes his stories of settlers, scouts, Army officers, fierce men on missions, and tough frontier women.

Frank Capra (1897–1991)

Capra is best known for his stories about little people asserting themselves and finally prevailing in the face of powerful, undemocratic forces. Some critics call these productions sappy, yet Americans keep renting them and viewing them.

In Capra's populist films—*Mr. Smith Goes to Washington* (1939), *Meet John Doe* (1941)—the frame is often crowded and bursting with energy. People smile, laugh, demand this or that, impinge. There is also a zippiness about the editing, a briskness in pacing. When people are alone they seem really alone—George Bailey in *It's a Wonderful Life* about to jump off a bridge at night during a snowstorm, or Jefferson Smith in *Mr. Smith Goes to Washington* brooding about democracy at the moodily lit Lincoln Memorial in Washington, D.C. But things pick up soon enough; people flow back into the frame. The little folk prevail.

Billy Wilder (1906–)

An Austrian who emigrated to the United States in 1933, Billy Wilder was one of the inventors and first practitioners of film noir, which we considered briefly in chapter 2. Noir is fatalistic storytelling. Men in urban, nighttime settings are haunted, pursued, doomed.

Two of Wilder's most famous noir films are *Double Indemnity* (1944) and *Sunset Boulevard*. Both have to do with women who entrap men and cause their downfall. Wilder and other noir directors developed dark, dramatic lighting styles to tell their naturalistic stories. Wilder also experimented with unusual camera angles and imaginative sets that reflected the states of mind and themes of his films.

John Huston (1906–1987)

Huston was the supreme ironist of American filmmaking. Many of his films are about adventure and quest, with the questers' eventually finding themselves undone by their own ambition. For instance, in *The Treasure of the Sierra Madre* (1948), three men are obsessed with finding gold in the mountains of Mexico. Two of them

5.6. *The Treasure of the Sierra Madre.* This master shot guides the filming of subsequent shots, such as close-ups of each of the three men. This film was made during the height of the studio system when classic style, and things like master shots, were in full flower.

end up renouncing their greed, but the third, played by Humphrey Bogart, gets himself killed by bandits. In *Moby Dick* (1956), the peg-legged Captain Ahab (Gregory Peck) roams the ocean in search of the white whale that chomped him. He ends up getting tangled up in his harpoon line and drowning.

Huston loved exotic settings and filmed them with fervor, capturing the essence of Africa and remote Kafiristan in vivid color photography. He was endlessly inventive, especially when it came to filming disappointment and death. The dust storm that concludes *The Treasure of the Sierra Madre* and blows Bogart's gold dust away, returning it to the earth from which it was so ill-gotten, is one of the most cinematic climaxes ever produced.

Alfred Hitchcock (1899–1980)

Hitchcock virtually invented the genre we now know as the thriller. At his peak in the late 1950s and 1960s, he turned out masterpiece after masterpiece—*Rear Window*, *Vertigo* (1958), *North by Northwest* (1959), *Psycho*—of suspense and endangerment. His characters are often helpless and clueless, wrongly accused, tortured by fateful events.

Hitchcock's camera work strikes many viewers as stiff and formal, and so do the performances of his actors. But commentators point out that these qualities fit Hitchcock's particular view that human beings aren't really free, aren't loose or spontaneous. They are just puppets whose strings Hitchcock loves to pull. Often his sets seem unnaturally bright and color-saturated. For example, when his characters drive cars, the interiors of the cars look as bright as tanning booths. As noted in chapter 2, the famous shower scene in *Psycho* unfolds in bright, flat light. Hitchcock was the one film director who did not demand that suspense unfold in the dark.

New Cinematic Style and the Move to Formalism

In the 1960s, two films with numbers for titles had an enormous impact on filmmaking worldwide. These were Federico Fellini's *8½* (1963) and Stanley Kubrick's *2001: A Space Odyssey*. In these films technique ran rampant. It wasn't demure and invisible, as it had been before. Instead it became the main reason for making the film at all. *8½* is about a film director who can't get his ninth film off the ground, largely because of a midlife crisis he is undergoing. His past haunts him, but he doesn't sit around and talk about it, he relives it in some of the most imaginative and surreal interiors ever devised. It's impossible to separate what is real from what takes place in the director's imagination. *2001* is about—who can say? A big slab of slick stone turns up on the moon, astronauts take off for Jupiter, a psychedelic light show ensues, and one of the astronauts has a vision of himself as a hundred-year-old man having breakfast in a hard, white bedroom, then the slab turns up again. The point is, this is pure formalism.

Americans probably took the lead in developing a more technique-conscious cinema. It goes by several names. "New cinematic style" is as good as any. The new style made it okay to put technique on display. Photography became proudly and self-consciously expressive, even intrusive; editing played bold tricks with time and space. For complex cultural reasons, the viewing public was now ready for flashy technique and heartily embraced new style. For example, viewers had no trouble understanding that a handheld, purposely jerky camera—unthinkable in classic style—meant that a character in a film was disoriented.

It isn't quite accurate to say that technique is now an equal partner with straight acting and storytelling. In fact, as I have said, classic style has remained the fundamental undergirding of film narrative to this day. But gradually new style has asserted itself. Audiences now know how to deal with it. They have no trouble accepting, for example, that characters physically isolated from each other (that is, each is alone) will sing successive lines from the same song in the same melancholy tone of voice, at the same time, in perfect sequence without missing a beat, as they do in Paul Thomas Anderson's *Magnolia* (1999). This is not realistic. Nor is it realistic for the film to conclude with a rain of frogs—millions of them falling from the sky and landing on cars, streets, and rooftops and in swimming pools—all over town. All the same, audiences go home feeling that they have seen a very important film, even if they don't fully understand it. The film is about so many things: life, loneliness, regret, redemption, and (somehow) the awesome nature of coincidence. Audiences do not question the unreality of the simultaneous singing nor the implausibility of a camera that follows a falling frog down from a great height until it smacks into the face of a man climbing up the side of a building. They don't scoff, "What a mess of a story!" Instead, they sense that these oddities have something to do with meaning, with truth; and they drive home (or back to the video store) taking pleasure in trying to figure out the truth of a film with such disparate elements.

Four Formalist Directors

Contemporary directors still tell stories in more or less traditional ways. But since the onset of new style, they have given themselves permission to mess around with set-making, shooting, editing, or mixing sound, to the point of intrusion. Technique never really gets in the way of story, but it's not invisible either.

Robert Altman (1925–)

Robert Altman is less a studio man than a true American independent filmmaker who occasionally, and reluctantly, gets mixed up with studios. The Europeans consider him an auteur, or film artist. He makes films that go against the grain, either in subject matter or in storytelling. His *M*A*S*H* (1970) is a war film without the usual patriotic drivel or violence. It's mainly about blood and how army doctors adjust to so much of it. The surgeons just go about their business, sawing and tying up, as if blood affects them not at all. This is not realism, as in *Saving Private Ryan;*

it's surface satire with deep psychology, another way of saying war is hell.

Altman's *McCabe and Mrs. Miller* (1971) helped transform Westerns just as *M*A*S*H* had changed war films. The plot has more to do with rough-and-ready capitalism than with traditional Western themes of rugged individualism and abiding vengeance. *Nashville* (1975) and *Short Cuts* (1993) tell not one but a multiplicity of stories, sometimes running parallel, sometimes intersecting, coming down to conclusions that resonate with each other. There is much of *Nashville* in *Magnolia*.

Francis Ford Coppola (1939–)

Coppola has made a couple of big, operatic films with ingenious formalistic sequences. For instance, as I mentioned in the last chapter, the famous baptism sequence in *The Godfather* is an impressive formalistic crosscutting of sight and sound, from the baptism of Michael's son to the rubbing out of competing mob bosses. We *hear* the priest say, "Michael, do you renounce Satan?" and Michael responds, "Yes," as we *see* Michael's hit men gunning down rival godfather Richard Conti on the streets of New York. Such a disjunction of sight and sound would not be allowed in classic style.

In 1979, Coppola made an important war film, *Apocalypse Now*, which many

5.7. *Apocalypse Now.* Far up the river, deep in the jungle: Another world.

feel is the cinematic equivalent of the Vietnam War itself. In tone the film is ambiguous, insane, and surreal. Stylistically, it's probably the least realistic war film ever made. Much of it takes place in a drug haze; contemporary rock music dominates the sound track. It's 1960s America, with all its indulgences and contradictions, transported to Southeast Asia.

Martin Scorsese (1942–)

Scorsese has consistently directed interesting and original original feature films. Like Altman and Coppola, he's an individualist, a renegade, someone who is not entirely comfortable in the Hollywood system. Typically he makes films about men, all kinds of men—taxi drivers, boxers, mob guys, ambulance drivers—and their haunted inner selves, their self-destructive tendencies. And he does this with confident, breathtaking visual flourishes. His sets are spectacularly detailed, his lighting always original. Like Coppola, he too likes disjunctions of sight and sound. It's instructive to compare two similar Scorsese films, *Taxi Driver* and *Bringing Out the Dead* (1999), which is about an ambulance driver. Both films are about tormented, profoundly moral men on the verge of cracking up because of the vice, corruption, and death they encounter daily. But the latter film is stylistically much more advanced. Scorsese could get away with a lot more. The colors and lighting, the phantasmagoric urban backdrops, the camera that swoops in from unexpected angles—the ingenuity of these techniques alone make the film worth seeing.

Woody Allen (1935–)

Allen is probably the least cinematic, the least formalist of these contemporary directors, but the times have given him permission to do what he damn well pleases. Most of his films are comprised of straight storytelling devoid of stylistic flourishes. He likes stories of urban living, coping, getting along, falling in love, finding yourself through love, fearing death. He turns all this into self-deprecation, satirizing the New York Jew who takes himself and life too seriously.

Allen hasn't been able to settle on a consistent visual style. In *Crimes and Misdemeanors* (1989), he was loath to edit. He photographs rather complex dialogs lasting many minutes, with two or more people and nary a single cut; the camera floats around from speaker to speaker, from living room to dining room, and back again. But in *Manhattan Murder Mystery* (1993), his camera is jerky and jumpy, his editing busy.

A few Allen films are delightfully formalistic. *Zelig* (1983) is a preposterously original film about a man who wants to fit in so badly that he can actually transform himself into people he associates with. The film feels like a narrated documentary. *The Purple Rose of Cairo* (1985) is about a Depression-poor woman who so loves movies that she can will characters to step off the screen and join her in real life.

5.8. *The Mask.* Jim Carrey's alter ego in love. The seamless joining of computer special effects and live action is typical of many contemporary formalist films. New Line Cinema.

Truth's Beauty

Truth is beauty, and beauty is truth, to paraphrase the English poet John Keats. Realism does not have a monopoly on truth, as one might suspect. Nor is formalism frivolous. It's just another way of arriving at truth. The kind of beauty that formalism creates has potential for getting at the truth as much as do starkly realistic styles. For truth is embedded in style itself. The invitation to detect truths residing in realist films goes something like this: *Here is life depicted pretty much as it really is. The truth lies on the surface for anyone to see.* Meanwhile, the invitation to detect truths residing in formalist styles might go this way: *Here is life abstracted, made magic or hideous beyond everyday experience, poeticized by unusual photography, editing, and sound. Certain truths can be brought out only by these means. So go dig.*

Ah, truth! What is it? Such a question will never be answered by me. But please indulge my nibbling around its edges in the second section of this book.

TRY THIS

Rent any realist film mentioned in this chapter. What truths lie on the surface and await your discovery? Rent any formalist film mentioned in this chapter. How might its poetry, its unreality, be interpreted to discover the truth of the film?

Story

And so we move on to the story, the oldest and in many ways the most complex of human inventions. Just as in the first section I hoped to deepen your appreciation of motion picture sight and sound, I hope in this section to give you a few new takes on the story, and in particular the *film* story.

chapter six

Drama

It's strange. You go to the movies, you want to be gripped. You want to be put through something. But why? Why would anyone want to feel tension, fear, uncertainty? If I came up to you and asked you, "Do you want to be frightened?" you'd think I was nuts. You'd want to get away from me. But if I added, "There's this great movie that's really scary—you ought to see it," you might give me a minute of your time.

So although we don't want life to scare us, it's okay for movies to scare us—or to put us through some kind of tense time. We are of two minds when we watch a movie like *The Blair Witch Project* (1999). We are scared, sure, but we also know it's only a movie. Me, I wasn't scared by *The Blair Witch Project*, I guess because I know too much about filmmaking for my own good. But I didn't leave the theater muttering, "What a relief. I wasn't scared at all." Instead, I was disappointed. I had really wanted to feel frightened.

The question is, just how do movies engage us? The short answer is that movies, after all, aren't fundamentally different from those other two forms of storytelling, the novel and the stage play. All three forms use many of the same tricks of narrative. Novels have the verbal edge. They can go on and on with lots of details, explanations, history, and analysis, which is what we like or don't like, according to our lights. Stage plays are "live"; real people are up there on the stage before us putting themselves on the line, risking, and we can surrender to the theatricality of it, or not. Movies can't employ as many words as novels, and they aren't live, but they still engage us. They have that visual edge. They—but to say more here brings me to the long answer. This chapter is about the long.

Types

As I said before, the proper term for a type of movie is "genre." But genre gets me into weightier matters I don't want to do here. (Turn to chapter 10 for some psychosocial angles on genre.) For now, let's take an informal look at a few broad movie types and what they imply for drama. There are three main types of movie stories: melodrama, comedy, and tragedy.

Melodrama

Melodrama refers to a hyped-up story in which the main characters are put through hell, then they are rescued, or they rescue themselves, so that everything ends happily. *Air Force One* (1997) is this kind of movie, and so are *Double Jeopardy* (1999), *Rambo: First Blood II* (1985), *The Game* (1997), and *Fatal Attraction* (1987). You can just feel the screenwriters engineering events and inventing characters to insert at just the right time in order to work the audience into a frenzy. The directors know every trick of casting, lighting, camera angle, movement, editing, and so on to tighten the screws on the main characters—and on viewers. Despite its predictability, you keep watching melodrama. You know that you are in the kind of film where everything will turn out fine in the end. You sense that because Harrison Ford or Michael Douglas is the lead, he is going to prevail. It's all show biz, commercial, and difficult to take seriously. When critics label such movies "melodrama," they aren't giving out any compliments.

Melodrama, then, is big box office. All of the films mentioned in the last paragraph did good business. In fact, they were like small, temporary businesses unto themselves. Making money is the primary reason all the talent comes together to make the melodrama. Studio executives have no compunction about intervening to change endings they feel will displease audiences and ordering new endings to be shot. Screenwriters and directors don't object much—they knew what they were getting into when they signed on.

This happened to *Fatal Attraction*, in which an attorney (Michael Douglas) has a weekend fling with an unstable woman (Glenn Close) who later stalks him and threatens his family. The story goes to great lengths to establish that Douglas's family was close and loving; he did not stray because the marriage was in trouble. In the original screenplay, Close commits suicide by slitting her throat. She does this to set Douglas up and make it look like he had murdered her. But the wife, played by Anne Archer, finds a tape recording in which Close explains her intention to take her life. She takes the tape to the police and Douglas is finally let go.

But test-market audiences felt that this ending was too bloodless. They wanted Archer to have her vengeance. So the movie's director, Adrian Lyne, dutifully reshot the ending to have Close enter Douglas's house with a big knife, reminiscent of slasher movies. Archer ends up shooting Close, and this is the ending that was affixed to the movie when it was released in theaters. Critic Roger Ebert was harsh on the Archer-kills-Close ending. He wrote, "*Fatal Attraction* is a spellbinding psychological thriller and could have been a great movie if the filmmakers had not thrown character and plausibility to the winds in the last act to give us their version of a grown-up *Friday the 13th*."

Comedy

Most comedy is technically also melodramatic but it feels so different from the *Fatal Attraction*–type of compromised product that I discuss it separately here. It's fruitful to think of three kinds of comedy: romantic, satiric, and farcical.

Romantic Comedy

Romantic comedy features attractive young people, a few good laughs, and a plot that puts some stresses and strains on the couple before they finally fall in love or forgive each for something horrid they've done, and finally reaffirm an earlier love. The ending implies that they live happily ever after. Here are three romantic comedies that more or less follow the formula of boy wins girl, boy loses girl, boy wins girl back:

- *Singin' in the Rain* (1952). Some people call this the best romantic comedy ever made. It's also been called the greatest musical ever made. It stars Debbie Reynolds and Gene Kelly, whose love for each other is enacted against the backdrop of late 1920s Hollywood, when the industry was making the transition to synchronized sound. Basically Gene Kelly, who plays a movie star in the story, has to learn some humility and choose Debbie over selfish, ambitious Jean Hagen, a silent-era star who can't make the transition to sound because her voice sounds silly. Debbie has been dubbing her voice for Jean's in picture after picture and getting no credit for it. The main thing that drives plot, however, is *nice*. Lina (Hagen) is not nice. Gene used to be nice but he's lost that in crass Hollywood. Debbie has always been nice and always will be, Hollywood or not. The film was made during a time in U.S. history when nice counted more than anything, or the movies made us believe it did. You see where Gene has to go to win Debbie.
- *Ever After* (1998). This is the Cinderella story made to seem halfway real by a very strong feeling of social stratification. Cindy (Drew Barrymore) really is working-class; in fact, she and her family are sort of low life. They have dirty fingernails. The prince meanwhile looks down his nose at the masses. The story follows the fairy tale. Somehow the prince and Cindy, who has tootsied herself out and cleaned her fingernails, meet at a ball and fall in love. Cindy finally has to leave, but not because her chariot will turn back into a pumpkin—there isn't any magic in this film. She returns to her shabby digs because she doesn't feel she's good enough for the prince, which is believable. But the prince can't get her out of his mind, combs the realm in search of her, finds her, and overcoming his classism, marries her.

- *Honeymoon in Vegas* (1992). Nicolas Cage is trying to honor his mother's dying wish that he never marry. All the same, he and Sarah (Jessica Parker) have some kind of serious, romantic relationship going, though Nicolas hedges on actual marriage. She finally gets him to fly to Las Vegas for the wedding, but before the ceremony can take place, Nicolas loses Sarah in a high-stakes poker game. Things look pretty bleak until (1) the guy who won Sarah (James Caan) reveals himself to be dishonest, and (2) Nicolas parachutes into a casino with a troop of wannabe Elvises, which is supposed to impress Sarah. It does. They finally marry. Nutty story.

A common romantic comedy plot formula is "meet cute," that is, scriptwriters think of clever ways for the boy and girl to meet:

- *Sleepless in Seattle* (1993). Meg Ryan has gotten herself engaged, but she hears Tom Hanks on national talk radio praising the merits of his dead wife. Meg is really moved by the depth of Tom's love and just has to meet him. She goes to great lengths to track him down—in far-off Seattle. Guess what?
- *Pretty Woman.* Rich business guy Richard Gere hires a classy prostitute (Julia Roberts) to accompany him to an important business lunch. Guess what?
- *Green Card* (1990). Andie MacDowell needs a husband in order to keep her nice, rent-controlled NYC apartment; Gerard Depardieu is an alien (that is, from France) who needs a wife to avoid being deported. Guess what?

Satire
Satire pokes fun, deflates, unmasks:

- *Bob Roberts* (1992). This is a film about a folk-song singing, right-wing senatorial candidate (Tim Robbins) who fools everybody in sight. The targets of the satire are voters and the media. Robbins directed.
- *Bulworth* (1998). A senatorial candidate (Warren Beatty) gets religion and speaks (actually, raps) the truth about everything from corporate campaign financing to the way African-Americans are patronized by politicians. Beatty directed.
- *The Player.* This is a film about a Hollywood producer who is threatened by a rejected screenwriter. Along the way, Hollywood is shown as power-hungry and supercilious. Bruce Willis sort of wraps things up with a great spoof of the kind of melodrama I described above. Robert Altman directed.

Farce

Farce is over-the-top, all-stops-pulled outrageousness:

- *A Fish Called Wanda* (1988). I'll just describe one scene. Kevin Kline wants to know where stolen jewels are located, so he ties up fish-loving Michael Palin, who knows where the jewels are. Palin won't talk. Kline stuffs french fries up Palin's nose as a kind of torture. Palin still won't talk. Meanwhile an aquarium is at hand. With poor Palin looking on, Kline starts swallowing goldfish one by one. That does it.
- *Bullets Over Broadway* (1994). Sold-out playwright John Cusak is backed by a rich mob guy just so his ditzy girlfriend Jennifer Tilly will have something to act in. Bodyguard Chazz Palmenteri hangs out at rehearsals, soon takes to critiquing the play, and—improbably, delightfully—ends up rewriting and directing it himself.
- *The Man With Two Brains* (1983). This is just one of several krazee komedies krafted by Steve Martin; others include *The Jerk* (1979) and *Bowfinger* (1999). One scene: Martin, a brain surgeon, falls in love with a talking brain in a jar in a rowboat.

6.1. *The Man with Two Brains.* Steve Martin as a parody of the mad scientist. He doesn't want to rule the world; he just wants to give people screw-top craniums so they can swap brains. Warner Brothers.

Tragedy

This is a broad category of films that do not end happily. Usually the hero gets killed off, but not always; people don't always have to die for the film to end on a dire note. The movie industry doesn't make many tragedies, on the premise that the public does not want to see them. This is doubtless the truth. Tragedies tend to be made by earnest independent and foreign filmmakers beyond the Hollywood nexus. They try to reach audiences willing to deal with the demands, dramatic and intellectual, of tragedy.

The main purpose of ending a film unhappily is to make a point. The death or bad fortune of the main character underscores some issue, some truth about human nature or society—what I call a *theme* later in this chapter and in chapter 10. This advantage is largely squandered in melodrama because when the hero is let off, everyone forgets what the original point was.

Classic Tragedy

In classic tragedy, the hero is (1) highborn, (2) possessed of a fatal flaw that brings about his death, and (3) caught up in a story of high moral significance. When he falls, a lot of people go down with him—his family, maybe even an entire state. *Oedipus Rex*, by the ancient Greek Sophocles, works like this. So do *Hamlet, King Lear, Macbeth*, and *Othello*, Shakespeare's big four. Very few movies follow this classic pattern, but then neither do many American or European plays or novels of note. The fact is, classic tragedy has been in decline for centuries. Most film tragedies in the classic mode are adaptations from Greek or Elizabethan theater, such as Orson Welles's *Macbeth* (1952), George Tzavellas's *Antigone* (1962), and Kenneth Branaugh's *Hamlet* (1996).

Two films with modern stories that do feel like classic tragedy are Sidney Lumet's *Prince of the City* and Sam Raimi's *A Simple Plan* (1998). In *Prince of the City*, Treat Williams plays a New York City cop who resists ratting on his partners for some pretty minor corruption. But guilt gets the upper hand, and he finally does tell all to an investigating unit. As a result, Williams brings down everybody around him. One of his partners even commits suicide. In *A Simple Plan*, rural type Bill Paxton and a couple of friends recover a lot of money from an airplane that crashed ages ago in a remote wooded site. They decide to keep the money instead of turning it over to the authorities. But Paxton displays a certain arrogance that puts his friends off and finally leads to the unraveling of their agreed-upon story.

These films are worth seeing for the unique, agonizing tragic *tone* that finally dominates them. You feel that the main characters are headed toward disaster. Unlike melodramas, where you expect the hero always to wiggle out of any jam, characters in tragedies are doomed almost from the start. You want them to do the right thing and avert disaster. *They* want to do the right thing but cannot. You know how matters will end, but you keep watching anyway. It's probably the high moral lesson that rivets you, that and something called "catharsis," an Aristotelian term

6.2. *A Simple Plan.* An independent film, that is, one made off-Hollywood. As Hollywood grows more commercial, discerning viewers look to the independent film scene for integrity and originality. Paramount picked up this film after it was completed, thereby minimizing its creators' financial risk. Photo by Melissa Moseley.

depicting the unique, soul-cleansing sense of pity and fear that viewers feel when they experience such drama.

Film Tragedy: More Visual Than Verbal
The best film tragedies create downer moods through sight and sound instead of through words. Few films are as visual as *Citizen Kane*, which among other things is about innocence and isolation conveyed in part through images of a glass paper-weight encasing a cabin in the snow, a child's sled, smoke rising from a huge chimney, and a fence with a "No Trespassing" sign.

It's hard to forget the end of *Chinatown* (1974), which many consider to be the best noir film ever made. It's authentic tragedy, visually rendered. Detective Jack Nicholson doesn't die, but the woman he loves, Faye Dunaway, does. This happens on a dark street in Los Angeles's Chinatown. Dunaway is the desperate daughter of a corrupt real estate mogul. She's trying to keep her daughter out of his clutches. She holds off the cops with a pistol, gets her daughter into her convertible, and drives off. One of the cops gets off a shot in her direction. It's one of those gratuitous shots stupid cops do in movies; they never hit anything. But this time the convertible stops in extreme long shot and rolls ominously to a stop a block away, its horn sounding incessantly. The cops, plus Nicholson and the incestuous mogul (played by John Huston), look at each other, dumbfounded, then run to the car to discover Dunaway slumped against the horn, the cop's bullet having blasted through the back of her head, the daughter screaming.

Other film tragedies conclude with subdued visuals. At the end of *The Godfather*, Michael's wife, Kay, wants to know—really know and not be lied to—if Michael, the new godfather, ordered the assassination of his sister's husband. Michael pretends to puzzle and pretends to puzzle and finally lies and says no. Duped Kay is satisfied and leaves the room, where her husband is doing business as usual with assorted mobsters. Kay lingers in the hall. Near silence: We hear only the murmurs of the mob guys in the room in the background. Then one of the mob guys walks to the door and closes it, almost in Kay's face. That's it. That's how one of the greatest films ever made ends, undramatically, with the closing of a door. No one dies but the sense is subtly tragic—Kay's exclusion, Michael's ruthlessness.

TRY THIS

Nearly all film tragedies have points to make, something to challenge us intellectually. Accordingly, see these films and challenge yourself:

- *The Age of Innocence* (1993). Intricately structured social life among young upper-class men and women in New York circa the turn of the last century. Directed by Martin Scorsese.
- *The Seven Samurai.* Seven professional swordsman agree to help residents of a poor farming village defend themselves against marauding bandits who show up every year at harvest time. Directed by Akira Kurosawa (Japan).
- *The Oxbow Incident* (1943). A rare, tragic Western about three men whom vigilantes rush to hang for stealing cattle. Directed by William Wellman.
- *Once Were Warriors* (1994). Domestic discord among descendants of New Zealand's indigenous people, the Maori, who face problems of racial identity and dignity. Directed by Lee Tamahori (New Zealand).
- *At Play in the Fields of the Lord* (1991). Rain forest, Indians, missionaries. Directed by Hector Babenco (Brazil).
- *City of Hope* (1991). A cross section of an American city and the various factions in conflict with each other. Directed by John Sayles.
- *The Godfather, Part II* (1974). Michael, the youngest son in *The Godfather*, is now the godfather. He consolidates his position, at a price. Directed by Francis Ford Coppola.
- *A Streetcar Named Desire* (1951). A sweaty guy (Marlon Brando), a pregnant wife (Kim Hunter), and a neurotic sister-in-law (Vivien Leigh)—all jammed together in a hot New Orleans apartment. Directed by Elia Kazan.
- *Gun Crazy* (1949). She likes guns, so does he. They're on the lam. Elemental. Directed by Joseph H. Lewis.

Conflict

All stories since the beginning of time have been based on conflict—suspense, tension, disequilibrium. If a caveman came home after a day of hunting and mentioned that he ran into a saber-toothed tiger during his rounds, his fellow cavies would want to know how he came through that, which meant he'd probably have to tell them some kind of story. If he weren't much of a storyteller, he'd say, "Oh, I just hid behind a rock." But if he were in possession of some narrative skills—and some bravery—he'd say, "Well, the trouble was, the rock was like way off, and I wasn't sure I could get to it, see? I wasn't sure if I should back off or go around. Then I remembered I had that club blessed by Ortlzog in that ritual we had last week. [Ortlzog is the God of the hunt.] So I went for it." Right away the guy has created an audience—and a conflict. Will his consecrated club avail him?

Let's consider three kinds of narrative conflict: conflict of plot, conflict of character, and conflict of theme. They inhabit every story, every film, every novel, and every play ever made.

Conflict of Plot

At their simplest level, all stories have conflicts of plot. In *Titanic*, the conflict of plot is about life and death: Will the upper-class Rose and the steerage-class Jack end up together, or will they drown out there in the cold Atlantic? We know the ship finally sinks, but we want Jack (Leonardo DiCaprio) and Rose (Kate Winslet) to be together, among the survivors.

In *Enemy of the State* (1999), the flashy melodrama directed by Tony Scott, we quickly come to care about Will Smith, a lawyer who is in jeopardy. There are bad guys in the government who think Smith has a videotape that will implicate them in the assassination of a U.S. senator. Smith doesn't know what is going on except that people are trying to kill him. He runs and runs. He is monitored by all sorts of high-tech electronic devices. Dozens of experts are arrayed against him. It looks hopeless.

In *In the Line of Fire* (1993), Clint Eastwood is an aging Secret Service agent who feels guilty about not throwing his body in front of the bullet fired by Lee Harvey Oswald, a feat that would have saved the life of President John F. Kennedy back in 1963. You'd think Eastwood would get out of the Secret Service and become a bartender or something. But he sticks with it—except that now he is sixty or sixty-five, and he huffs and puffs to keep up with presidential limos. The plot is set in motion by one of those genius madmen (played by John Malkovich), who is bent on assassinating the current president during an exclusive fund-raising dinner. Clint is there too. Is he too decrepit to act fast and save the president? Stick around.

Conflict of Character

In these three films (*Titanic, Enemy of the State*, and *In the Line of Fire*), conflicts of character are usually just as interesting to discerning viewers as your big ship going down in the North Atlantic or your giggling nutcase out to off a president. We should rejoice when a movie bothers to develop characters who have interesting personal problems to work out. We ought too to appreciate the screenwriter who can blend conflict of plot with conflict of character. Damn few do.

Returning to the caveman scenario, we sense that the hunter has a personal problem: He doesn't want to come off as a wimp. How he comported himself as a man when confronted by the tiger, and how he *narrates* this, are just as important to his listeners as how he actually dealt with the long-toothed feline. In *Titanic*, Jack doesn't really have a personal problem. Screenwriter James Cameron makes Jack brave and resourceful, and he's likeable, so the audience can relate to his character. But it's Rose who has the personal problem. It isn't just that she doesn't want to marry the domineering, arrogant Cal Hockley (Billy Zane). To call off the marriage would disappoint her mother and apparently leave them penniless. This is real pressure.

Will's personal problem in *Enemy of the State* is at first pretty basic. He has to keep his wits about him and not give up—and also find out what is going on. Later in the story, he has to learn to trust ex-spy Gene Hackman. Plus, Gene has to trust Will. When you can't tell who is good or who is bad, trust does not come easily.

6.3. *Titanic.* Roles for independent women like the character of Rose descend from a distinguished line of feminist-influenced films. A sample from recent decades: *An Unmarried Woman,* 1978 (the devastation of divorce from the woman's point of view); *Private Benjamin*, 1980 (rich, spoiled brat of a girl enlists in military and discovers how she wants to be in the world); *Yentl*, 1983 (young woman refuses to be excluded from circle of male Jewish scholars); and *The Silence of the Lambs*, 1991 (young woman FBI agent stands up to intimidating serial killer). Twentieth Century Fox/Paramount.

TITANIC

In *In the Line of Fire*, Eastwood has personal problems of long duration that I have already alluded to. He feels guilty about not taking action to save President Kennedy and he's aware of his own aging. Also, he wonders if he isn't too old to attract women, namely fellow-agent Rene Russo, who is much younger than he. Screenwriter Jeff Maguire has fun with the Eastwood persona, making him something of a rube who uses crude, sexist language that at first puts Rene off.

TRY THIS

Here are five adventure films which in spite of their melodramatic story lines have characters who are more than just sticks. They are complex and face daunting personal problems. See the films and track the development of personal conflict.

- *Bullitt* (1968). San Francisco police detective doesn't think much about putting himself or others in harm's way. His girlfriend does. Directed by Peter Yates and starring Steve McQueen.
- *The Man Who Would Be King* (1975). Two Brits try to scam high priests of Himalayan kingdom out of great wealth. Directed by John Huston and starring Sean Connery and Michael Caine.
- *Dog Day Afternoon* (1975). Guy holds up a bank to get money for his friend's sex change operation, ends up having to hold employees and customers hostage for hours. Based on a true story. Directed by Sidney Lumet and starring Al Pacino.
- *Deliverance*. Four men from the city on a white-water canoeing trip. They run into a lot of trouble, from nature, from mountain folk. Directed by John Boorman and starring Burt Reynolds and Jon Voight.
- *The Silence of the Lambs* (1991). Young, green, female FBI agent is assigned to interview mass murderer to learn what he knows about another mass murderer on the loose. Directed by Jonathan Demme and starring Anthony Hopkins and Jodie Foster.

Conflict of Theme

Theme has to do with broad, overarching lessons, realities, truths. All stories have themes, even dumb ones like *Speed*—which is founded on the immutable truth that you can get killed driving too slow in Los Angeles. Often screenwriters don't even know they are infusing their stories with themes. That's okay. We'll do the infusing ourselves. We'll probe to discover ideas resident in the drama, or we'll simply read them into the story, an option I suggested in the Introduction.

How might the caveman story be processed intellectually? Arching above character is this thematic conflict: Are we really alone in the world to prevail or does survival depend on divine assistance? What kind of cave-wimps need special, sanctified clubs blessed by a god to fight big cats?

As for *Titanic*, the conflict of theme has to do with what might be called the modern woman, just emerging in 1912, whom Rose personifies. Was it possible for intelligent, willful, tuned-in young women to live independent lives in that pre–World War I era? James Cameron doubtless had this large issue in mind as he drafted the story. He had to make sure Rose lived in order to keep the theme, and its possibilities, alive.

In the Line of Fire suggests several conflicts of theme, all related to character. Here are two, which I have stated as questions:

- Do women really, really, deep down, prefer tough old chauvinists like Clint over younger, more sensitive men?
- What about aging and self-doubt? How do older men deal with it?

In *Enemy of the State*, the conflict of theme has to do with the loss of privacy in a high-tech, high-surveillance society. Writer David Marconi very cleverly rigged the story so that all forms of communication, even a pay phone at a 7-Eleven, are plugged into Central Monitoring. We can't make a move without being watched. Plus, the computer guys who watch the monitors have absolutely no feeling about what they do. They don't think twice about directing helicopters and hit men to move in on Will and kill him. Also rising to theme: The new intrusive technological society is amoral. It doesn't give a Pentium damn about us. How are we to survive in such a world?

Enemy of the State offers another important conflict of theme that blends with the conflicts of character I mentioned before: To beat the system, people have to link up, trust each other, and fight back. Will they?

Resolution

Just as every story has a conflict—several, in fact—every story has to resolve its conflicts. Resolution is the noun form. Resolution comes at the end of the story. Resolution coincides with climax, which is a much more elemental term having to do with actual drama and action. Climax: Bang, bang, the bad guy is killed, end of story. But *resolution* is more thoughtful, more intellectual, as I keep saying, more thematic, and has to do finally with idea, not just plot or character.

Assume that the caveman started putting his story together in his mind during his return to the cave. He might have had two clubs, one blessed by Ortlzog, one not. Last time out he killed a warthog with the blessed club. This time he wants to know if he can bring something down with the unblessed club. This is outrageous. He knows he's sticking his neck out—literally. He knows he's breaking the rules. He's bidding for the kind of independence of thought and action that so concerns Rose—and which makes waves. He confronts the saber tooth and takes a couple of swings with the unconsecrated club. He knocks it down. He keeps clubbing away and finishes the job. That is the climax. Tonight the clan will feast on tiger. But the resolution is grander: This thing about having to depend on a consecrated club is a crock. It's a racket the witch doctors run. In fact, maybe the whole god thing is a crock. Ooh! Blasphemous!

Titanic resolves in Rose's favor. She lives. Along with hundreds of others, she gets rescued by the passing ship *Carpathia*. She carries on. Her modern way of looking at things is the theme that comes from the resolution. It's really her story. She's the one who carries on beyond the old *belle epoch* and into the new more democratic era.

The way the *Enemy of the State* ends seems to be telling audiences that they don't have to be afraid of technology. It's pretty bad, to be sure, with all that scary monitoring going on, but if people stick together, they can finally prevail.

And as for the Clint story, Clint finally comes through, stops the assassin's bullet—he wears a bulletproof vest and comes out okay—and wins the admiration (and maybe even the love) of ball-busting Rene. Theme: Old guys still have what it takes to get the job done and appeal to younger women.

Believability

I hope you don't buy all of this. It's not for me to judge the truthfulness of these themes I've ferreted out. As viewer, that's your job. I happen to like the theme I cooked up for the caveman's story, and I also think Cameron was onto something real when he scripted *Titanic*. But to me the way the conflicts of theme resolve themselves in *Enemy of the State* and especially in *In the Line of Fire* amount to a lot of wishful thinking. As I suggested before, melodrama is usually thematically suspect. Screenwriters spin resolutions in certain directions to send audiences away happy, not necessarily to be true to themselves. See chapter 10 for more ideas about theme, along with its fellow travelers, myth and countermyth.

TRY THIS

Some films that you might look at as practice in detecting conflicts of character and theme are *Jurassic Park*, *Hook* (1991), *Sling Blade* (1996), *Thelma and Louise* (1991), *Raging Bull*, and *The Truman Show* (1998). And here are some lesser-known films whose screenwriters and directors sought, I believe, to create interesting characters and believable, important themes. Rent these for the same reason:

- *The Sweet Hereafter* (1997). Bus bearing school children skids off icy road and sinks in a lake. Some children drown. Directed by Atom Egoyan.
- *Kolya* (1996). He's middle-aged, single, and settled comfortably into his life as a musician, with a goodly supply of available women, until his ex-wife dumps a ten-year-old kid on him. This takes place in Czechoslovakia when the USSR still ran the country. Directed by Jan Severak (Czechoslovakia).

- *Nobody's Fool* (1994). An aging flake tries to make amends with his family. It could be too late. Directed by Robert Benton and starring Paul Newman.
- *The Straight Story* (1994). Improbably but delightfully, an old man rides a power lawn mower at a speed of maybe ten miles per hour for a hundred miles or so on back roads, to be with his dying brother. He hopes he can patch up some bad feelings they have for each other. Directed by David Lynch and starring Richard Farnsworth.
- *Platoon* (1986). Vietnam. A good sergeant, a bad sergeant, and a private caught in the middle. Directed by Oliver Stone, starring Willem Dafoe, Tom Berenger, and Charlie Sheen.
- *Wall Street* (1988). Wall Street. A greedy father figure, a more down-to-earth father, and an ambitious son who has a lot to learn. Directed by Oliver Stone, starring Michael Douglas, Martin Sheen, and Charlie Sheen.

Point of View

We considered point of view in chapter 4 as a basic editing procedure that shows how movie characters react to things they can see going on. Now we return to the topic in a much broader, narrative sense. Basically, there are two ways to tell film stories, from multiple points of view or from single points of view. Each approach has tremendous implications for drama.

Multiple Points of View

Most films are told from omniscient or multiple points of view. "Omniscient" means that the writer is all-knowing, like a god. She can deliver us back and forth from the point of view of this or that individual or group to the point of view of another individual or group. The writer utilizes the shifts in points of view to slip in information vital to the telling of the story and the building of drama.

For example, the point of view of *The Fugitive* keeps shifting from that of Harrison Ford, wrongly accused of murdering his wife and on the run, to that of Tommy Lee Jones, the marshal who relentlessly pursues him, and back again. Ford, Jones, Ford, Jones, back and forth. When we view events through Ford's point of view, we naturally share his confusion, but, as he pokes around Chicago's Cook County Hospital, we also participate in the important discoveries he makes regarding who actually killed his wife and for what reason. The story takes us just so far within Ford's sensibility, then it cuts to Jones and his crew and their sensibilities. The more Jones learns about Ford's whereabouts, the more we fear for Ford. But the more Ford discovers, the more we realize that he is closer to solving the crime and exonerating himself. The shifting point of view also develops Jones's gradual awareness of Ford's innocence. It matters when these points of view change. Cut too soon and not enough information is conveyed. Cut too late and the scene grows slack. Point of view then is an important narrative device for cranking up the drama.

6.4. *The Fugitive.* Dramatic plotting. Harrison is doubly vexed; not only does he have to elude Tommy Lee Jones and his team, he has to solve the crime of who murdered his wife. Photo by Steven Vaughan. Warner Brothers.

Occasionally we are placed in the point of view of Jeroen Krabbe, the evil doctor who is behind the murder. But Krabbe doesn't seem guilty or evasive in these scenes. Indeed, he seems like a nice guy, a good friend to Ford. This is clever writing. Screenwriters Jeb Stuart and David Twohy don't reveal any more than they have to about Krabbe until near the end. The story comes down to the climactic hotel laundry-room scene where Ford, Jones, and Krabbe are all present. All points of view converge. By this time Ford knows Krabbe is the perpetrator, and so does Jones. All that remains is the traditional *mano a mano* (hand-to-hand visceral release) that is formula thriller. So Ford whacks Krabbe with a pipe. Everyone in the audience feels pretty good about that. He had the right.

Thelma and Louise, written by Callie Khouri, works the same way. Khouri alternates between the point of view of Thelma and Louise, who actually become radicalized against men during their daring escape, and the point of view of Harvey Keitel and the FBI agents he works with in hot pursuit of the women. It's a clever shifting of points of view. Just as Thelma and Louise inch toward their extreme feminist position, we cut to Keitel, the redeeming male figure, and his awareness of the unfairness the woman confront. Back and forth, a delicate balance.

It's the same for romance. In *You've Got Mail*, we spend a few minutes with Tom Hanks, a few minutes with Meg Ryan—Tom, Meg, Tom, Meg. When we are with Tom, we get his perception of Meg, always wrong; and when we are with Meg, we get her perception of Tom, also wrong. This is the entire source of the humor and the drama. They are all wrong about each other until nearly the end of the film, when the plot untangles, they discover who they really are and who they are to each other, somehow falling in love in spite of everything.

Only the audience knows the big picture. The audience stays ahead of Jones in *The Fugitive* and Tom and Meg in *You've Got Mail*. We take pleasure in knowing we are three steps ahead of most characters, but we also want the characters to finally acquire ampler points of view. They almost always do.

The conflicts of themes of two films with enormous reputations are based not only on multiple points of view but on conflicting points of view. *Rashomon* (1950), the Japanese masterpiece written by Shinobu Hashimoto and directed by Akira Kurosawa, amounts to four accounts of a rape and murder. The accounts don't at all agree with each other. The theme of the film finally comes down to this: We structure reality to suit us. Perception of reality is self-serving. In *Citizen Kane*, a reporter interviews six people to find out what the gazillionaire meant when he uttered "rosebud" on his death bed. No one close to him knows. But the inquiry gives the interviewees an opportunity to say what they think about the controversial Kane. Each person has a different assessment. Some have affectionate memories, some bitter. Some take the long the view, some the short. The various points of view remind you of the old parable about the blind men who feel an elephant to discover its essence. One feels the elephant's trunk and reports that the animal is very much like a snake; another feels the elephant's leg and is quite sure the elephant is much like a tree trunk; and so on. None then has the full view of the elephant. Reality based on limited knowledge distorts or is unknowable. *Citizen Kane* says this too.

Single Points of View

However, there are times when drama in film storytelling is enhanced by keeping the point of view limited to a single character. Screenwriters do this when the plot turns on withholding information from a main character and, correspondingly, from viewers. For example, Jack Nicholson, the detective in *Chinatown*, is present in every scene of the film. There are no scenes without Nicholson. We do not cut to villain John Huston to see what he is doing, and we don't share in any information that cutting to Huston might yield. We are never ahead of Nicholson. There are times when he is ahead of us, and we have to do some quick thinking to catch up. There is truth to be discovered both by Nicholson and by ourselves as viewers. The discovery of truth provides the story with drama. Finally, at the end of the film, the truth comes out for all of us.

Chinatown is what I often call a metaphysical film, meaning the whole thrust of the narrative is to discover what is real. For most of the film, no one, viewer or main character, can tell what is going on. This is probably the best *thematic* reason for basing a story on a single point of view. *The Conversation*, which also appeared in 1974, is similarly structured around a single, relentless point of view, that of Gene Hackman, a surveillance expert. Hackman tries to remain neutral when he tape records a conversation with murderous overtones. Later, his conscience bothers him. There are many other people in the film but the story never shifts to them. If it did, the drama would deflate.

A much underrated film called *Mike's Murder* (1984) is told from the point of view of Debra Winger, who can't figure out why Mike, the tennis instructor she had fallen in love with, was murdered. The story takes place in West Los Angeles, which director James Bridges renders as corrupted by power and money. Poor Debra is only a naïve bank teller. She is out of her league in plunging after Mike's murderer. Mike was worldly, mixed up with drugs, and kept company with shady people. Before long, Debra discovers more than she wants to know. Unseen murderers go after her. We never do come face to face with them, which leaves one with the strong impression that director Bridges meant the murderers to represent evil itself.

Another reason for keeping point of view limited is to make the main character seem distant, larger than life, maybe even mythical. Thus a minor character tells the story and the main character is purposely kept in the background. This is the method of *The Great Gatsby*, both novel and film. The novel, written in 1925 by F. Scott Fitzgerald, occupies a large place in American letters. The movie (1974) isn't as great as the novel, but it's respectable. It stars Robert Redford as the mysterious Jay Gatsby, a self-made millionaire doomed to love a rich and classy twit of a woman (Mia Farrow). The story comes down to Gatsby's death. It is told, however, not from Gatsby's point of view but through the eyes of Nick (played by Sam Waterston), a young man who happens to live next door to Gatsby. Nick floats in and out of Gatsby's life, is fascinated by him, and narrates what he can to us, but his distance and lack of knowledge have the effect of keeping Gatsby appealingly vague.

Two films with wrenching shifts in points of view are Alfred Hitchcock's *Vertigo* and David Mamet's *House of Games*. Both are based on scams. In *Vertigo*, James Stewart is set up to believe that the soul of a beautiful woman (Kim Novak) has been taken over by a woman long dead. Kim acts strangely. She visits a museum and gazes at a portrait of the dead woman. She turns up at the woman's grave. She is moody and distracted. When she jumps into the San Francisco Bay, Jimmy is there to rescue her. He then falls in love with her and does everything he can to bring her back to what he thinks is reality. The story is too complex to summarize here. The main thing is the fine supernatural tone Hitchcock creates, which runs through nearly the whole film. Then Jimmy catches on to the scam, and the mood suddenly changes. Also, the point of view shifts to Kim for a few scenes. You feel like you have been kicked in the ribs. You thought you were in one kind of movie, then you find yourself in something else. This, too, is a metaphysical film in which point of view is the grand setup.

In *House of Games*, a wealthy, prominent psychologist named Margaret Ford (played by Lindsay Crouse) is scammed out of a lot of money in an elaborate scenario involving a half-dozen men. Actually, she fancies the world of grifters more than is good for her, and the scammers know this and exploit her for it. For most of the movie she thinks she is just a kind of observer of another scam, when really she is getting sucked into being scammed herself. So far, the story has been told strictly from the psychologist's point of view, which also has the effect of keeping the viewer in the dark. The story never cuts to the scammers without Dr. Ford's being present. But after a time Dr. Ford starts to doubt. She enters the back door of The House of Games, the bar where everything started. Mamet is careful to keep the point of view—the cinematic point of view—limited to what the psychologist sees and hears. And what she sees and hears are the men seated at a table, divvying up the money they got from her and congratulating each other on their cleverness. It's a wrenching moment. And Dr. Ford feels raped, morally and mentally.

Cinematics and Drama

We return now to cinematics to gain a feel for the effects of cinematography, editing, and sound on film drama. (In fact, all of these chapters about story will end with a consideration of how motion picture sight and sound have a bearing on our understanding and enjoyment of the film story.) First, let's look at how cinematics helped build drama in the three films we considered earlier.

The Boat Goes Down (*Titanic*)

Cameron combines live action, real people, studio mock-ups, and computer effects to get the stern of the great boat finally pointing straight up and down as it sinks in the Atlantic. It's the verticality that so impresses, terrifies, and saddens, for hundreds of people still on deck just have nothing to hang on to. They fall, not always into the water but onto railings, posts, cleats, vents, doors, and bulkheads. All this is done in respectful extreme long shot. When a body hits something solid, there is the softest of thuds. Cameron wants you to see this melancholy sight, but he doesn't want to overplay it. It's awful enough as it is. By keeping the shots wide and the sad events rather distant, he purposely mitigates the drama while inviting you to contemplate the tragedy.

The only tight shots are of Rose and Jack clinging to the railing at the very end of the ship's stern, the same railing from which Rose nearly leaped to end her life earlier in the story. Jack keeps his head, instructing Rose to take a deep breath and hold his hand tight. The ship finally goes under; cut to underwater shots, flailing bodies, muffled sound, Rose and Jack kicking. They get separated; then Rose surfaces in medium shot. No sign of Jack. A panicky man splashes to Rose and hangs onto her like a buoy, pushing her head underwater. Cut to Rose underwater, kicking, wide-eyed. Cut to surface, man still using her submerged head as a buoy. Then cut to Jack, not far away. He swims to the man and slugs him off. Rose surfaces,

6.5. *Titanic.* This was the most expensive film ever made, eating up over $200 million, but the money was generally well spent. Most of it went into worthy special effects like this one, instead of the mindless gimmicks of other, much overpriced, Hollywood products. Twentieth Century Fox/Paramount.

and they embrace, dog-paddling. The camera then pulls away for an extreme wide-angle shot that shows hundreds of people bobbing in the water. This shot is reminiscent of the great pull-away shot in *Gone With the Wind* (1939), when a confused Scarlett O'Hara beholds the many casualties of the Battle of Atlanta strewn across the city square. (See chapter 1 for production still.)

Near the very end of *Titanic*, Rose, age 101, gets a moment to herself on Brock Lovett's ship. She walks to the stern and takes something from her pocket. It's the "Heart of the Ocean," the big jewel Hockley (her fiancé) gave her back in 1912. We have lost track of the jewel. Then the film cuts to Rose, age 18, on the *Titanic*, her fear mounting, the ship sinking. She reaches in her coat pocket and discovers the jewel for the first time. Hockley had put it there, thinking that Rose would survive the disaster. Now, in the present, Rose drops the jewel into the ocean. This is nice editing, even if the symbolism is a bit contrived. It's also pure cinematics: communication through images and the editing of images. Later, the elderly Rose goes to bed. Having unloaded the jewel, she seems relieved and at peace. The camera pans away from her in sleep to the framed photographs she insisted on bringing. At last we see what kind of life Rose has made for herself apart from Hockley. Not for her was the life of leisure. Instead, we see her in the photos as a horsewoman, a fisher-woman (with a really big fish), and an aviatrix—action and independence. The photos at once resolve the conflicts of character and theme.

Some viewers might find the photos a contrivance. But photos are often used in films to convey information about the past—photos and newspaper clippings. They have become a respectable cinematic convention or a lazy screenwriter's fall-back, depending on your point of view. The trick is to insert them naturally into the story. Someone searches an office for information and notices photos set out on a desk or finds a scrapbook with clippings. Much is gleaned from such photos and clippings; their presence in such scenes is believable. But why would a 101-year-old woman want to pack a clutch of framed photos for an ocean trip?

The Great Chase (*Enemy of the State*)

I have nothing but superlatives for the chase in the middle of *Enemy of the State*. It's one of the most visual, most cinematic, and most meaningful of all movie chases. Like many movie chases, it's a metaphor. It stands for: You can't get away, superior forces are arrayed against you, you are alone. You are completely dependent on your wits to survive. The chase is a test of character. You don't give up. It's a matter of principle.

Movie chases also provide opportunities for ever-changing *mise-en-scènes* and settings. For this alone they are fun to watch. Will's chase starts in a hotel room.

6.6. *Enemy of the State*. Run, Will, Run (Will Smith, that is). In film, the chase is a grand, cin-ematic metaphor for real-life hounding—by an ex-husband, by the IRS, by whatever. Photo by Linda R. Chen. Buena Vista.

The bad feds come down the hall with guns. This is serious. Will goes out the window. He's way up there, ten or twelve stories. He leaps from balcony to balcony (actually, a stunt man did the leaping). He ends up on the street, running, running. But he is monitored by a satellite in space—a new twist in the literature of movie chases. The satellite beams signals back to a van where bad computer feds interpret the signals and radio orders to a bad SWAT team in black helicopters. Next Will is in a car tunnel. The bad SWAT guys are still right behind him. Where can he go? He drops into a sewer, then bobs up again in the middle of a lane of fast traffic. Meanwhile a tunnel technician who is also plugged into the all-seeing, Big-Brother surveillance system monitors Will's progress with video cameras and reports to the bad computer feds. This is big-time paranoia—that is to say, much of the film's premise has to do with that feeling we get every now and then that every one is against us. The visuals are striking. Tony Scott uses a lot of low angles, tilts, big jerky full-screen close-ups of Will's face in utter terror, large blotches of bright yellow and orange, lots of telephoto photography that blurs backgrounds, plus abstracted computer images of Will's progress red-dotting down alleys, plus cutaways to the satellite relentlessly beep-beeping, plus fast cutting, plus just the right mix-in of dramatic music. But let's give even more credit to editor Chris Lebenzon and sound designer Tom Myers for putting this all together.

Clint Figures it Out (*In the Line of Fire*)

Just before the climax of *In the Line of Fire*, there is a classic example of crosscutting that explains how Clint figures out that Malkovich is present at the presidential fund-raising dinner and will soon draw his gun on the president. The sequence consists of three lines of action: (1) Malkovich putting his plastic gun together under his table (it had to be plastic to get by the metal detectors); (2) Clint scanning, scanning, scanning the assembled diners, hoping to spot Malkovich behind a disguise; and (3) The president making his way to the podium to deliver a speech, pausing on the way to shake supporters' hands. Also cut in are shots of Clint looking down at a table seating chart trying to figure out if one of the names might be the altered name of Malkovich. The cutting gets faster and faster. Clint, Malkovich, president. Clint, Malkovich, president. ClintMalkovichpresident. At last Clint figures it out: He spots a guy who could be Malkovich in disguise and matches him to a name on the seating chart. But Malkovich is already on his feet, aiming his plastic gun at the president. Clint has only one choice, to throw his body in the line of fire, as I said before, which he does laterally and in slow motion. Anne V. Coates was the editor of *In the Line of Fire*.

So it's all over. Clint and Rene sit on the steps of the Lincoln Memorial in Washington, D.C. The shot is from behind them as we see the reflecting pools in the midground. Clint and Rene cuddle and coo. It's obvious she likes him, admires his courage, and appreciates his intelligence and resourcefulness. But is Clint too old to cut it with Rene? The backdrop provides resolution. For beyond the pools,

6.7. *In the Line of Fire*. René Russo and Clind Eastwood. Conflict of character soon to be resolved.

in the exact center of the frame, the Washington Monument looms proud. Get the picture?

 TRY THIS

Here are some thrillers with exciting cinematics. Check them out. Follow the tricks of photography, editing, and sound that contribute to drama.

- *Badlands*. Guy kills and robs, his girl goes along with him. Because of the unique treatment of this familiar plot, the result is an art film. They hightail it across the flat Dakotas toward a mountain that never gets any bigger. Directed by Terrence Malick and starring Martin Sheen and Sissy Spacek.
- *Charade* (1963). Probably the classiest thriller ever made. Feels like Hitchcock. Set in Paris. Man of many identities helps woman recover fortune stolen from dead husband. Great sequence in promenade with Cary Grant and Walter Matthau hiding behind huge pillars, trying to shoot each other, and distraught Audrey Hepburn out in the open, not knowing whom to believe. Also a love story—but aren't they all? Directed by Stanley Donen.
- *Cliffhanger* (1993). This is an up-and-down thriller based on a mountain rescue plot and some really bad guys who try to get a climbing expert to take the plunge. We don't get many thrillers based on up and down. Directed by Renny Harlin and starring Sylvester Stallone.

- *Patriot Games* (1992). Ex-CIA agent gets mixed up with an Irish terrorist plot. Main terrorist then takes revenge by attacking ex-agent's home and family. Pay attention to the London murder-kidnapping scene in which Harrison Ford gets involved. It's superbly shot and edited. Directed by Phillip Noyce.

6.8. *The Graduate.* Drama cinematically resolved by movement, costuming, and facial expression. Dustin Hoffman reaches the church after the marriage ceremony is over. No big deal. He snatches Katharine Ross away from all the straight people in the church and locks them inside with, appropriately, a cross (seen in the background). Embassy Pictures.

chapter seven

Characters

C ertainly one main reason we go to the movies or rent a tape is to follow the lives of some interesting fictional characters. If the characters in the movie are played by stars we happen to like, that's even better. Stars or not, if the characters turn out to be boring or unbelievable, we are disappointed. On the other hand, if the characters are unique and capture our imagination, maybe we don't require such a slam-bang story. The uniqueness of the characters somehow drives the story and makes it interesting. When this happens, which is not often, we feel we've gotten our money's worth and then some.

It happens in *Forrest Gump*, in which character is everything. The role of the title created by Tom Hanks *is* the story. On the other hand, in high-concept action movies like *Independence Day* (1996), character matters far less. What viewers probably remember most about that movie is the shadow of a colossal alien spacecraft creeping across the land and the blowing up of the White House. They probably don't remember—or don't want to remember—the comic-strippiness of the characters: Bill Pullman as the U.S. president who happens to be a decorated jet fighter-pilot. He saves Earth by flying computer whiz Jeff Goldblum into the guts of the alien mother ship so that he can upload something that explodes—after Bill and Jeff have safely rocketed away, of course. But we don't want to be too hard on movies like this: We see them not to ponder the human condition, but to marvel at special effects.

Characterization in most movies falls somewhere between the extremes of the originality of *Forrest Gump* and the cartoonishness of President Whatshisname, the jet pilot. This chapter covers a lot of that ground.

Main Characters

Every movie story has at least one main character, and sometimes more than one. Often the title of the story names the main character—*Bambi* (1942), *Barton Fink*, *Batman*. The story's climax or resolution is all about the main character. He or she survives, prevails, or loses everything. It is the main character who risks the most, strives the hardest, and touches us the deepest.

Some stories have two main characters: funny sidekicks Stan Laurel and Oliver Hardy in *Way Out West* (1937), Annie and Bart on the run in *Gun Crazy*, immigrant lovers Tom Cruise and Nicole Kidman in *Far and Away* (1991). All films with two names in their titles also have a pair of main characters: *Bonnie and Clyde*, *Oscar and Lucinda* (1997), *Thelma and Louise*. In *Star Wars*, Luke, Han, and Princess Leia could all be considered co-main characters, though Luke might have a slight edge. It's probably his story more than the others'. The main character of a movie is the person whom the story is most about. The whole plot turns on him.

Protagonists and Antagonists

Protagonists are the proverbial good guys in movies. We sympathize with protagonists and wish them well. We want them to prevail. Opposed to protagonists are *antagonists*, who are the perennial bad guys. Audience affection does not go out to them. In most movies, especially ordinary ones, protagonists are main characters, while antagonists tend to be secondary characters (with secondary billing). As you probably sense, protagonists and antagonists are constantly struggling with each other.

Mel Gibson is the main character and protagonist of *Braveheart* (1995). We want his rebellion against the antagonist tyrant King Edward I to succeed. Keanu Reeves is the main character and the protagonist of *Speed*, and we want him to dispatch madman Dennis Hopper and thereby save Sandra Bullock and the Los Angeles transit system. James Stewart is the main character and protagonist of *It's a Wonderful Life*. We want him to resist the meanie of Bedford Falls, Mr. Potter, and thereby save the town for tract houses, which Stewart's loan company will conveniently finance.

Psychologist Sydney Harriet feels that the reason so many novels and movies divide the world into sharply delineated good guys and bad guys is that this is pretty much what we do in our everyday lives. He points out that "We tend to see the world in black and white, up and down, us and them, Giants and Dodgers, Fords and Chevrolets, Macs and PCs, inner city and suburbs, good and evil, saint and sinner, nice guy and jerk, Madonna and whore." Screenwriters know this and exploit our need to structure the world by these binary oppositions.

There is nothing wrong with making movies with such simplistically polar-opposite characters, nor should moviegoers feel guilty for enjoying movies with clear-cut protagonists and antagonists. Though we know that people in the real world are a mix of good and bad, we never tire of seeing a movie like *Back to the*

7.1. *Braveheart.* This movie is more satisfying than most historical fare, partly because the role of William Wallace, played by Mel Gibson, has some depth to it. The movie took a couple of Oscars. Photo by Andrew Cooper. Icon-Ladd.

Future (1985) so that we can root for good guy Marty McFly in his across-the-decades struggle with the brutish Biff.

Clear-cut good guys and bad guys make for fun viewing. But it's also satisfying to see a movie with characters who are more psychologically complex and maybe more lifelike than your stock heroes and villains. For example: A pair of highly-respected Chinese films, *Raise the Red Lantern* (1991) and *Xiu, Xiu, The Sent-Down Girl* (1998), feature young women who are not exactly goody-goody. In the first film, Songlian (Gong Li) is a beautiful but unhappy concubine who is cruel to her servants and is responsible for the execution of an older concubine. In the latter, Xiu Xiu (Lu Lu) is a city girl whom the communist government has sent out to the countryside to learn horse wrangling from a lonely but kindly eunuch. She is mean to the eunuch and sleeps with any passing man she thinks can help her get home. Yet Songlian and Xiu Xiu are not bad, not antagonists. We manage to sympathize with them despite their faults. They seem real. We wish them well. Unlike Hollywood screenwriters, the creators of these characters do not ask that we like them, only that we understand their plights.

Most film critics and discerning viewers value complexity of character. Probably much of the appeal of Clint Eastwood is the complexity of some of the roles he has played. In his *Dirty Harry* films, Eastwood, though certainly meant to be a protagonist, also comes off as something of a fascist who takes the law into his

7.2. *Enemy of the State.* Barry Pepper, left, has the kind of chiseled looks and crisp moves that directors like for secondary roles that must be established in seconds. He was one of the bad feds in this film, but he was the good sniper in *Saving Private Ryan*, kissing his crucifix to aim true. Photo by Linda R. Chen. Buena Vista.

own hands. Good guys aren't supposed to do this, but since he's after people, or "punks," even worse than himself, some of us give him permission to be dirty. But others of us do not. Dirty Harry, then, provokes discussion about means and ends. Few film characters do that.

The original *Dirty Harry* (1971), directed by Don Siegel, succeeded in getting some psychological as well as ideological complexity into Harry's persona. Harry may be the way he is in part because he is sexually repressed and in even larger part because of court rulings in the late 1960s and early 1970s that seemed to favor criminals over victims. In this sense Harry isn't just your standard screen fascist. He stands for much more and ends up a protagonist with social and political resonance. Much the same can be said for Sylvester Stallone's portrayal of John Rambo, especially in *Rambo: First Blood II*. These characters may be reprehensible and even laughable at times, but at least they provoke discussion. No one ever discussed whether the Biff character in *Back to the Future* stood for anything. He simply is what he is.

Round and Flat Characters

"Round character" is a term borrowed from literary criticism. A round character strikes viewers as three-dimensional, filled-out, realistic, surprising, lifelike, multi-faceted, even appealingly inscrutable. The opposite of "round" is "flat"—two-dimensional, cutout figures who usually are not interesting to watch for any length of time.

There are lots of flat characters in movies, but few round ones. If you see nothing but hyped-up thrillers, adventure yarns, and romantic comedies, you will not see many round characters at the movies. To experience roundness of character, you have to see unique films like the following:

- *Raging Bull*, which is about a boxer who abuses his wife and goes crazy when he suspects his brother of having sex with her.
- *Vagabond* (1985), a French film about a homeless, drifting woman who lives by a tough survivalist ethic.
- *Nights of Cabiria*, the recently rereleased masterpiece about a streetwalker who, despite being dumped on all her life, pathetically still has faith in a better tomorrow.

A round character may be more complicated than your best friend is when she is in the middle of a divorce. The life of the fictional film director Guido Anselmi, played by the great Italian actor Marcello Mastroianni, is the focus of Federico Fellini's *8½*. Guido's life is layered with so many aspects of past and present, good and bad, that few viewers can say with certainty that they really understand him. At the same time, they appreciate repeated viewings of a film like this in order to understand the character better.

One of the most round and compelling characters in recent films is Johnny in Mike Leigh's *Naked* (1993), played by David Thewlis. Film critic Desson Howe warns that "not everyone will enjoy *Naked*, an uncompromising film about the war between the sexes and the bleakness of existence." Johnny is dirty of garment, smelly of body, and foul of mouth, and he treats women terribly, but it's his incredible intelligence and wide-ranging philosophical view of things that make him such an interesting character. Here is how Johnny responds to an innocent question:

LOUISE: How did you get here?

JOHNNY: Well, basically, there was this little dot, right? And the dot went bang and the bang exploded. Energy formed into matter, matter cooled, matter lived, the amoeba to fish, fish to fowl, fowl to frog, frog to mammal, the mammal to monkey, to monkey to man, *amo amas amat, quid pro quo, momento mori, ad infinitum*, sprinkle on a little bit of grated cheese and leave under the grill 'til Doomsday.

See a film that promises to be rich in character. You might choose one of the films mentioned above, or you might be able to glean this by reading the blurb on the video box. Note complexity/originality/roundness in its characters. Ask yourself: What makes these characters so refreshing? How are they hard to understand? What about their being hard to understand makes for interesting, challenging viewing?

Thematic Characters

As we saw in the last chapter, some films are driven by *themes*, which are the underlying messages or truths of stories. However, some film themes are not so underlying. They appear on the surface of the narratives for all to see, and they are embodied in the pronouncements and actions of main characters. Such a character is Jefferson Smith, the greenhorn U.S. senator in *Mr. Smith Goes to Washington*. The theme of this entertaining Frank Capra movie from 1939 has to do with the classic conflict between government for the public good and government for self-serving special interests. Smith, who embraces a Boy Scout idealism about government (he was, in fact, a kind of Scout troop master) is on the side of the public good and defeats corrupt forces through sheer will, endurance, and energetic standing up for the rights of the people—literally, as he filibusters on his feet for days. No one misses the theme of the film, and no one fails to see how the Smith character embodies it.

Other films like this include the following:

- *Boyz N the Hood* (1991), with Larry Fishburne as a father struggling to protect his teenaged son against ghetto violence.
- *Dances with Wolves*, in which Director Kevin Costner plays a nineteenth-century Army officer who lives with Native Americans and comes to stand for the theme of respect for indigenous cultures.
- *Born on the Fourth of July* (1989), the essential anti–Vietnam War film with Tom Cruise in the heavily thematic role of Ron Kovic, the paraplegic vet whom the government has abandoned.

Mythic Characters

Related to characters who embody important themes in films are characters who stand for abiding cultural myths that society, or culture, just naturally transmits. Whether these myths are false or true is not really the issue. Instead it's the way these myths find their way into film stories on an instinctual level and often suffuse the lives of the characters, much as thematic characters embody themes.

The Rocky character patented by Sylvester Stallone embodies the myth of the underdog. We love this myth. We love it as much in the world of boxing as we loved it as children when our mothers read us "The Tortoise and the Hare." To root for the underdog is as American as roast beef on Sunday afternoon at Grandma's. What's more, underdogs always prevail in our mythology. The meek inherit the earth. They try harder. Favorites get arrogant and let down their guard, and then underdogs sneak up on them. So we pretty much know that Rocky is going to come out of his fight with champ Apollo Creed with great dignity, and he does. Stallone, who wrote and directed the first *Rocky*, must have sensed somehow that he was tapping into the deep feelings viewers bring to the movie.

Much of the popularity of Capra's *It's a Wonderful Life* is based on myths about the American small town. These myths conflict. On the one hand there is what I call a countermyth about small towns: They restrict you, they keep you down. People in small towns cannot be all they can be. Thus, as we noted in chapter 1, the George Bailey character played by James Stewart wants to get out of Bedford Falls and go away to college to become an engineer. But the family business keeps him in Bedford Falls. Things look bad when George's Uncle Billie misplaces a lot of money that could result in the family business's being taken over by the town's rich old codger, Potter. But guess what? True to another myth of small towns, all of George's friends come through for him and collect enough money to keep the business out of Potter's hands. This myth is positive and uplifting: People in small towns care about each other and help each other out. George, who considered taking his own life over the money thing, regains his faith in life itself. He becomes the embodiment of the grandest myth of all, that life is worth living.

Many myths are not just regional or national. They are global—or what is called "archetypal"—because human beings everywhere share them in a kind of genetic way. One such worldwide myth is the Cinderella myth. This rags-to-riches story is echoed in *The Scent of Green Papaya* (1993), a film made by Hung Tran Anh. It tells the story of a humble girl, Mui, who comes to live as a housekeeper with a wealthy, though troubled, Saigon family. Her connections with the family result in her meeting Khuyen, a writer who is well-to-do, tasteful, and kind. Soon they fall in love and are married.

Epic Characters

An epic is a novel or a movie that sweeps up a big chunk of the history of a people, together with their hopes, dreams, and fears. It's like myth, only more historical and more directly connected to the particular consciousness of nations. By far the epic movie best known to viewers is the durable *Gone With the Wind*, a story that straddles the Civil War, told from the South's point of view. On one side is the antebellum South, portrayed as a gracious, aristocratic society too naïve for its good; on the other side is the post-war South, sadder but wiser, less aristocratic but a good deal more practical. Several characters embody these epic qualities. Leslie Howard as the kindly Ashley Wilkes and Olivia De Havilland as the forbearing Melanie Hamilton represent everything sublime about the Old South. Meanwhile

Scarlett O'Hara (Vivien Leigh) undergoes important changes with epic significance. Before the war she is charmingly irresponsible, self-centered, and mainly out of touch; after the war, she displays a shrewd business sense and singleness of purpose that captures the spirit of the South's rebuilding itself.

Films with heavy doses of theme, myth, and epic often make for good viewing, but to some viewers their main characters fall short of being round, if roundness is a virtue in film characterization. They don't often surprise us or seem to have lives of their own. Usually, though, viewers don't care. They know what kind of film they are in for and enjoy it for what it is. Character comes in second.

Characters Who Change for the Better

Some of the most compelling characters in film undergo important changes in values and outlook, and these changes often benefit not only the characters themselves but their larger societies. We admire such characters because we realize how difficult it is for adults settled in their ways to change.

In Steven Spielberg's *Schindler's List*, the main character, German industrialist Oskar Schindler (Liam Neeson), starts out a morally shady character. As World War II rages, he gets the idea of opening a porcelain factory using Jewish slaves as labor. Since he doesn't have to pay these workers, he stands to make a lot of money. But about a third of the way through the film, Schindler has an amazing change of heart and realizes the awful crime against the Jewish people that he is perpetrating. He then uses his power and authority to fool high-ranking military officers and government officials, saving several thousand Jews from the gas chambers.

Schindler's story is one of personal redemption. And so is the story of Terry Malloy, the young longshoreman of Elia Kazan's *On the Waterfront*. Terry, a discredited boxer who is a favorite with the local waterfront mob, is implicated in the death of a fellow dock worker. He goes back and forth in his conscience between staying "D and D"—that is, deaf and dumb about the murder—and doing the right thing, which is to testify against the mob at the crime hearings. When he finally does testify, he saves the wider waterfront society as well as his soul.

Characters Who Change for the Worse

The endlessly fecund *Citizen Kane* tells the story of a man whose life traces the self-corrupting effects of money and power. Charlie Kane, who came into a fortune young in life, buys a failing New York newspaper and makes it profitable. At first, he wants to use the newspaper to run stories on the side of the oppressed and to break industrial trusts in the tradition of turn-of-the-century political progressives. But as he ages, his interest in the poor, always paternalistic at best, wanes as he becomes obsessed with the uses of his own considerable influence. He buys shiploads of European sculptures and paintings with no real feeling for their artistic worth. He builds an opera house for his wife, Susan, a mediocre singer, and forces her to pursue her "career" long after the press has humiliated her. He finally

7.3. *Schindler's List.* You see this typewriter a lot in this film. It's more than a prop, it's what in film lingo is called an *icon*, or sacred object. The more accountant Ben Kingsley works at it, the more Jews will be saved. Photo by David James. Universal.

builds an enormous castle to his ego and takes Susan there, where the two grow more distant in sitting rooms the size of basketball courts. Weary of his manipulation, Susan finally leaves him, and Kane later dies, a bitter, broken, and baffled man for whom, in the end, wealth and power come to nothing.

Honored nearly as much as *Citizen Kane* are *The Godfather* and *The Godfather, Part II*, which together also profile the life of a powerful figure made tragic by his own excesses. The character of Michael Corleone has something of Kane's youthful idealism and dedication to do right. At the long wedding scene that opens the first film, the fresh-faced Michael tells his fiancée Kay the story of how his father, a Mafia godfather, once secured a signature by making the signer "an offer he couldn't refuse"—namely, the contract would bear either ink or blood. Michael then tells Kay, "That's not me. That's my family." But later on, Michael, the youngest of three brothers, displays such shrewdness and courage that he eventually ascends to the position of godfather himself. In *Part II*, Michael becomes obsessed with total control and revenge and goes so far to get it as to engineer the deaths of two people very close to him.

Good Characters under Pressure to Change

Some characters in films refuse to change in the face of the pressure aimed at getting them to change. The screenwriter has no intention of engineering their change; in fact, their constancy is usually a large part of the point of the film. Julia Roberts plays the title role in *Erin Brokovich* (2000). She's a mouthy, miniskirt-wearing woman with wild hair who works in a law office and is under considerable pressure to dress more conservatively and moderate her language. But it's her self-confidence and tenacity that lead her to dig up a lot of bad stuff about a big power company. She convinces her easygoing boss, played by Albert Finney, to set everything aside and represent hundreds of people whom the power company has made ill. Eventually, prodding Finney and a new partner every step of the way, Erin sees the case all the way through to a favorable ruling.

In *The Nasty Girl* (1990), a German film directed by Michael Verhoeven, a schoolgirl played by Lena Stolze accidentally discovers some information that clearly implicates her Bavarian community in some Nazi-era wrongdoing. When later she threatens to publish her findings, the city fathers become edgy and pressure the girl, now a woman, to abandon her research. But the woman perseveres, resists the pressure, and finally gets the town to acknowledge its past crimes.

But these are easy calls. The screenwriters engineer matters so that we just know that Julia and Lena are doing the right thing. *Leaving Las Vegas* (1995), the Nicolas Cage comeback vehicle directed by Mike Figgis, is much more problematic. Cage is a hopeless alcoholic who retires to Las Vegas to drink himself to death— willingly, proudly. He doesn't want to reform. Even when he falls in love with a sympathetic woman (Elizabeth Shue), he continues on his course of self-destruction, and Elizabeth finally respects this decision. The film has provoked much discussion. Many critics liked it because of its staunch refusal to turn into a cheap *When a Man Loves a Woman* (1994), in which drunk Meg Ryan finally quits drinking and gets her life back. Other viewers think Cage is simply stupid. Why would he want to kill himself after finding the love of his life? But ponder this: Cage took an Oscar for best male actor, and Figgis was nominated for best director.

Characters Who Should Change

In Abel Ferrara's *Bad Lieutenant* (1992), a hopelessly corrupt New York City police officer (Harvey Keitel) does bad thing after bad thing. He steals dope from addicts and uses it himself. He stops a pair of teenage girls and talks filthy to them. He has no connection with his wife and children, though he sleeps under the same roof with them. He has no friends, and none of his colleagues on the force will have anything to do with him. He is utterly alone with no hope of redemption—except at the very end when a saintly nun shows him the way. Then it's too late.

A film called *The War Zone* (1999) is about an English family torn asunder by incest. There is a mother, a teenage son, a teenage daughter, and a baby. The daughter silently bears the father's assaults. The son catches on and confronts the father, who denies everything and whips the boy for accusing him. We so want the father to change. But Roth suggests that the infant will be the father's next victim.

The War Zone was produced and directed by the commendable British actor Tim Roth. Another British actor, Gary Oldman, took time out from his usual roles as movie bad guys to return to the south side of London to write and direct *Nil By Mouth* (1997), which is about wife beating. We want the husband, played by Ray Winstone, to change, too, as in a Hollywood movie. But the man is just too limited, too self-absorbed to look at himself. He isn't going to change.

TRY THIS

All the main characters in the films listed below change in one way or another. Rent a few and see how.

- *Born Yesterday* (1950). Ditzy woman in an abusive relationship with a businessman who rips off the government. Directed by George Cukor and starring Judy Holiday and Broderick Crawford. (Remade in 1993, starring Melanie Griffith and Don Johnson. The original was nominated for five Oscars and won one. The Griffith-Johnson version won nothing, deservedly so.)
- *Wings of Desire* (1988). Angel tires of angelhood, wants to be human again. Directed by Wim Wenders and starring Bruno Ganz (Germany).
- *The Little Mermaid* (1989). Mermaid tires of merhood, wants to be human. Directed by Ron Clements and John Musker.
- *Men With Guns* (1997). Idealistic physician-professor in unnamed Latin American country journeys to politically troubled countryside to see how his former students are doing. They aren't doing so well. Directed by John Sayles.
- *Boiler Room* (2000). Young man struggles to regain his soul in pressure-filled job of selling worthless stocks to unsuspecting clients. Directed by Ben Younger and starring Ben Affleck and Giovanni Riblsi.

Character Relationships

Films aren't just about people; they are also about the relationships people create. Often characters have no real identity or personality apart from other characters, but the relationships they create, though incorporeal, are nevertheless very real. Often, in fact, a relationship is the movie.

Couples

In films as in life, couples bond for a great variety of reasons. While many couples bond for the best of reasons—love, avocation, soul-letting—a surprising number of relationships rest on negative foundations, such as power-tripping, domination, a willingness to be exploited, a need to control, and so on. Here are some films with interesting character relationships.

Bonding for Survival: Heartland

This is a Western movie, but it's not about Indians, rustlers, or poker games. It's about a married couple trying to make a go of a small cattle ranch in Wyoming circa

1910. Stewart (Rip Torn) and Elinor (Conchata Ferrell) marry for what seems to be the worst reason: They need each other in a practical sense. Stewart needs a woman to share his bed and Elinor needs Stewart's frontier know-how to make the land she laid claim to pay off. They are often out of sorts with each other during the long winter of the middle of the story. Spring comes. They learn that they have lost most of their stock to the harsh winter. But as the film closes, the real reason for their staying together emerges. One of the heifers is in the middle of a breech birth and could die. Together, they work to save the calf and the mother. Each appreciates the other's efforts. Their love, if love it is, is at best based simply on mutual respect. That is enough.

Love Dies (and Does It Ever): War of the Roses *(1989)*
This movie starts out with Michael Douglas and Kathleen Turner loving each other, as couples usually do when they get married, then the marriage goes bad and love fades, as so often happens. However, the real hate (and the real movie) starts when Michael and Kathleen get around to the property settlement. And then it's total war. They live in a well-appointed, yuppie house with lots of good stuff to destroy, and the destruction has the purpose of making sure the other person doesn't get any good stuff in the settlement. This sly, underappreciated movie is a great satire on the materialism of marriage and the craziness of divorce. It was directed by Danny DeVito.

Splattering Blood: Natural Born Killers *(1994)*
This is the ugly, hard-to-watch Oliver Stone film that satirizes—it isn't so hard to watch if you take it as satire—just about everything in sight: krazee killers on the run, the blood-thirsty media who legendize the pair, the public who can't get enough of it. Mickey and Mallory (Woody Harrelson and Juliette Lewis) drive across the country, murdering whimsically and indiscriminately, making sure they leave one person alive at each slaughter site to tell the press who wrought the mayhem. Maybe *Natural Born Killers* is inspired more by other movies than by life, in par-ticular *Bonnie and Clyde* and *Badlands*. To me, though, the movie could be a metaphor for the incredible thoughtlessness of some young couples. They marry badly, consume stupidly, have babies pointlessly, and on rare occasions go nuts with guns. The relationship is based on a kind of mutual mental shutdown. They just don't look at each other and ask, "What the hell are we doing?"

Willfulness: Camille Claudel *(1988)*
If murder links Mickey and Mallory, art forms the basis of this film's relationship between the famous French sculptor Auguste Rodin and his mistress-model-collaborator Camille Claudel. Camille (Isabelle Adjani) is a woman possessed. She is not only driven to create great art in stone, particularly renderings of hands, she wants to be acknowledged as an artist in her own right. But Rodin (Gerard

Depardieu) dominates her and takes credit for her work. The times are on Rodin's side. Women's art was seldom recognized or appreciated in France in the 1890s, or anywhere else for that matter. The relationship between Camille and Rodin is presented as a conundrum because it both supports and oppresses Camille. Ultimately, she must escape Rodin's domination. The feeling of being cheated drives her personality and the story.

Men

It's called "the buddy movie," and it's about men in close relationships. These men don't talk about each other or how much they like each other's company. Instead, the relationship is based on some third thing, some mission, some professional matter, some complication of plot that draws them together and bonds them.

In *The Sting*, Paul Newman and Robert Redford come together for the purpose of pulling off an elaborate, movie-long scam against a fat-cat underworld figure. The audience, too, is scammed. All the scamming and counterscamming just draw Newman and Redford closer to each other.

Newman and Redford worked together again when they made *Butch Cassidy and the Sundance Kid* (1979), with George Roy Hill directing. In this Western, they are pursued all the way to Mexico by lawmen. They die together because it is an honorable and manly thing to do. Of course they do this with guns blazing because that is the way men go out, at least in Westerns. Thus the men bond in death and love doing it.

This romantic and improbable theme suffuses one of the greatest buddy movies of all time, *The Wild Bunch*, in which William Holden, Ernest Borgnine, Warren Oates, and Ben Johnson, desperados on the run, decide to die all at the same time for the sheer glory of it. They do this in the plaza of a Mexican village when they are badly outnumbered by a contingent of Mexican soldiers who have the drop on them. There is a magnificent pause as Holden, Borgnine, Oates, and Johnson exchange knowing smiles that say, Okay, guys, this is it. See you in Hell. Then the rain of bullets commences, and of course the fearless four go down, smiling to the end. This was hot stuff in 1969, and the editing is still wonderful, but today the scene plays macho-silly.

Another great buddy Western is *Ride the High Country* (1962), in which an awareness of the passing of the Old West, real or imagined, bonds two aging gunmen, played by Joel McCrea and Randolph Scott. Sam Peckinpah directed both *The Wild Bunch* and *Ride the High Country*. However, the greatest portrait of all of male bonding is found in *Lonesome Dove* (1989), a six-and-a-half-hour, rentable, made-for-TV epic starring Robert Duvall and Tommy Lee Jones. When you have so much screen time to work with, you can set up a lot of plot; insert a couple of women to temporarily distract the men; and create situations in which one man has to help the other, hates the other, or drags the other's one-legged body all the way from South Dakota to Texas to the town of Lonesome Dove. You can learn all you need to know about men from this movie, which was adapted from the Larry McMurtry novel by William D. Wittliff and directed by Simon Wincer.

Women
Women don't have such a wonderful genre as the Western for exploring relationships among themselves because, overall, Hollywood has had a male bias in telling stories and creating great parts. Women actors often remark about the paucity of good parts in movies for their gender. All the same, many notable films have been based on strong woman-to-woman relationships.

Bonding through Suffering: The Color Purple *(1985)*
This film is based on the famous Alice Walker novel about black women in the early decades of the twentieth century. Though technically emancipated, they still endure virtual slavery and abuse from assorted black men and whites in a world where black women are at the very bottom of the social order. Celie (Whoopi Goldberg) is plain and unassertive. She is "married"—I put the word in quotes because she is more a maid and semen receptacle than a wife—to cruel "Mister" (Danny Glover); she doesn't even learn his name until halfway through the picture. Shug (Margaret Avery), is an attractive and independent alcoholic juke joint singer and probable prostitute who has worked a spell on Mister for years. She is a complex figure: outwardly buoyant, inwardly burdened. And Sophia (Oprah Winfrey) once prided herself on not working for whites, but when she stands up publicly to a respectable woman in the community, a constable cracks her over the head with a pistol. She ends up a brain-damaged, compliant wretch, a de facto slave for the very woman who humiliated her. Despite the considerable differences between these three women, they bond through their misery. Shug sees inner beauty in Celie. The women connect through tender, satisfying sex, seemingly rare in Shug's life and before this utterly absent in Celie's.

Celie's bonding with Sophia is incredibly brief—a sympathetic exchange of glances in a store where Sophia is shopping for the white woman. Their glances communicate identically: *We connect because we suffer.* The women finally come across as brimming with spirituality, nurtured by suffering. This is a common theme in Walker's writing, and Steven Spielberg, who directed *The Color Purple*, understands it.

The Power of Storytelling: Fried Green Tomatoes *(1991)*
In this film, Kathy Bates plays a lonely, repressed Southern housewife. While visiting a nursing home, she meets an elderly woman (Jessica Tandy) who, over a period of weeks, tells her the story of a pair of irrepressible women who ran a restaurant and went their own way during a time (the 1920s and 1930s) in the South when women were not supposed to be so uppity. As you might suspect, Tandy was one of the indomitable women—the other is played by Mary Stuart Masterson. Tandy

apparently feels that she can impart to Bates some of the vitality that defined her own youth. She perceives that vitality and independence are the very things Bates needs in her life. This narrative works wonders on Kathy's character, who successfully starts tackling her own problems, namely excessive weight, a drudge husband, and a weak will. To show that she is now more assertive, director Jon Avnet sets up a wonderful scene in which she does battle over an empty stall in a crowded parking lot. Before, Kathy would have yielded the stall to another driver. But after having benefited from the story of the two rambunctious women, Kathy's character plays "parking lot chicken" and wins.

Switching Minds: Persona (1966)

Persona, written and directed by the Swedish director Ingmar Bergman, is a difficult film that most people have to see more than once to even begin to understand. It's about two women, one a famous actress, the other her nurse, who have retreated to a seaside cottage in Sweden. The actress, played by Liv Ullmann, has now ceased to speak, and no one knows why. The nurse, played by Bibi Andersson, instinctively feels that if she talks a lot to her patient, maybe Liv will come around and start talking in return. Bibi reveals herself to have had a troubled past filled with much longing and regret. There are certain visuals based on double exposures of the faces of the two women that suggest that the women exchange personas. Each may have what the other lacks. All this is complicated by the fact that the story seems to be about the making of a film about Vietnam, which was getting ugly at the time—a film within a film. Probably the professions of the women are a key to their relationship. Nurses heal, actresses act. But Bibi doesn't heal and Liv doesn't act. Or maybe Bibi does heal because Liv may be acting in her silence. Not easy. You watch *Persona* with the feeling that Bergman is venturing beyond the limits of film, or the patience of viewers, in trying to get to the bottom of this relationship.

Female Buddy Film: Thelma and Louise

I mention this film again here because it's one of the only woman-woman films that feels like a man-man buddy film and also like a Western. As I explained in chapter 6, Thelma and Louise are on the run and end up going over to a radical feminist point of view: They don't need men in their lives. This is a remarkable direction for a pop movie to take. It's not surprising that a lot of men hate the movie.

The Exclusion of Men: Entre Nous (1983)

This is another radical feminist film, completely bold and original. Two women (Miou-Miou and Isabelle Huppert) seem simply to tire of their husbands, and of men in general, and make a life with each other. French Director Diane Kurys does not really present them as lesbians; the intellectual possibilities are so much greater if they are not. Does it require a woman director to bring out subtle aspects of a woman-woman relationship?

7.4. *Persona.* In 1960 this movie was voted one of the ten best films of all time by an international jury of film critics and professors. The poll was taken by the prestigious British film magazine *Sight and Sound*, which takes the poll in the first year of every decade. *Citizen Kane* has headed the list every decade since 1960. *Persona* was dropped from the list in 1980, to be replaced by the likes of *The Godfather* and *The Godfather, Part II*. Which film is the true classic? Maybe not *Persona*, because it hasn't stood the test of time, though it (and Bergman) were certainly honored to have been on the list for twenty years. Meanwhile *Citizen Kane's* reputation as a true classic seems much more secure, if the *Sight and Sound* poll means anything. United Artists.

TRY THIS

Here are more films based on compelling character relationships. I've slipped in two new categories, father to son and mother to daughter.

- *Tumbleweeds* (1999). Mother and daughter on the road. In spite of various hardships and spats, they remain essentially close. Directed by Gavin O'Connor.
- *Gas Food Lodging* (1992). A mother in a spiritless, truck-stop town struggles to raise her daughters "respectable." Directed by Allison Anders.
- *Distant Voices, Still Lives* (1988). An art film—actually a pair of art films—about a father who uses his fists to work his will on wife and children. Directed by Terence Davies and starring Peter Postlethwaite (United Kingdom).
- *Cinema Paradiso* (1988). A boy who loves movies learns much about life from a projectionist father-surrogate. Directed by Giuseppe Tornatore (Italy).

7.5. *Entre Nous.* Subtle, multilayered. No one makes relationship films with more baggage than the French. So that's two photos in a row from dense European films. Are the Europeans then just superior at creating sophisticated characters? Not quite. The only foreign films that make it to America are those aimed at the cinemagentsia. It's natural selection more than cultural superiority at work.

- *Affliction* (1997). Has the male lead of the story turned out to be alcoholic and dumb about relationships because he was abused by his father, or is he this way because, more fundamentally, he is afflicted by the Male Condition? Directed by Paul Shrader and starring Nick Nolte (in the lead), James Coburn (as the father), and Sissy Spacek.

Cinematics and Character
Here is a sampling of films in which character is defined or enhanced through thoughtful cinematics.

Changing Frames in *High Noon*
In *High Noon*, Marshal Gary Cooper has to shoot down one last bad guy. The bad guy grabs Gary's wife and uses her as a shield. This happens on the main street of a town that looks deserted. Tension mounts. Can Gary figure out a way to shoot the bad guy? Will any of the townspeople come out from hiding to help him? Yes

7.6. *The Conversation.*
Costuming that com-
municates. You just
know this scene isn't
going anywhere,
romantically speaking,
she with her socks, he
with his coat and tie.
Paramount.

to the first question, no to the second. Finally the wife, played by Grace Kelly, makes a move that allows Gary to shoot the bad guy. Now Gary and his wife run to each other and embrace. A close-up shows Grace's relief. A reverse angle close-up shows Gary, also relieved. But near the end of the close-up, Gary starts to register disgust. His eyes dart left and right. Editor Elmo Williams and Harry Gerstad then cut to a wider frame as the cowardly townspeople at last emerge from hiding, looking sheepish. Then the editors cut back to a tighter shot of Gary as he removes the badge from his shirt and throws it in the dust. Cut away to badge in the dust. And at last I come down to the shot I really want to emphasize: Williams and Gerstad cut to an extreme high-angle shot of Gary and Grace and the people of the town encircling them. The people are shy, and they keep their distance. It's a great frame and a great piece of composition for showing the people's shame.

High-Class Frame in *Roman Holiday*

The respected German-American director William Wyler must have felt that medium shots and long shots imparted dignity to his characters. His *Roman Holiday* is about a European princess—a *real* princess—who runs away from her hotel while visiting Rome. She longs to live like ordinary people, at least for a time. She meets a reporter who shows her around Rome, only she doesn't know he intends to exploit her and get a good story in the bargain. Very quickly the pair fall in love.

The princess is played by the naturally regal Audrey Hepburn, the reporter by all-time movie nice guy Gregory Peck. These actors, under Wyler's firm direction, render their characters incredibly decent and honorable. In the end, the princess goes back to her hotel, and the reporter decides not to do the story, which is exactly the proper thing to do. Wyler used close-ups very sparingly in this film. Too many would have felt invasive and inappropriate for Hepburn and Peck. Medium shots, lots of them, keep the audience at arm's length from the chaste couple. It's the best frame for such a classy movie.

Low-Class Frame in *Nil By Mouth*

But Gary Oldman in his *Nil by Mouth* uses so many close-ups that we feel we are practically sitting in the laps of the characters, who are working-class men in South London. They are vulgar, self-centered, abusive to women, and uncertain about their manhood. The filming style is ragged. The film feels gritty and real, and means to rub your nose in so much male ego. Close-ups here are the ideal frame for these purposes.

7.7. *Nil By Mouth.* You probably didn't know that, for a lot of prestigious British films released in the United States, actors are coached to level their accents and render their lines more like Americanspeak in order to break into the big market. But *Nil by Mouth* does not aspire to prestige or bigbuckshood. Director Gary Oldman's Neanderthals speak only pure, uncompromised South Londonese, which ain't easy to understand. Some scenes you have to rewind and play again to catch what is said. It's worth it. SE8 Group.

Skinned Knuckles in *Blue* (1993)

Polish director Krzysztof Kieslowski directed this masterful formalist film about a woman trying to resensitize herself after her husband and child were killed in an auto accident. Early in the film she doesn't feel anything, neither grief, nor loss, nor pain. But Kieslowski does not use many words to convey this. Instead, images convey the woman's numb state of mind. She walks along a sidewalk and presses her knuckles against the iron bars of a fence. She stops and looks at her knuckles, the skin scraped off, bleeding. But her face is impassive. The images say it all: She's trying to *will* pain through her own actions. But at this point—nothing.

Time Compressed in *The Miracle of Morgan's Creek* (1944)

In this Preston Sturges classic set during World War II, Trudy Cockenlocker (Don't ask!), a teenager played by Betty Hutton, feels it is her patriotic duty to show servicemen on leave in her town a good time. She borrows her friend Norval's car and heads out to a local dance hall. Before the night is over, she drives carloads of soldiers back and forth to a clutch of dance halls and country clubs. She is seen as a good dancer, gleeful, energetic, very pretty, and a magnet to the servicemen. Finally, after too much to drink, she passes out. Editor Stuart Gilmore compressed all of the scenes with the servicemen—and what must have been miles of film footage shot over several nights—to only three minutes of screen time while also rendering Trudy as a vigorous character, which was Sturges's intent. But Gilmore had to be careful. In deference to the times, he had to exclude footage that might portray Trudy as loose and oversexed and instead make her simply enthusiastic. Most viewers feel he succeeded, though they can sense Sturges, who undoubtedly guided Gilmore, winking at them. By the way, later in the story Trudy turns up pregnant. Bold for 1944!

Space, Crosscutting, and Character in *Never Cry Wolf* (1983)

Crosscutting is such a fundamental and powerful editing tool that it can be used to advantage in nearly any dramatic situation. The climax of *Star Wars* depends entirely on the deft crosscutting of Marcia Lucas of shots from a half-dozen locations and lines of action: the rebel base, the Death Star, two or three rebel fighter pilots, two or three bad-guy fighter pilots, and Luke, Han, and Darth Vader in their own fighters. But most crosscutting in movies is far less dramatic than this. In the pensive Carroll Ballard film *Never Cry Wolf* the naturalist Tyler tries to explain to two Eskimos why he is studying wolf droppings. Ballard directed Charles Martin Smith, who plays Tyler, to be likeably condescending in his scientific explanation. For their part, the Eskimos listen intently and often ask questions, but they really have no idea what Tyler is talking about. Finally, at the end of Tyler's lecture, one of the Eskimos says "Good idea." He is mocking Tyler, displaying a sophistication most viewers would not have expected. But Tyler is oblivious to the Eskimo's irony. Space and the editing technique of crosscutting intensify the cultural distance. The

7.8. *The Miracle at Morgan's Creek.* Trudy and her disapproving father. Wacky film, wacky composition. Also see pages 20–23. Paramount.

three sit in a small makeshift shelter and could have been framed in an integrative medium shot. But Ballard had Tyler sit at some distance from the Eskimos to suggest spatially the cultural gap between them. And because of the cuts back and forth from Tyler to the other two, the naturalist seems isolated, not just professionally, but culturally as well. As a scientist he'd no doubt be isolated from lay Westerners, too. This is a good technique for a film about the loneliness of intellectuals.

 TRY THIS

See a film rich in cinematics. You can tell this from the trailer you saw last week. The trailer seems to showcase a lot of cool camera work and editing. As you watch, note how cinematics contributes to character. Keep track of frame and photography, editing, sound.

chapter eight

Settings

t matters where a film story is *set*. Setting spins story. Imagine *E.T.: The Extraterrestrial* set in Harlem or Hong Kong. What a different story that would be! Setting isn't just place. It's also season and era. It can be physical, geographical, or social.

Season

Here is a selection of films in which season contributes importantly to story.

Summer

The title of *Summer of '42* (1971) introduces two settings: summer and war. There is also a third setting, a Virginia beach vacation community. Credit writer Herman Raucher and director Robert Mulligan for weaving these settings into a compelling story. A teenager (Gary Grimes) has a crush on a woman (Jennifer O'Neill) six or seven years his senior. This is a crucial age difference: the boy is virginal and immature, the woman has been matured by marriage and the fact that her husband serves in the war under combat conditions. Then she learns her husband has been killed in action. She mourns in a strange way: She immediately takes the boy to bed, but only once. Then she leaves him with a note that explains nothing. To the boy, it is all a mystery. What is the point? Maybe that people have very personal ways of mourning. The three settings displace the story from the normal. The war setting, though far off, nevertheless impinges on the woman; the recreational setting creates a kind of spell and gives the boy permission to fall in love; and since it is summer, the boy is further liberated from the usual demands of schooling to find time to turn his attention to the woman. The sexual encounter would not have happened at all if one of the elements of setting, or maybe two, had been missing from the story.

Something of the same thing happens in Frank Perry's *Last Summer* (1969), which is also set in a beach community during summer. A half-dozen teenagers explore life among themselves. School is out. No more sitting and learning. Now it's poking around in each other's lives and learning about sex. If the story weren't summery or beachy, the young people wouldn't have learned as much about each other, about life.

Spike Lee's *Do The Right Thing* (1989) is also set in summer, but it's a summer with a far different feel. It's a long, hot summer day in a black community in Brooklyn. People get out of their hot apartments, sit on stoops, roam the streets, interact. Heat stokes emotions. A white-owned pizza restaurant engenders hard feelings. You can feel the heat leading down to violence. If this important film had been set in the winter, it would have been a far different story.

Winter

But the Coen brothers' *Fargo* is set in winter, and you can't help but wonder why. Winter forces people into thick clothing. They look a little ridiculous. Marge, the chief cop investigating a triple murder, is so padded out she can scarcely drop her arms to her side. She doesn't look like she could stand up to the amoral punks she

8.1. *Do the Right Thing.* Films set in inner cities are nearly always fraught with palpable anger, frustration, danger, but the suburbs have their problems, too. See pages 212–17. Universal.

has to track down. The snow covers everything. It's sad, it evokes loneliness and isolation, it creates hazardous driving, and yet there is something pure about it, too. The locals of Brainard, Minnesota seem just fine with it. The punks are sort of out of their element in it, though it's hard to say just what their element is.

 TRY THIS

A few more films in which season figures: *The Ice Storm* (1997), *The Sweet Hereafter, Black Robe* (1991), *Spring Break* (1983), *Big Wednesday* (1981), *Beach Blanket Bingo* (1965), and *Stand by Me* (1986). See one or two of these films and consider how season spins the story.

Era

Era, or period, films try to capture the times—how people live, what they value, what they are willing to die for, and so on. But you can't help being on guard. Is the presentation of era authentic, or has it been fudged by Hollywood and made to seem more appealing or romantic than it really was? Does it matter? If it does matter, how does it matter?

8.2. *Fargo.* It isn't easy to film scenes in the snow. Cold reduces battery life by about one-half, and motion picture cameras and tape recorders run on batteries. Tents with heaters must be set up for cast and crew. Also, snow that is supposed to look pure for filming can't be sullied during rehearsal. Is it worth it? The Coen brothers must have thought so. Polygram.

8.3. *Spartacus.* This film was made during a time when movie theaters were losing out to TV. People were staying home to watch *I Love Lucy.* So the big studios decided they could lure people back to the theaters with a type of spectacle that TV couldn't match. Hence the bloat: this three-hour, 70 mm, full-color, panoramic armies-coming-over-hills extravaganza from Universal.

Classical

Spartacus (1960) is one of the better-known Roman-era or "sword and sandal" movies to come out of Hollywood. It was directed by the thirty-one-year-old Stanley Kubrick, who was just finding his wings. *Spartacus* tells a poignant story about a slave revolt that failed. A lot of characters died, including the male lead, played by Kirk Douglas.

Though this film has many admirers, it's still a Hollywood product and maybe is not to be entirely trusted. Sharper contemporary viewers can't help wondering about its authenticity. Did Rome really look like that? Did people really talk in that stilted way? ("Thus it is written, thus it shall be done.") It's such a big film, maybe too big. One wonders: What would a little film set in ancient Rome be like—one in which a boy and a girl simply meet in the marketplace? Ernest Hemingway once wrote a short play about three Roman soldiers in a tavern in Jerusalem after the crucifixion. They feel guilty; one says, "He looked pretty good in there today." It's just a little play. There would not be a part for Charlton Heston.

Medieval

There aren't many films made about medieval times. Renowned Swedish filmmaker Ingmar Bergman made two: *The Seventh Seal* (1957) and *The Virgin Spring* (1959);

both are highly acclaimed. In these films the medieval ambience is extremely convincing. Bergman's set designer P. A. Lundgren, who crafted the look of both films, built taverns, stables, inns, and churches that seem painfully real. You think: Did people really live so crudely?

But the realism extends beyond the mere look of these two films. In his scripting and directing, Bergman also took pains to make people think, feel, and speak medieval. Religion competes with superstition for the main focus of life. If there is a plague in the land, it's because so many people have sinned. The remedy: The afflicted don sackcloth and lash themselves with whips. As you watch these two films, you really experience medievalism, both the look of it and the way of it. Max von Sydow plays the lead in both.

Renaissance

Today's best known renaissance film by far is *Shakespeare in Love* (1998), directed by John Madden. The ambience of Elizabethan England is strongly felt in the film. Streets, shops, and theaters are closely detailed, and costumes are sumptuously authentic for the upper classes and suitably unwashed for the lower classes. I like the ink pot into which Will dips his pen—it looks real to me—and his ink-stained fingers and blotchy manuscript. I was almost convinced that I really was watching the great bard in the act of creation.

I should say a little about the story for the two or three of you who have not seen the film. Will—short for William Shakespeare—is played by the youthful Joseph Fiennes. He's blocked. The play he's struggling with—*Romeo and Ethel, the Pirate's Daughter*—isn't going anywhere. Then Joseph meets well-to-do Olivia (Gwyneth Paltrow), falls in love, and in days has penned his masterpiece, *Romeo and Juliet* (1595).

Many viewers probably do not appreciate how the film story picks up some conventions of the Elizabethan stage. For example, Olivia took a big risk in playing a boy because there were laws against women taking parts in plays. Screenwriters Tom Stoppard and Marc Norman have fun with the switcheroo whereby a male member of Will's acting company plays Juliet while Olivia plays Romeo, though no one as yet suspects her of being a woman. In Elizabethan theater female characters played by men often disguised themselves as men. Follow?

In the movie, Olivia's nurse—actually more maid than nurse—is her accomplice, standing guard as Olivia trysts with Will in her bedroom, helping her get into costume for her activities at the Rose Theatre. The sympathetic nurse was a common plot element in the dramas of the time, including *Romeo and Juliet*.

At the same time, the film takes liberties and gets contemporary. Early in the story, Will sees a shrink, not just for writer's block, but also for a sexual problem. The shrink times the session with an hourglass. Complains Will, in metric Freudspeak: "It's as if my quill is broken."

The 1950s, or Thereabouts

Judging from their popularity, we currently love films about the 1950s, just as a few decades ago we were enamored of films about the American West. Both kinds of movies traffic in nostalgia for bygone days and perceived better times. They also provide entertainment that mixes pleasure and pain. Westerns invited audiences to luxuriate in plots of rugged individualists bending vast distances and bad men to their will. Today, we delight in films about the 1950s with their simple depiction of straightforward family values and clear-cut lessons of right and wrong. But a kind of pain accompanies the viewing of these films. So much has been lost. Housing tracts and shopping malls now sprawl across once sacred, wide-open spaces; family values today are complicated by such contemporary social developments as spousal abuse and deadbeat dads. Westerns and fifties movies both feature types of heroes that are perceived as being absent from today's society. Westerners achieved dignity by completing movie-long acts of bravery and integrity, while characters in fifties movies win audience respect by the quiet, every day heroics of staying married and bringing up kids good and straight. Films about both eras deal in myth—myths of the West, myths of simpler times. We don't see them to learn anything about history or sociology; we see them to lament the passing of venerable ways of being in the world, whether those ways ever really existed or not.

Really typical in this way is *My Dog Skip* (2000)—straight, literal, never winking. The weightiest issue in this movie has to do with whether the kid, played by Frankie Muniz, is ready for a dog. Mom (Diane Lane) says yes; Dad (Kevin Bacon), no. Guess who wins? Dogs in this kind of story usually save the day. At first they are despised by either Dad or Mom, then early one morning while the household sleeps, the dog smells smoke, yaps and yaps, wakes everybody up, and—you know the rest. *My Dog Skip*, which was directed by Jay Russell, doesn't have anything like this, but Skip does save the embittered soul of the WWII vet (Luke Wilson) next door by licking him in the face. Before, Luke had a perpetual scowl; afterwards, he manages to smile, thanks to magic dog slobber. Me, I felt that every turn of this piece of nostalgia was predictable. Take that as criticism. But I probably missed the point. People who like this movie like it because it is predictable.

Most screenwriters mining the rich fifties vein endeavor to be more original. *Pleasantville* (1998) is one of the most creative fifties-era films ever made. Thanks to a magic TV repairman (Don Knotts), nineties teens Tobey Maguire and Reese Witherspoon involuntarily time-travel back to the town of Pleasantville, which exists only in a black-and-white sitcom made in the 1950s—the kind of thing that now plays only on Nick at Night or The Family Channel. The people in Pleasantville have been sensually leveled. They don't know how to feel deeply about anything because the scripts they are in don't give them chances to, or if feeling deeply happens to figure, the characters are made to feel badly about it. But the way the story sets us up, Pleasantvillers feel vaguely deprived and *want* to have deeper reactions to life; they just don't know how to go about it. Maguire and Witherspoon soon discover that their mission is to give the sense-starved Pleasantvillers nineties-style sensations. So because of them, a repressed housewife, played by Joan Allen, does a taboo thing: One quiet afternoon she satisfies herself while taking a bath. A soda jerk (Jeff Daniels), who really wants to be an artist, cuts loose and starts painting some wild stuff, the likes of which no one in town has ever seen before. Whenever characters do indulge themselves this way, they become colorized—not dull Ted-Turner colorized, but full, rich, Technicolor colorized. Remember: Pleasantville is a monochromatic community. So when Joan Allen is seen in vivid pink against her black-and-white bathroom, she knocks you out. As sensuality spreads through the entire town like Commie subversion, nearly everything that can provoke the senses takes on color. It's a great metaphor in the same tradition as the use of color in *The Wizard of Oz*. Color equals adventure, risk, life. In spite of myself—remember how back in chapter 1 I had harsh things to say about color being used this way?—in spite of myself, I like this film, ably written and directed by Gary Ross.

Quite obviously, life in the fifties was not really as two-dimensional as American movies about the period insist. *This Boy's Life* (1993), directed by Michael Caton-Jones, is far more loose, more real. Set in the late 1950s, the film deals with a single mom (Ellen Barkin) and her troubled, rambunctious teenage son (Leonardo DiCaprio) who both do some very un-fifties things. First, Ellen marries a man (Robert De Niro) whom she doesn't really love, pretty much because he

8.4. *The French Lieutenant's Woman*. At last, peace of mind. It took Meryl Streep, shown here as the nineteenth-century woman, the whole film to find it. United Artists.

has a little money and offers security. The price she pays is giving up her independence to the dominating De Niro. Who ever heard of issues like this creeping into a movie about the 1950s? For his part, Leonardo takes up with a young gay guy, though Leonardo himself is not portrayed as gay. It's not sexual preference that draws the boys to each other, but complex outlooks on life that Leonardo hasn't been able to get from the dumb-ass chums he used to hang with. The main focus of the film, however, is the abuse, physical and verbal, that De Niro heaps on Leonardo. Mom is conflicted. Does she stay with Robert for the security, or does she take her son and get the hell out of the situation? None of this is the stuff of screenplays about the 1950s.

I have to say, though, that the real reason *This Boy's Life* is set in the fifties is that it's actually biography—about the childhood of novelist Tobias Wolf who just happened to grow up in that decade. All the same, the film turns out to be a damn interesting use of an era about which we have too many misconceptions.

Down to the Present

As I noted in chapter 4, *The French Lieutenant's Woman* has two settings: Victorian England and contemporary England. In the former, the main character is a social outcast because she's suspected of having an illicit relationship with a French officer. She has been driven a little crazy by her melancholy and isolation. In the contemporary setting, an actress (played by Meryl Streep) plays the part of the French lieutenant's woman, and we obtain a behind-the-scenes rendition of the Victorian story's filming. When film is not being shot, the actress is unburdened, free, in a time and society in which "illicit" means little. Indeed, the film star, who is married, has an affair with the actor who plays the French lieutenant (Jeremy Irons). The Victorian story makes it clear that unmarried women had few life choices: They could be teachers, factory workers, or prostitutes, but not respectable *and* promiscuous. The woman in the contemporary story has unlimited choices—but she finds that she cannot duplicate in her own life the passion her fictional character finds with her fictional lover. Setting *is* the point.

TRY THIS

Here are some more films that illuminate eras—or eras that illuminate films.
- The Roaring Twenties: *The Great Gatsby, Splendor in the Grass* (1961), *The Gold Rush*
- The Great Depression: *King of the Hill* (1993), *The Grapes of Wrath*
- The 1970s: *Five Easy Pieces* (1970), *Night Moves* (1975), *Alice Doesn't Live Here Any More* (1974)
- The Vietnam era: *Coming Home* (1978), *Apocalypse Now, Platoon*

How does each of these films illuminate an era, and vice versa?

8.5. *Easy Rider.* The outsider film, a potent narrative type. Other outsider characters: The tramp in *The Gold Rush*, Beldar and Prymaat in *The Coneheads* (1993), Sean Thornton in *The Quiet Man* (1952), the four canoers in *Deliverance*, Lawrence in *Lawrence of Arabia*, Jean in *Jean de Florette*, Gino in *Lamerica*, and Carl in *Sling Blade* (1996).

Setting as Journey

Here are glosses on six films based on journeys. All are ultimately about America, and all are about searches for meaning.

Easy Rider (1969)

Low-budget and shot from the hip, *Easy Rider* follows two bohemian biker outsiders, played by Peter Fonda and Dennis Hopper, on a journey from Los Angeles, where they made a lot of money selling drugs, to Mardi Gras in New Orleans, where they do drugs and have sex. These guys are really into *freedom*. They think about it a lot and talk about it as much as anything else—actually they don't talk much at all. They pick up a renegade lawyer (Jack Nicholson), and he talks about freedom, too, and how it frightens people. The trouble is, they are traveling in the Deep South, where intolerance lurks. This film is unfair to the South, which does not have a monopoly on intolerance. Director Dennis Hopper and writer Terry Southern were probably trying to say something about the whole country by using the South as an example. And geographically, the story couldn't have been set anywhere else because one has to go through the South to get to New Orleans. This film feels a little dated—we probably do better now at reconciling freedom with responsibility—but it was an anthem to bohemian youth in its day.

Bright Angel (1991)

This is a strange, cruel road movie, virtually unknown and unseen, which I believe to be a near-masterpiece. It's about a youth (played by Dermot Mulroney) whose family life is so unsettled that he leaves home and journeys across the face of bleak, unfriendly Montana. He picks up a rootless girl (Lili Taylor) who flinches at life just about as much as he does. Soon she sucks him into a bad, underworld mission that leads to disaster. The boy survives, wiser and better prepared. This is not a happy view of the American West. It's bereft of myth or romance. Instead, it is a *vision* film; that is, it poses a particular view of America with which you may or may not agree. The vision was spun by director Michael Fields and writer Richard Ford.

Stranger Than Paradise (1984)

A lot of people who watch this film feel boredom or disgust. It relies entirely on the *sequence shot*, as it is sometimes called, in which each scene is covered in one long-running long shot showing people from head to foot but never moving in for medium shots or close-ups. The main characters, a young woman (Eszter Balint) and two young men (John Lurie and Richard Edson), are seen only at a distance, which makes it hard for viewers to cozy up to them. The young woman has recently arrived from Hungary, and the men are Brooklyn deadbeats. They have zero-sum relationships—they don't seem to respond to each other on any level. They are

8.6. *Stranger Than Paradise.* Contemplation of bleak, mute Lake Erie. The trio doesn't find answers to the questions they don't know they have. The Samuel Goldwyn Company.

8.7. *Stagecoach.* Normally the West is too big to bring peoples from different mythic backgrounds together for very long. But in the stagecoach, Easterners and Westerners rub elbows, bruise psyches, and soon learn they don't want to live in the same space together. United Artists.

near-zombies, depressed and isolated. Yet they need each other in a sexless, unutterable way. They embark on a journey across America, first to snow-covered Cleveland for an icy view of Lake Erie, then to Florida for banal palm trees, motels, and sand. They are obviously searching for something in America, in themselves, but they don't know what it is, and they don't find it. They don't even know they are searching. This is a film poem, an art film written and directed by Jim Jarmusch, and it has a tremendous reputation among independent filmmakers. I dare you to see it.

Stagecoach
Classically Western, *Stagecoach* is about the redemption that the West offers if you have the right frame of mind. The story is about seven people who are traveling west in a stagecoach across vast Monument Valley in the arid Southwest. Of the seven, three are from the East and four are Westerners. The latter include an alcoholic physician run out of the last town; a reformed hooker, also run out of the town; and an escaped convict (played by a young John Wayne) who seeks vengeance. These characters embody mythic qualities contrasting East and West, as follows:

If the East embodies:	*then the West represents:*
collectivism	individualism
legalism	pragmatism
compromise	integrity
absolutism	relativism
damnation	redemption*

As the plot of *Stagecoach* unfolds, the doctor redeems himself by delivering a baby while the prostitute redeems herself by assisting. John Wayne falls in love with the prostitute (played by Claire Trevor), but he knows nothing of her past. For her part, Trevor falls in love with Wayne but can't bring herself to tell him of her former profession. Later, when the stage reaches its destination (the rough-and-ready town of Lordsburg), Wayne gets his revenge by shooting three bad guys, and Trevor finally tells him of her past. But it ain't no big deal for Wayne: He still loves her—because this is the West, where you can be forgiven your past. Then the marshal, sensing that ad hoc justice was served by Wayne's vengeance, lets him and Trevor escape to Wayne's ranch by the river to start a new life.

8.8. *The Wizard of Oz*. In addition to possibly representing symbolic searches for the self, film journeys also offer changing settings, each with potential to be particularly cinematic. Just look at the Emerald City looming in the distance. Who wouldn't want to go there? MGM.

*Adapted from Horizons West by Jim Kitses.

The Adventures of Huckleberry Finn (1939, 1960, 1981, 1985, 1993)

Mark's Twain's novel *Huckleberry Finn* has been called the essential American work of fiction about youth. Published in 1884, the story is based on the journey of a boy and a man, Jim, floating on a raft down the Mississippi. Huck is an orphan, an unwashed, unlettered outsider, living by his wits and despised. Jim is a runaway slave. They make shore now and then and have various adventures with devious adults who scare Jim and make terrible role models for Huck. The irony of the story is the same as that of *Easy Rider:* The deeper Huck and Jim penetrate the South, the more likely they are to encounter intolerance and the more likely it is that Jim will be caught and returned to his owner in Missouri for harsh punishment. The novel is also a chronicle of Huck's maturing. He finally comes to regard Jim a man, a human being, and not a slave or a "boy."

Unfortunately, the many movie adaptations of the novel touch only slightly on these serious matters. Most were designed as entertainment and not especially as mirrors held up to America. The darker issues are only dimly glimpsed. An authentic Huck and Jim film has yet to be made.

The Wizard of Oz

Dorothy's journey, too, is ironic. She longs to get out of drab, unfeeling Kansas, just as so many youths through the decades have longed to escape their colorless home

8.9. *E.T.: The Extraterrestrial.* Director Steven Spielberg has often been accused of laying it on too thick. How many cops, technicians, scientists, workmen, gear, lights, and fog machines does it take to check out a little guy from outer space? But excess may work here if you believe that Spielberg's intent was to poke fun at overreacting adults. Universal.

8.10. *Gone With the Wind*. Flowers, flowing dresses, handsome young men formally posed, cunning shadows—these convey, in a single shot, something of the grace and naïveté of the South before the Civil War. Now go back and look at figure 1.1. MGM.

lives and check out New York City, San Francisco, or other places perceived as magical. But dumb Dorothy—after coming to maturity in colorful Oz, what does she do? Her fairy godmother gets her to regress to her old, naïve self, intoning such silliness as, "If I ever go searching for my heart's desire, I can find it in my own back yard!" and, "There's no place like home." Dorothy clicks her ruby heels—and is back to black-and-white Kansas she goes. Terrific.

Settings in Foreign Films

A major reason for seeing foreign films is to tune in to their settings. Foreign settings may puzzle you for a while, but if you are patient, you can learn much. I call viewing foreign films *celluloid anthropology*. Only the film medium—not books, not plays, not even travel—has the power to place you in the living rooms and bedrooms of people from other lands. Only foreign films might capture

- the gruff voice of in-charge Japanese males (*Yojimbo*, 1961)
- the shyness of Australian men around women and the bonding of Australian men, or mates, a legacy from Australia's woman-scarce colonial past (*Gallipoli*, 1981)

- the loquaciousness of angry Italian women (*Stolen Children*, 1992)
- the offhand, no-big-deal treatment of sex in Scandinavian films (*My Life As a Dog*, 1985)
- The surprising worldliness of Spanish women (*All About My Mother*)

Lamerica (Italy, 1994)

Hailed as one of the best films of the nineties, *Lamerica* is set against the collapse of the Soviet communist empire in the late eighties. It takes place in Albania, always poor and made even poorer by the economic chaos following the fall of the communist regime. Two Italians go to Albania and scam the government into giving them money to set up a shoe factory. They plan to take the money and run. But they need an Albanian as a corporate figurehead to make the deal legal and enable them to get the money. They settle on a doddering old man who has just been released from prison and won't suspect anything. But the old man gives them the slip and takes off across Albania in pursuit of his hazily remembered youth. All this is background, preliminary to the spiritual center of the story when one of the hustlers plunges into rural Albania in search of the old man and comes face-to-face with poverty for the first time in his life. He undergoes a transformation, a profound understanding of the yearning of the poor who want to escape destitute Albania and emigrate to affluent Italy, a kind of stand-in America to them. Lamerica feels like a documentary. In fact, director Gianni Amelio shot a lot of footage of real peasants, farms, and villages, then intercut them with set up scenes. The cast is largely amateur.

The Blue Kite (China, 1993)

Now the setting is communist China during the 1950s and 1960s when the government was intervening in the life of just about every Chinese family, busting them up, humiliating people who did not toe the party line, sending people hither and yon for training and "education." *The Blue Kite* is about one such family and the havoc and disruption visited upon it. Production was halted a few times when government censors didn't like the way the story was going. But the film got finished and had wide distribution outside China.

Reviewers feel that the film is hard-hitting and uncompromising. I don't quite agree. I sense director Tian Zhuangzhuang's efforts to keep a lid on the production by moderating the responses of affected family members and by muting the anger and despair—all to slip past the censors. Or is this understatement simply characteristic of the Chinese people's behavior in the face of adversity? I don't know. You watch the film to sort it out; you become the celluloid anthropologist.

Central Station (Brazil, 1998)

This film reveals a lot about the people of Brazil in both urban and rural settings. It is a journey story; the destination is self-discovery. The central character is a woman, Dora, played by Fernanda Montenegro, who works at a card table in a main train station in Rio where she charges a fee to write letters for illiterate people. She's not a young woman; she lives alone and seems to have no prospect of a relationship with a man. She has grown cynical: She may or may not eventually write the letters, and she often throws away the ones that she does write instead of troubling herself to take them to the post office. Then a boy of ten, Josue (Vinícius de Oliveira), comes into her life. At first she sells the kid to an underground outfit alleged to slaughter children and sell their organs. She buys a television with the money, then feels bad about that and gets the kid back. Now Josue longs to connect with his father, who he thinks lives way out in the country, many miles from Rio. The woman agrees to take him there. We don't know why. *She* doesn't know why. They journey across a treeless, prairie-like setting, through villages—some old, some recently built, in and out of bazaars and churches, inquiring after the father. The people of the countryside are deeply religious; Dora starts to soften, to feel. She shakes off her Rio cynicism. She doesn't talk about this, nor does the film dramatize it. She just starts to change, gradually, before our eyes. Dora becomes a human being, a caring mother figure, a benefactor, and she finally leaves Josue in good hands.

This film, nominated for an Academy Award for Best Foreign Film, was directed by Walter Salle, who I feel was faithful to the two Brazils of the story.

Jean De Florette (France, 1986)

For a time, this was the highest-grossing French film released in the United States. It's actually a two-part story that concludes with its sequel, *Manon of the Spring* (1986). If you see the first part, you will not rest until you get your hands on the second. It's about a cheerful hunchback, Jean, who inherits a farm in provincial France and thinks he can farm it profitably by scientific methods. He has two obstacles: The people of the region despise him as they despise all outsiders, especially educated outsiders; and the weather will not cooperate. Jean (Gerard Depardieu) and his wife and daughter work hard to make the farm productive, but a jealous older man (Yves Montand) sabotages their efforts by secretly sealing a crucial spring on Jean's property. In this year of drought, the rain clouds do not make it over the ridge that separates the village and a fertile agricultural region from the drier valley where Jean's farm is located. Geography and weather figure dramatically, but it's the anthropology that stays with you. You can't recall small-town Americans as cruel as these French provincials are—not that you don't believe the film. You do.

En Coeur en Hiver (A Heart in Winter, France, 1993)

This film is set in Paris, and I include it here to contrast with *Jean De Florette*. The characters are very sophisticated, urbane, intellectual; the story is about love and the lack of it. The French have a particular way of telling love stories, wrapping relationships in a great deal of talk, analyzing why lovers act and feel as they do,

8.11. *The Gods Must Be Crazy.* This film from Botswana is unusual in that we don't get many films from places like Africa, Asia, or South America. Often they are based on cincmatics, storytelling, and ways of living that differ markedly from our own. Usually, when we are open-minded, we are rewarded. Twentieth Century Fox.

suspecting each other's motives, discounting surface civility. A good deal of this film takes place at tables in cafes. I don't want to make the film sound dull because it isn't, providing you are willing to plunge into the subject of romance with the same intellectuality that director Claude Sautet intended.

The Gods Must Be Crazy (Botswana, 1981)
This is a completely offbeat film about the gentle—nobody gets hurt—clash of several cultures in Africa. To start matters off, someone throws a Coke bottle out of an airplane. It lands near an African bushman who thinks the gods cast it down on him (or for him—he can't tell which). He's never seen anything like it before. He takes it back to his village to show around, and no one there has any idea what it is, either. They blow into it. They taste it. They plink it. But they can't figure out what the hell it is supposed to do. Finally, they get the idea that it must be returned to the gods, who just happened to drop it on earth by mistake. This sends the original finder off on a long journey to find the rightful owner. Another journey film! All this is played for gentle laughs. The movie looks naïve and simple, even primitive, and picks up charm because of it. It was lovingly written, produced, and

directed by Jamie Uys, a Botswanan who has never been heard from again. It's a gem of a film, dropped from the sky for us Westerners.

TRY THIS

Here are a few foreign films (or films with foreign settings) based on journeys. What do the travelers really seek? How are the settings meaningful?

- *Landscape of the Mist* (Greece, 1988). Two Greek children, offspring of a prostitute, travel alone at great peril to Germany in search of their father. Directed by Theo Angelopoulos.
- *The Adventures of Priscilla, Queen of the Desert* (Australia, 1994). Three male cross-dressers who support themselves by lip-syncing disco tunes in outrageous costumes travel in a bus named Priscilla to gigs at various all-male outposts in the Australian middle-of-nowhere. Directed by Stephan Elliott and starring Terence Stamp.
- *La Strada* (Italy, 1954). Young, wide-eyed woman is a kind of moral barometer registering cruelty and immorality while others around her, more worldly, sense nothing wrong. She travels with a crude circus man across an impoverished post–World War II countryside. Directed by Federico Fellini and starring Giulietta Masina and Anthony Quinn.
- *Pele the Conqueror* (Sweden-Denmark, 1984). Aging, weak-willed man emigrates with his son from Sweden to Denmark, both becoming indentured to a wealthy farmer. Nineteenth-century setting. Much poverty. The son alternately loathes the father and tries to bolster him. Directed by Bille August.
- *Sankofa* (1994). A beautiful Ethiopian model who has forgotten about (or never knew) the brutal history of slavery that stains her country is transported by a kind of spell to the United States before the Civil War, where she lives the harsh life of a slave. Directed by Halle Gerima.

Cinematics and Natural Settings

It's easy to overlook the considerable contributions of cinematographers, editors, and music composers in establishing setting. Below are short takes on six films in which one or more of these three artists created settings where nature figures prominently.

Never Cry Wolf

We considered this film briefly in the last chapter, with regard to character. We return to it now to consider the cinematics that director Carroll Ballard employed in presenting the near-tundra conditions of northern Canada during a late winter, spring, and summer. Charles Martin Smith, playing the naturalist, is investigating the fate of caribou. The film's cinematographer (Hiro Narita) renders the sparse

8.12. *Never Cry Wolf.* Tyler, the young biologist, has just been dropped off in the middle of a wintry nowhere. He watches the plane disappear into the distance. Few films establish solitude as effectively as this one does. Sound makes an important contribution: After the drone of the plane fades away, Tyler stands in terrifying silence. Buena Vista/Disney

setting as something like abstract art in which deep meaning resides. At first there is snow everywhere. The snow does for Canada what the vast expanses of sand do for Arabia in David Lean's *Lawrence of Arabia*; that is, the snow makes people look small and insignificant. Later, as spring approaches and the snow melts away, Narita composes gently curving lines of horizon with layers of rock and sky. A flock of geese flies parallel to the ground, describing a dotty line that then becomes an arc, wondrously changing before our eyes. Rocks are shot at just the right angles to create pleasing compositions with ground and sky. Colors are muted—soft browns, grays, gray-greens, muted blues. It's all very beautiful, inviting meditation. Individual blowups of shots could hang in galleries. During his time in the quiet wilderness, Smith establishes a new, more respectful relationship with the outdoors, which, apparently, he had rarely visited before. He drops his detached scientific posture and surrenders to nature. We see him in contemplation, alone, puffing his pipe outside his shelter. Editors Peter Parasheles and Michael Chandler cut away to Narita's artful nature shots, then back to Smith. The crosscutting establishes the relationship in purely cinematic terms: no spoken words. The effect is finally spiritual.

The Mark Isham music also makes a large contribution. It's subtle and un-Western. You feel the presence of Inuits (Eskimos) in the music. The music recapitulates how they taught Smith about wolves and the land; it transports viewers to a mythic, primal state when humans and nature existed in harmony.

The Black Stallion

This film was also directed by Carroll Ballard. Much of it, too, takes place in a wilderness setting, which in this case is an uninhabited coast of Africa. It's a boy-and-his-horse story. The two are shipwrecked and nearly drown but finally bob up together on the shore. They form one of those close boy-animal relationships that you can believe only if they happen to develop in children's stories. The horse, an Arabian, is tangled up in his reins, and the boy cuts him free. A snake nearly strikes the boy; the horse tramples the snake. Boy and horse bond.

If Ballard went for spirituality in *Never Cry Wolf*, here he goes for magic. His cinematographer, Caleb Deschanel, was fond of filming boy and horse in the surf against the setting sun. The effect makes the waves shimmering gold while the boy and the horse become silhouettes. The boy befriends the hungry horse by offering him kelp on a giant shell. The horse whinnies, stomps, tosses its head, and finally approaches the shell. Editor Robert Dalva crosscuts: the boy watches, the horse acts up, finally surrendering. Dalva keeps the pacing slow. This is a paradise, a timeless island; there is no need to hurry. Later there is a dreamy underwater sequence when we see the boy's legs churning through waist-high water, then the horse's legs, also churning, following. It's a purely visual way of communicating that the two have bonded.

Then, as you might imagine, the boy finally mounts and rides the horse. Deschanel films this from every possible angle, capturing the long shadows of horse and boy on the sand as well as their reflection in a pool of shallow water. Later, when the boy and the horse are returned to the States, they have a chance to race a famous thoroughbred in a challenge match. It's the most elegantly filmed horse race in the history of the movies. Deschanel uses a very wide-angle lens to exaggerate perspective and make it seem impossible for the boy and the Arabian to catch the thoroughbred, which is in the lead. Then the magic takes over. Dalva crosscuts footage of the race and footage of the horse-and-boy shadows from their rides along the beach back in Africa. You just know by the crosscutting that the magic will return. It does. Soon the black stallion overtakes the thoroughbred and wins the race.

The music was composed by Carmine Coppola, who used an assortment of instrumentation ranging from harp and African stringed instrument to full orchestra with brass and tympani. In this case, less is more. The most magical music comes from the harp and the African stringed instrument, heard mainly during the island section of the story. The music is so subtle that you scarcely hear it; you *feel* it. You see the movie a second time just to reexperience Coppola's magic.

Snow Falling on Cedars (1999)

This film is about the murder trial of a Japanese-American wrongly accused of killing a Caucasian-American. The setting is an island in the Puget Sound near

Seattle where Caucasian- and Japanese-Americans live by fishing and raising strawberries. Relationships between the races have always been strained there.

It's a small town with a rural feel. Nature crowds it. Cedars are all over the place, and the always-felt ocean crashes on rocks. A lot of snow falls on the cedars. Director Scott Hicks certainly wants to make some connection between the goings-on of the trial and the natural setting. Hicks's hallmark is darkness: The courtroom is dark, even when the trial is in progress; people somehow get out a newspaper in dark offices; and the omnipresent cedars stand against dark backdrops. Coloration is dark green, gray, and black.

Cinematographer Robert Richardson's rendering of the cedars and the snow that accumulates on them is especially arresting. Richardson is partial to close-ups of trees, limbs, cedar needles, and rocks, while backdrops are kept blurred. The frames are lovely in a dark and sad way. They, too, could hang proudly in galleries. For a reason I can't quite explain, these visuals evoke something like haiku poetry, as does the title of the film. Maybe this is the connection Hicks wants to make: Japanese-American defendant and haiku-like photography.

Or maybe it's the music, also brilliant, by James Newton Howard, who likes percussive effects. Atonal sequences ripple through the visuals, casting their own spell. It's an enchanting blending of nature photography and music. Frankly, in my view, it isn't much of a story, but the film is certainly worth seeing for the photography and music.

Heartland

One more time for this underrated masterpiece set on the Wyoming prairie at the end of the nineteenth century. The principals, Clyde and Elinor, have a hell of a time with the weather. The winter is merciless; the land remains frozen for months and months. To film the vast prairie, cinematographer Fred Murphy preferred extreme long shots. In the autumn, before winter settles in, we see Elinor riding her horse on a neighborly errand, crossing the empty land as a small boat might make slow progress through an angry ocean—the frame makes her look so small and insignificant. The land is so empty that when someone runs across anything at all, it becomes disproportionately important. For instance, Elinor's daughter finds a shoe in a deserted cabin and says, "Look, Mama, a shoe!"

You can't ignore the prairie, which is enormous, oppressive, uncaring. In the trough of winter, Clyde has to go out on horseback to seek a midwife. Murphy films him in extreme long shot as he makes his way slowly through a swirling snowfall at night, the man and storm melded by a diffusion of dim light. Editor Bill Yahraus cuts these shots short, then cuts back to Elinor in labor in the cabin. The crosscutting produces drama: Will Clyde get caught in the blizzard? Will Elinor have to give birth without assistance?

But it's the folk-songish music by Charles Gross that lets you know that things will be all right in the end. There is no hint of tragedy in the music, no minor keys sounded. Instead, Gross employs simple string instrumentation and cheerful ditties so that nothing stays downbeat for long. Nor do Clyde and Elinor admit defeat, despite setbacks.

Aguirre: the Wrath of God (German, 1972)

This film, written and directed by the German Werner Hertzog, is about a contingent of sixteenth-century Spanish conquistadors who entertain notions of conquering Peru. They come for the Crown, for the conversion of heathen souls, and for gold. Among them are about a hundred soldiers and a handful of priests, noblemen, and pampered ladies. The film opens with a spectacular extreme long shot that shows the band, led by head conquistador Gonzalo Pizarro, wending its way precariously down a steep mountainside and into the jungle below. It's a descent into hell; Pizarro's people have evidently never heard of camping gear. They wear the absolute wrong clothing—chest armor, steel helmets, heavy robes, thick velvet dresses. The ladies are carried about in sedan chairs, and a tagalong aristocrat has his own throne. When the contingent gets to the bottom of the mountain they encounter a rushing river. They don't know what else to do but make a couple of rafts, float, and vainly claim everything they see for Spain, as if anyone were listening.

To make a long story short, the jungle wins. As photographed by Thomas Mauch, it is dark, dense, foreboding, and unforgiving. The contingent is always climbing clumsily over big rocks. It doesn't belong here. The river rushes and tumbles so fast that the rafts seem out of control. Unseen Indians take out the soldiers and priests, one by one, with poisoned darts. The rafts, made of soft wood, become waterlogged and start to sink. Water sloshes over ankles. Everyone looks bedraggled, ridiculously attired, unprepared, and out of place. They execute each other for silly crimes. Finally only two remain, a captain, Aguirre (Klaus Kinsley), and his daughter Inez. He has made himself delusional with dreams of gold and power. He says he will found a new empire here in the jungle, using his daughter to produce subjects. But the visuals show him to be a fool, for by now the raft, the only raft left, has floated into calm water that leads nowhere else. Little spidery monkeys descend on the raft, leaping and running across the soggy logs, bouncing off Aguirre's shoulders. He tries to swat them away, but they keep coming, like the Furies. It's one of the most strikingly original sequences of man overcome by wilderness ever photographed.

Bambi

Everything about this full-length, animated Walt Disney movie is calculated to spell "Home run!" in the hearts of Mr. and Mrs. U.S.A. and their children. At the same time, the story is skillfully told and prophetically on the side of nature; it feels very progressive for 1942. It was the *Lion King* of its time.

Our interest here is mainly in the depiction of wilderness, which changes with the seasons and with the drama. As Bambi is born, the forest setting is lovely—dark in the background but never dreary, warm and light-struck in the foreground where we see gathering families of rabbits, field mice, bluebirds, and skunks—little, cuddly creatures—all come to behold the birth of the Prince.

Winter comes. At first the snow is benign and fun as Bambi and his rabbit chum Thumper explore a frozen pond. The setting is white, innocent and benign, pure. Then comes the poignant sequence in which Bambi's mom gets shot. Traditional Hollywood suspenseful music transforms the wintry setting into something dark and sinister. Now skies turn gray and trees black; overall illumination dims. Bambi crawls back into the gloomy thicket, baffled and alone. When he ventures out he at last beholds his stately father. He's one of those stiff-spined dads who feels that it's wrong for children to show emotion. Demeanor is all. As he instructs Bambi, he is shot (photographed, that is) from a low angle against a black background. So much swirling snow intrudes that the father is scarcely seen at all, which makes him all the more regal and distant. He finally turns and walks away, Bambi following.

After this it's spring, and all of Bambi's forest buddies are finding mates. The forest takes on much color and brightness with leaves and flowers. Backgrounds lighten. In time Bambi pairs up with the fluttery-eyed Phylline. Petals fall. A churchlike choir hums hymnic approval. But before Bambi can call Phylline his, he must battle a dark, rival stag. Clash, clash. Dramatic Hollywood music. The background goes black again, the combatants are rim-lit in red. Naturally, Bambi wins, but two more challenges remain. There is a forest fire that turns the forest into a gray-and-red holocaust; later, a pack of dogs pursues Bambi and Phylline. Bambi stumbles, and his father appears to admonish him: "Get up!" This he does, as a future King must.

The film ends as it began, in early summer, with Phylline, the new queen of Woodlandia, having given birth to twins. The wilderness offers gifts of soft pastels and sprightly music. Goodness and purity prevail.

You don't have to give credit to people working on an animated film in the same way you give credit to people who helped shape a live-action film. David Hand is listed as the director, while Frank Churchill and Edward Plumb did the music. As for the all-important coloration, it's hard to determine which of the four animators—Milt Kahl, Eric Larson, Franklin Thomas, and Oliver M. Johnson, Jr.—should be accorded credit for that stupendous achievement. Maybe all.

TRY THIS

Here are some films in which the natural setting figures importantly. Rent a few and note the cinematic techniques used to render nature. Also pay attention to what the natural setting means.

- *The Last of the Mohicans*

- *My Brilliant Career* (1979)
- *Deliverance*
- Any two *Robin Hoods* (there are fourteen)
- *Snow White and the Seven Dwarfs* (1937)
- *Badlands*
- *Blue Lagoon* (1980)
- *Dances With Wolves*
- *Jeremiah Johnson* (1972)
- *McCabe and Mrs. Miller*
- *Mr. Johnson* (1991)
- *The Searchers*
- *Strangers in Good Company* (1991)
- *Walkabout* (1971)
- *Picnic at Hanging Rock*
- *White Fang* (1991)

chapter nine

✿

Tones

All movies strike tones—at least one tone, usually more than one. It's just as important to "hear" tone as it is to note anything else. Miss the tone, and you will often miss the point of the film.

Tone is like mood. It may be the same thing. Certain films are suffused by particular moods—doom, hope, corruption, salvation. Tone may be easier to understand because of our familiarity with the phrase "tone of voice." In *Toy Story 2*, the cowgirl Jesse is skeptical of how much Andy loves Woody (Andy is a kid, and Woody is his toy cowboy), because Woody has ended up in a 25-cents bin at a yard sale. Jesse says, "Sounds like [Andy] really loves you," but she says this sarcastically. Her meaning is in her tone of voice and in the sneer on her face.

The 1997 Bruce Willis movie, *The Jackal*, has nearly the same content as a 1973 film called *The Day of the Jackal*. In both pictures a professional assassin eludes police and the military long enough to make a serious attempt on the life of a head of state. The earlier film, directed by Fred Zinnemann, is a terse, lean thriller about the efforts of French authorities to track down the assassin, played by Edward Fox. Character is developed subtly and swiftly through behavior, props, costuming, and a few choice words. There are one or two chases, as befits a thriller, but they are modestly produced. The climax is swift and blunt and contains no moralizing. The film feels objective. The tone of the film is that of a documentary.

The remake, directed by Michael Caton-Jones, is bigger and showier. Willis's weapons make louder explosions and blow more stuff up. Willis puts on some pretty mean faces; Fox, in the earlier version, doesn't put on any faces at all; he is disinterested in what he has to do, which makes him more scary than any faces he could put on. Fox is double-crossed by a special-weapons supplier, so he kills the man quietly with one of those fast twists of the neck that killers in movies are so adept at. When Willis is double-crossed by a weapons expert, he blows the guy up with a big rocket. Willis's *Jackal* strikes a different tone, that of a high-tech thriller with a really, really cool guy. Nearly the same plot but different tones equals different viewing experiences. Fox's *Jackal* is more ambivalent—we like Fox, and then we don't like Fox. But Willis's *Jackal* is straight-up, unsubtle action adventure. And since Willis is so established in the public mind as a can-do, good-guy hero, adoring audiences uncritically grant him wide moral latitude.

Up Tones

Movies with what might be called "up tones" are very familiar and probably make up 80 percent of all movies produced. These are films that end happily. Also, they are nearly always genre films—types of movies that are made over and over because they are predictable, audience-pleasing, and thus bankable. Below, briefly—because we don't need to dwell on what we already know—are some common types of up-tone pictures.

9.1. *The Day of the Jackal.* We'd probably have more respect for the hackneyed contemporary remake if it would display some of the restraint of this fine film. Universal.

Adventure

These are exotic action movies in which the men are brave and the women beautiful. Increasingly, though, the women are just as brave as the men, though they are still beautiful. Recent successful adventure movies include *The Mask of Zorro* (1998) and *The Mummy* (1999). Dominant tone: swashbuckling.

Thrillers

Thrills and chills and spills. The plots are always melodramatic—lots of high drama, then a happy ending. Always predictable. Recent thrillers: *Double Jeopardy* (subgenre: avenging woman) and *End of Days* (subgenre: high-tech sci-fi). Dominant tone: nerve-wracking.

Feel-Good

These are sentimental movies intended to send you away from the theater feeling good about just about everything but especially about life. At first this optimistic view is in question. Someone is cynical or loses hope. But the scriptwriters turn everything around. Hope rises. Climaxes bring tears to our eyes and leave us believing that people are good after all, and so is life. We just have to go through some bad times first.

Casablanca (1942) takes place during World War II; in fact, it was made in the middle of the war and was meant as a kind of propaganda piece. Humphrey Bogart is the cynical owner of a nightclub in Casablanca, where Nazis are in control. He refuses to help an important member of the Allied underground, saying, "I stick out my neck for nobody." Then the wife of the underground agent, played by Ingrid Bergman, floats into the nightclub. (She and Bogart had an affair some years before in Paris.) Bogart softens and helps the agent and Ingrid escape, and in doing so regains his humanity. We feel good: Bogart has a heart after all, and so should all Americans.

In *Meet John Doe*, a fascist figure (Edward Arnold) has set up a broken-down baseball player (Gary Cooper) as the figurehead for a political movement leading to the presidency. He plans to rule the country with an "iron hand," i.e., be an American Hitler. He fools everybody but Cooper, who tries to expose him. But Arnold, who has all the power, succeeds in discrediting Cooper. Cooper's thousands of followers, dedicated to the decency of the common man, disavow him in a poignant scene; he is booed and hooted at in a baseball stadium, in a driving rainstorm. It looks pretty bad for a time—the fascists really are going to take over and deliver the United States to the Nazis. But Cooper saves the day single-handedly by nearly committing suicide—he'd promised earlier to kill himself on Christmas Eve if people didn't start caring about each other more. The leaders of the John Doe movement happen to be present as Cooper is just seconds away from throwing himself off a tall building. Also present are Arnold, Cooper's girlfriend, and a newspaper editor. By Cooper's action, they all now know John Doe to be honest, and talk him out of it. Everyone is so happy. Viewers feel terrific. Our faith in the goodness of human nature and the American Way is restored. Merry Christmas.

When a Man Loves a Woman is about an alcoholic woman played by Meg Ryan. In spite of the many problems her drinking causes her family, her husband (Andy Garcia) loves her and continues to love her through thick and thin, and finally, as we knew all along because this is a Hollywood movie, she starts going to AA and gets her life back. Everyone feels grand. Love conquers all. The dominant tone of feel-good movies, then, is *Everything's gonna be all right.*

Against All Odds

This type of up-tone movie is about underdogs or people who are up against so much that their situation looks hopeless. Audiences readily identify with these people because now and then they feel overwhelmed by life themselves. This is the kind of story that made confident tortoises pitted against flaky hares world-famous.

It probably wouldn't occur to you that a movie starring Paul Newman as a Boston lawyer would have much in common with the famous tortoise-and-hare boxing movie *Rocky*. You remember Rocky. He's washed up. He works for the mob, breaking the legs of people who won't make their loan payments. Then, against all odds and by a convolution of plot I won't go into, he gets a shot at the world champion. Paul is an alcoholic lawyer reduced to chasing ambulances. When

9.2. *Meet John Doe.* John Doe is booed and actually arrested. The guy laughing is the fascist who threatens to take over the country. One of the most poignant moments in the Capra oeuvre.

he is sober, he tries to talk people into suing other people or corporations. It's dishonorable, borderline unethical work. Then, like Rocky, he gets his big chance. A friend gives him an easy case getting the wheels turning for an insurance company to pay a claim having to do with the death of one of its policyholders on the operating table of a big Catholic hospital. But Paul stays sober long enough to poke around and find big-time malpractice. He talks the survivors into letting him file a suit against the hospital and the surgeon for very large money. Tortoise-like, he goes against one of Boston's slickest, smoothest law firms. He seems certain to lose, but like the tortoise he perseveres. He digs up evidence, gets key people to testify, and wins the suit, against all odds. This film is *The Verdict*, and Sidney Lumet directed it in 1982. Like all against-the-odds films, it strikes a tone of Never, never give up.

The Hurricane (1999) alters this formula somewhat. Denzel Washington is an ex-boxer doing a life sentence for murders he didn't commit. He educates himself in the law while doing the time, but his appeals get just so far, and he's finally stymied. He resigns himself to doing the long time. Then a boy, a woman, and two men, who are a kind of family, learn about his plight and start working in his behalf. They even move to the prison town to be in a better position to plan legal strategy with Denzel, who is now refortified. They are up against the corrupt police system that stacked the deck against Washington in the first place and an equally corrupt state judicial system that doesn't want to admit error. It comes down to one last shot in a federal courtroom. The miracle happens: The judge, played by Rod Steiger, considers new evidence and frees Washington.

This film sounds a different tone: *miraculous*—because, based on what the movie provides us, Washington should not have prevailed at all. We really don't know that much about the family that comes to Washington's rescue. We don't know what motivates them. It's not easy to condense stacks of evidence for cinematic presentation, so this part of the film is suggestive rather than explanatory. From Washington's point of view, the family that helped him is a miracle. We leave the theater with miracle ringing in our ears.

Down Tones

Two common types of films that ring downer tones are film noir and what I call *the fear of the big*.

Film Noir

We have looked at film noir from various perspectives in other chapters—in chapter 2 in terms of low-key lighting, in chapter 5 in connection with some films Billy Wilder made, and in chapter 6 when we considered the tragic mode of storytelling. Now let's consider the mood of noir and how it might affect you as a viewer. When you are in a noir film, you feel uneasy, off balance, unsure. You dread what will happen to the main character, who is headed for disaster. You want him (it's always a man) to quit the job, get out of town, dump the woman. She is nothing but trouble. You wish he would smarten up. But, no. The dominant mood is dread.

You feel this way while watching the classic *The Big Heat* (1953). It stars Glenn Ford as a police lieutenant whose wife gets blown up when Ford starts looking into civic corruption. Ford leaves the force a bitter man bent on vengeance. You like Ford but you fear for him. He's up against the likes of Lee Marvin, who thinks nothing of throwing hot coffee in Gloria Graham's face. Ford isn't as poised and assured as, say, Mel Gibson in *Payback*, who is the very portrait of cool. When you watch *Payback*, you know everything's gonna be all right because the film is a kind of comic strip. But you don't know that about Ford. He is more complex than Gibson. His hatred and need for vengeance could be his undoing. Gibson can control his world of bad guys. Ford's world is more iffy, and Ford himself is more problematic. Thus, dread—and the down tone.

A similar dread-full world is created by *Devil in a Blue Dress* (1995), which has a very interesting twist of character: This time the noir hero is an African-American man played by Denzel Washington. (Denzel gets around in this book.) It's tough enough for white men to make it in noir worlds. But when you are black and have to endure 1940s-style pandemic discrimination, you are doubly handicapped. Washington also has one more strike against him: He has no experience in detec-

9.3. *The Big Heat.* Glenn Ford (left) may be too hotheaded for his own good. Universal.

tive work. He has no experience in the world of crime. He takes a job locating a classy white woman who has disappeared. This alone could get him in trouble. The title intensifies the dread: Washington plunges toward a kind of devil.

The Fear of the Big

Movies have often exploited Americans' natural distrust of the big. In *The Parallax View* (1974), big government is willing to knock off reporter Warren Beatty for investigating the suspicious death of a U.S. senator. *Three Days of the Condor* (1975) stars Robert Redford who tries to figure out why his intelligence section was wiped out—that is, everybody was shot to death—apparently by another section of government, a renegade CIA offshoot. *All the President's Men* is the story of the Watergate scandals of the seventies made spicier by a strong suggestion that the lives of reporters Bill Woodward and Carl Bernstein could be in jeopardy if they don't lay off. More recently, *The Rock* is a story about a man (Sean Connery) who has been illegally imprisoned for many years. They—government people—let him out only when he agrees to lead an elite team against some military men who are holding San Francisco hostage with lethal rockets. And as we saw in chapter 7, *Enemy of the State* is one of the scariest evil-government movies of all: It posits that the government is watching us and gathering data about us from every conceivable source, including the phone booth at 7-Eleven.

Counterbalancing movies depicting big government as evil are movies in which evil is big business. For every American who believes government is out to get him, there's another who believes that big corporations are bent on destroying his soul. Anticorporate films include a wide range of genres: *The Apartment* wants to be a romantic comedy. True, Jack Lemmon and Shirley MacLaine eventually fall in love, but they are so corrupted by the big, manipulative insurance company they work for that they have trouble discovering each other. *Alien* (1979) acts like a sci-fi flick, and it is; everyone remembers the alien creature. But everybody also forgets that the entire story is set up by a megacorporation that wants the alien brought back to Earth in order to replicate its blood for its weapons division. Everyone on the *Nostromo* is dispensable. The android Asher is coolly efficient in the way he bumps people off. He's a stand-in for the amorality of the corporation. Not many sci-fi movies are as cynical as this one.

The dominant mood of these fear-of-the-big movies is either *paranoia* ("They're out to get me!") or *suspicions confirmed* ("I always knew Microsoft runs everything").

Mixed Tones

As good as some of the aforementioned movies are, they are very predictable. You may find films with mixed tones or moods to be far more original and compelling. These films make you think. You don't forget them easily. You leave the theater and head for the drive-through with the movie still ringing in your ears. The voice from

the black box says, "You want that supersized?" but you don't hear. You turn to
your date and say, "What did we just see?"

Here is a miscellany of such films.

Sullivan's Travels (1941)

This film is about a famous film director (played by Joel McCrea) who is tired of
making mere entertainments. He wants to do a film with a real social conscience.
To find out how poor people live, he plunges into the life of a penniless bum. Soon,
though, his producers track him down and supply him with a 1940s-version
Winnebago with lots of food and comforts. Sullivan hypocritically goes along with
this for a time, but to his credit he runs away again and rejoins the poor. He finally
ends up in a church in a poor black neighborhood, surrounded by poor parishioners
who are watching a Mickey Mouse cartoon. They laugh heartily. Sullivan laughs,
too, and undergoes a transformation. He realizes that people don't want message
films. All they want from movies are laughs. So he goes back to Hollywood, makes
funny films, and at last feels fulfilled.

For me, this film strikes a curious tone. Is it a satire, or is it straight? For years
I thought it was a satire, but then I learned that the director, Preston Sturges, really

9.4. *Sullivan's Travels*. Preston Sturges not only wrote but also directed this film. It was made
at the height of the rigidly controlled studio system era when it was rare for a screenwriter to
direct his own script. When writers do direct their own handiwork the result, then as now, is
often appealingly idiosyncratic. MCA TV.

meant for it to be taken at face value. Well, I just don't want to believe that. I want to believe that what Sturges really had in mind was to criticize Hollywood's tendency to go for the easy, ha-ha money; he wanted to show how directors justify their selling out. If *Sullivan's Travels* is a straight film, it's monotonic and less interesting for that. If I can think of it as satire, it becomes multitonic and all the more interesting.

My Name Is Joe (1998)

This film by British filmmaker Ken Loach is a love story. No, it's a story about an alcoholic, Joe (Peter Mullen), trying to stay sober. It's both. His girl loves him, and because she loves and supports him, we expect him to quit drinking, as Hollywood would have it. But this is not *When a Man Loves a Woman*. The tone is quite different. To be sure, Joe goes to AA and has a sponsor, but he is also mixed up with a small-time British mob. A friend on a soccer team Joe had organized is in trouble with the mob, and Joe tries to help him. Meanwhile Joe meets a woman, Sarah, played by Louise Godall. They date, fall in love, etc. Only this is not Meg Ryan. She's pretty, but not pert-Meg pretty. She's more real. She's a social worker who admires Joe for staying sober.

But Joe does something that causes the soccer friend to get killed, and, feeling terrible about the incident, he goes back to drinking. If this were a Hollywood movie, there would be a scene where Sarah throws her arms around Joe and says, "Oh, Joe, don't blame yourself!" and he would get back on the wagon and stay on it, and they would live happily ever after. But it doesn't go this way. Sarah shows up at the funeral for the friend, but she keeps her distance. She's not so quick to take Joe back. And Joe is so ashamed that he stays away from Sarah. The funeral ends, Joe walks away, Sarah drifts near Joe and walks in his direction. But they do not touch nor look at each other. And that's all. The End. You don't know.

This film rings several tones: *personal responsibility*, *immersion in society*, *interdependency*, and (because of that last scene) *ambiguity*. There is another important tone sounded, too, which has to do with Joe's history of beating up women. Sarah knows about this, yet sticks with him. She isn't stupid. She has *faith*. She feels it, and we hear it. *Faith*, then, is another important mood of the film.

Groundhog Day (1993)

Is this a comedy? It must be. It stars Bill Murray. But it's also a kind of sci-fi or fantasy film, because it's based on the idea of a man's reliving one day over and over again. It's a love story, too, because Andie MacDowell finally falls in love with Bill. *Groundhog Day* is all of these, and each facet of the story strikes its own tone.

The story is about a self-centered TV reporter (Murray) who goes out with a crew on February 2 to the town of Punxsutawney. He aims to do a light story about a groundhog whose appearance, or lack of it, predicts whether or not winter will persist. There are a few laughs in this because Bill Murray makes us laugh no matter what kind of story he shows up in, but it's the same-day-over-and-over-again part that really starts to interest us. Think of it: If you could live yesterday all over again, you could cash in on your knowledge in many ways. You could get rich. But Murray uses his knowledge of yesterday, Groundhog Day, to impress his TV producer (MacDowell), whom he has long wanted to bed. Two or three Groundhog Days after this, Murray achieves his goal.

Then the story takes a complex moral turn. In reliving the same day over and over, Murray also confronts himself and his many faults. He starts to change. Groundhog Day by Groundhog Day, he corrects a bit of the selfishness he exhibited before. He becomes a better person. So the possibility of *change*, as a mood, gradually replaces the *self-serving* feel of the first part of the film. Mood, feel, tone—it gets pretty complicated, and we are grateful it is.

Crimes and Misdemeanors

This film has a lot of characters, one of whom is responsible for a heinous crime. Martin Landau plays a wealthy ophthalmologist who has his mistress murdered by a hit man and, for a time, feels terrible about it. He confesses to his rabbi and goes about trying to make amends with his conscience. Meanwhile, in a separate story, Woody Allen is an obscure filmmaker at work on a film about an obscure Israeli philosopher. To support himself, Allen agrees to do a promotional video about a

9.5. *Groundhog Day.* Probably no single device of plot generates so many narrative types as the love story. It plays well against war (*A Farewell to Arms*), against peace (*The Best Years of Our Lives*), against political revolution (*Reds*), against comedy (*There's Something About Mary*), against tragedy (*The Seven Samurai*). Columbia.

famous though fatuous TV producer (Alan Alda). While making the video, Allen falls in love with a woman (Mia Farrow) from the fringes of Alda's life. But bad luck intervenes. The philosopher, who ironically has written about hope, takes his own life. Farrow rejects Allen for Alda. Finally, at the end of the story, Landau and Allen happen to meet at a party. They get into a strange, abstract conversation about sin and salvation. Allen does not feel good about his life, but it is obvious that Landau is okay with his; he has overcome his guilt. He got away with the murder, both legally and spiritually. Meanwhile, all Allen had committed was a misdemeanor when he came on to Farrow while a married man. But he pays more for his misdemeanor than Landau for his crime. Farrow, who had been taking him for a ride, leaves him for the better-heeled Alda, who is in a good position to help her advance in her career. So the bad are not punished, while the not-so-bad suffer. Justice is not poetic; the philosopher knew nothing. There are many tones here. You can't tell which are meant to be straight and which satiric.

Unforgiven (1992)

In this film, Clint Eastwood is a retired gunman who gets involved in a kind of quest to find and punish two men who slashed the face of a prostitute. He gets a friend (Morgan Freeman) to help him. Later, a gun-crazy kid (Jaimz Wolvett) out to make a reputation joins the pair. There is a pretty good sum of money involved. So far, this feels like a conventional Western. But the mood shifts when Freeman starts to show uneasiness. First, when we finally do see the face of the prostitute we note that she was not cut all that badly—her eyes were not gouged out, nor were her breasts disfigured, as we were led to believe. Instead, her face bears only two shallow cuts, which seem to be healing fine. Second, Clint picks off one of the bad guys by shooting him in the gut. But he's just a kid. He lies helplessly in the dirt, dying, crying out for help. Freeman doesn't say anything, but we can tell from his face that he doesn't like shooting a man so young and leaving him to die. Was what the kid did *that* bad? Later, Clint's ambitious, young, gun-crazy sidekick shoots the other bad guy while he's sitting in an outhouse—a chickenshit act. Later he feels guilty about what he did. Clint is starting to regret the whole outing, too. He admits that it's a hell of a thing to kill a man. The dead man loses everything he's got. Morgan has already abandoned the quest by this point, but when he's caught and strung up by the town's psychopathic sheriff (Gene Hackman), Clint gets crazy himself and goes on a rampage. He outdraws everyone in the bar and ends up shooting Hackman point blank in the face.

A lot of viewers miss the point of *Unforgiven*, which is to say that they miss the main mood of *irredeemable psychopathology*. This is an anti-Western. It's not about traditional, Western-style heroism; it's about crazy gunmen who are compelled to kill. It was a tremendous box-office and critical hit, winning four Academy Awards and making it practically impossible for anyone to make a straight Western ever again.

9.6. *Crimes and Misdemeanors.* It's hard to know what is going on in this film. Is it satire? Is it straight? Both? If so, where, when, which? How does Allen get away with mixing this story of a hapless documentary filmmaker and a wannabe TV producer, with . . .

. . . this completely different story, about a rich eye doctor who rubs out his lover because she makes trouble? Orion.

The Conversation

This is a dense film about surveillance in modern society. It stars Gene Hackman as an extremely competent professional bugger. He and his crew can record conversations in seemingly impossible situations. But he has several personal problems. First, he is morally detached from his profession. He doesn't want to know what the conversations he records will be used for. Second, he is a loner—suspicious of everybody, afraid of being bugged himself, and unable to connect with a woman who cares for him.

This is an art film about character and morality, not a thriller like *Enemy of the State*. Makers of art films are vastly more interested in exploring characters and ideas, often in cinematically compelling ways, than in creating primitive suspense. The challenge for viewers watching *The Conversation* is to figure out the connection between Hackman's profession and his self-imposed isolation.

As the story unfolds, Hackman starts to develop bad feelings about one particular conversation he recorded. He thinks it will be used to murder someone. He goes into deep guilt and actually tries to stop the murder from happening. But as it turns out, he is wrong, which is a large part of the meaning of the film: You can't always tell what is going on. Multiple tones are heard: *professional responsibility, loneliness, regret, redemption, the nature of reality itself and how you discover it.*

TRY THIS

Here are some more films with intriguingly ambiguous or complex tones. Rent, watch, and listen.

- *1900* (1977). This is the story of two men born on a large farm on the same day in the year 1900. One is born to the farmer's owner, the other to a family living and working on the farm. The two men's lives take radically different directions. Listen for the epic tone of social class conflict. Directed by Bernardo Bertolucci, starring Robert De Niro and Burt Lancaster (Italy).
- *Babette's Feast* (1987). For complex reasons, a woman who was once a master chef leaves her native France to cook for a community of puritanical old folks in Denmark. They abstain from indulging their senses. Babette then wins the French lottery and spends every centime of it doing a feast for the sense-starved seniors. Tones: *self-denial, sensory rebirth, profound gratitude.* Directed by Gabriel Axel (Denmark).
- *3 Women* (1977). Three women interact in a barren, dreamlike California setting centered on an old-folks home. Note how the tone of the film shifts back and forth from the real to the unreal. Directed by Robert Altman, starring Sissy Spacek, Shelly Duvall, and Janice Rule.
- *Happiness* (1998). A half-dozen interwoven stories about men and women trying to find—what? Love? Someone to dominate? Someone to confide to? Happiness? The dominant tone is *desperation*. Directed by Todd Solondz and

starring Lara Flynn Boyle, Philip Seymour Hoffman, and Camryn Manheim.

- *Dogma* (1999). Wild, crazy, irreverent look at Catholicism with a plot having to do with two outcast angels who want back in. You can't miss the satire. Directed by Kevin Smith and starring Ben Affleck and Matt Damon.
- *Irreconcilable Differences* (1984). A sprawling comedy about a couple who become great successes in Hollywood and neglect their ten-year-old daughter. Broad farcical tone. Daughter sues them for divorce. Directed by Charles Shyer and starring Drew Barrymore, Ryan O'Neal, and Shelly Long.

Cinematics and Tone

Now let's see how cinematographers, editors, and sound recordists and mixers combined their arts to create distinctive tones in three of the films discussed above: *My Name Is Joe*, *The Conversation*, and *Unforgiven*.

The Realist Style in *My Name Is Joe*

In chapter 5, I discussed the contrasting film styles of realism and formalism. I pointed out that each has its own way of arriving at truth. *My Name Is Joe* is a realist film. Its director, Ken Loach, has made a number of films about working-class people and the problems they face. He's on the side of the poor and is critical of the aspects of big business or big government that tend to oppress the poor. Given this subject and Loach's attitude toward it, he would come off as pretentious and even hypocritical to spend a lot of money on expensive sets or special effects. Thus he keeps his production values simple and inexpensive, because these suit his subjects and the tone he usually strikes. Joe, Sara, and everyone else in *My Name Is Joe* live on the edge. They are "on the dole" or work with the poor. The film was shot in real apartments, medical centers, and bars on locations in Edinburgh, Scotland. If the rooms of these locations seem cramped, it's because they are. Working-class people live out their lives in small rooms.

Most of the optics are "normal"; that is, Loach avoids the distorting effects of wide-angle or telephoto photography. If you take the trouble to note how Loach lights his interiors, you will not find much that is fancy. No deep shadows, no alternating areas of light and dark. Instead, rooms are functionally lit and often go nearly dark if the camera follows someone walking away from a lamp or a window. The editing (by Jonathon Morris) is also functional, though certainly competent. Editing never intrudes, never becomes "arty." It functions to keep events clear and swiftly moving.

There is a moment in the film that exemplifies low-cost, realist filmmaking. Joe is driving to another city to make a drug pickup. As he drives, we see close-ups of him. He's thinking about Sara and a possible better life with her. Most big-budget American productions would film the close-ups by hitching Joe's car to a truck with a specially rigged camera on a crane cantilevered over the hood of the car, allowing tight, front-angle shots of Joe through a glareless windshield. Or they'd rig a camera on the side of the car and shoot through a side window, also made free of glare with a sheet of special material and a special lens. Loach eschews such frippery. It just costs too much money and takes too much time to set up. Instead, he merely had a cameraperson film inside Joe's car, as you and I would think to do. In fact, I used to film like this when I made films on zero budgets. I had three choices: I filmed the driver from the front passenger seat in a side-angle close-up; I filmed the driver from the back seat catercornered from the driver for a kind of three-quarter, rear-angle shot; or I had my friend Karl, who is five feet four inches tall, scrunch down on the floor of the front seat for a dramatic low-angle shot of the driver with, maybe, an occasional pan to the passenger. Loach utilized the first two options and saved himself a lot of time and money. I never heard of anybody who walked out on the film because it lacked a crane shot. People have walked out on my films, but when I asked them why, they never said, "Because you didn't use a truck with a crane." My point is that much of the working-class feel of the film is derived from its simple, realist style.

The Formalist Style in *The Conversation*

But Coppola worked far differently in *The Conversation*, which is essentially a formalist film; that is, intrusive cinematic means are occasionally brought to bear on the story. The film was made at the height of the so-called American film renaissance, which lasted roughly from 1965 to 1980, when young filmmakers explored bold new techniques of shooting, editing, and mixing sound. *The Conversation*, a fine film in its own right, owes much to *Blowup*, another film about figuring out reality which I mentioned in chapter 3.

In the opening shot of *The Conversation*, Coppola signals that sound will play a main role in the story. This is an extreme long shot taken from the roof of a department store in San Francisco. The camera looks down on Union Square, where the couple, the "target," are walking and talking. At this point we do not hear their words. Instead, we hear a strange, fluttering electronic sound, both harsh and beautiful. Soon the sound starts to resolve into something resembling human speech, which is the conversation of the couple as the recordist atop the department store adjusts his equipment to maximize the signal. But the speech is never quite intelligible in these opening shots. The sound becomes a metaphor for the film: *You can't quite figure out what is going on.* And the main tone of troubling reality is sounded.

Later in the film, this intriguing sound is mixed into the sound tracks for scenes that contain nothing that could produce the sound. In these scenes, we see Gene Hackman puzzling. Will the couple really be murdered? Would he then be responsible? What is the truth? What is real? Pairing a sound from one scene with the visuals of a completely different scene is vintage formalism. The sound could be in Harry's mind, or it might work as a kind of electronic music, setting the mood.

The Conversation also includes a subdued musical theme for piano by composer David Shire. It's a mix of classical and blues and swims into the film as a kind of scene connector, inviting viewers to ponder the mystery. It could also be a clue to Hackman's personality, the classic part referring to his rigidity, the blues part suggesting his aloneness. In fact, Hackman does play the saxophone alone in his apartment now and then, an aspect of the story that may seem contrived. Formalists always run that risk.

The film has lots of long shots of interiors. Coppola shows Hackman walking around in his spartan apartment, drifting in and out of frame. If he walks into the kitchen, the film does not cut to show him in the kitchen. It keeps the camera on the living room, on space without people, which is an unusual thing for a film to do. You can't help pondering Hackman's isolation in the space the shot gives you. If the film had cut to the kitchen, we would see Hackman doing something, and the mood of spiritual vacancy would be destroyed.

Hackman's studio takes up only a corner of an entire floor of a vast, empty warehouse. The setting is cold, cool, and again vacant. There are chain-link space dividers that throw harsh shadows of grids. Set designer Dean Tavoularis intended to show bleakness and succeeded. The client (played briefly by Robert Duvall) and his corporation are housed in a sterile-seeming building of preformed concrete, hard, cold, and efficient. We see Hackman venturing up the stairs in the building in extreme long shot, again placing him in an empty, spiritless setting. The hotel where Hackman hears (or thinks he hears) the murder of the client had to be San Francisco's ugliest at the time the film was made, the garish Jack Tarr. (It has since been remodeled and humanized.) The actual murder is made visual in a most ingenious and fitting way. Hackman takes a room next to the room where the couple he had recorded said they had to be at this certain hour on this particular day. Each room has a balcony, and the balconies are separated by translucent Plexiglas slabs, like shower door material. As Hackman hears screams and moves to the balcony, he glimpses a bloody hand against the Plexiglas and a smear of blood, but the face is too far away from the Plexiglas to be in focus, so he can't really see who is being murdered. This is the visual equivalent of the stuttery electronic sound of conversation that also could not be clearly made out. Both allude to the metaphysical mystery from Hackman's point of view. (Check out chapter 6 for the dramatic implications of telling a story from a single point of view.)

Later Hackman lets himself into the apartment where the murder took place and finds it spotless, the blood all wiped away—except when he flushes the toilet, a lot of blood and guts come up. You may not like this toilet blood-and-guts scene. It also seems contrived, as is the last scene of the film in which Hackman completely dismantles his apartment—ripping out light fixtures and prying up the hardwood floorboards—in search of a microphone he never finds. Unsuccessful, he sits in the middle of his utterly trashed living room and plays blues on the saxophone. As I said before, the trouble with formalists is that they sometimes go overboard. They need someone to say, "Francis, really now, back off. Can't you do without this scene?" Coppola had the same problem later, when making *Apocalypse Now*, which some feel is overproduced. No one told the emperor that he had no clothes.

Meteorology and Insane Gunplay in *Unforgiven*

At the end of *Unforgiven*, Clint Eastwood strides into Greeley's bar and, in a psychopathic spasm, kills a half-dozen men, including the sheriff. Meanwhile a storm rages outside. It's a most cinematic storm. Thunder punctuates nearly every snarling utterance Eastwood makes and every ugly thing he does. Eastwood says, "Who's the owner of this shithole?" Thunder. Greeley speaks up. Eastwood shoots him. Thunder. Then Eastwood shoots five patrons who try to draw on him. Thunder. Seconds later, during a period of calm, a frightened writer from the East wants to know in what order Eastwood killed the men. Eastwood says, "I lost track, but you'll be the last." Thunder. Lightning, lightning. A wounded guy makes the mistake of groaning; Eastwood shoots him. Thunder and lightning. Eastwood sticks his head out the door of the bar and yells, "Anybody out there shoots at me, I'll kill him and burn his house down and kill his wife and friends." Thunder, lightning, thunder.

It has rained before in the story, and also snowed, but both events were subdued compared to the crashing and flashing that accompany the ugly killings at the

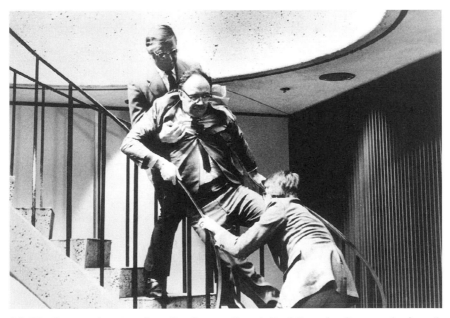

9.8. *The Conversation.* As a formalist director, Francis Ford Coppola often goes for formalism in frame composition. Also see pages 20–24. United Artists.

end. Before, Clint's craziness was muted. But when he finally goes totally nuts, so does nature.

Go to a video store and rent a film with a strong tone you can't get out of your head. It still rings in your ears. You want to know, *how the hell did they do that?* So you rent the film again and find out, by noting the cinematic means employed to strike the tone that won't go away.

Or do the same thing for one or more of the films listed below, whose dominant tones I have taken the liberty of naming.

* *Breaking the Waves* (1996, Danish)   Steadfast love
* *The Grey Fox* (Canadian)   Mastering change
* *Cinema Paradiso* (Italian)   Regretting change
* *The Straight Story*   Atonement
* *Lost World*   Melodrama
* *Sunset Boulevard*   Decadence
* *Psycho*   Unnatural attachment
* *My Life as a Dog* (Swedish)   Preadolescent angst
* *Stand by Me*   Coming-of-age seriousness

9.9. *Kolya.* This film strikes warm. It's about a middle-aged single man, settled and comfortable in his life as a musician, with a goodly supply of available women. Then the kid gets dumped on him and his life changes. This is a Czech film that won the Oscar for best foreign film in 1997. Nearly always, if the Academy has a choice between giving an Oscar to a warm film or a cool film, it opts for warm—not that there is anything wrong with warm with this particular film.

chapter ten

Meanings

his book has touched on *meaning* in one way or another in every chapter. Now a final chapter is needed to pull matters together and define the concept of *meaning* in film itself.

From Tone to Meaning

Actually, the last chapter was all about meaning, at least the kind of meaning you might derive from detecting tone. The moment you give a film's tone a name, you are just inches away from an intellectual relationship with the film. Your understanding of the movie is far greater than that of the guy next to you, who, when the final credits roll, says only, "Dude, scary movie." Here are some leaps from tone to meaning, based on films discussed in the previous chapter. First, you "hear" the dominant tone, and then you articulate a more complete statement of meaning.

- Film: *The Day of the Jackal.* Tone: detachment. Meaning: This film, with its lean, objective method, seems beyond morality. We admire the assassin's professionalism, and yet it's scary the way assassins go about their business with such moral neutrality.
- Film: *The Jackal.* Tone: High-tech cool. Meaning: It's cool the way assassins, who are also cool media heroes, go about their business with such mastery of high tech.
- Film: *The Mask of Zorro.* Tone: Swashbuckling. Meaning: Believe that one man, scaling walls effortlessly, swinging on lamp ropes, deftly sword fighting, looking handsome as hell, can single-handedly make fools out of the tyrannical rulers of old California and lead a people's revolt.

- Film: *The Hurricane.* Tone: Miraculous. Meaning: Believe that when we are down and out, it could happen that someone, somewhere—maybe even people we have had no connection to before—will take an interest in our predicament and be our salvation.
- Film: *Devil in a Blue Dress.* Tone: Dread. Meaning: When we get sucked into bad things and led down paths we'd rather not follow, we wonder what the hell is going on and how we got ourselves into such a mess; but we are helpless, alone, and finally doomed.
- Film: *Alien.* Tone: Manipulation. Meaning: Corporations will stop at nothing to acquire the knowledge they need to manufacture their products, even bad products like weapons.
- Film: *Sullivan's Travels.* Tone: Satire. Meaning: Big-time moviemakers are hypocrites for yearning to make socially conscious films, because in the end, they always go back to making mindless movies for the big bucks.
- Film: *My Name Is Joe.* Tone: Ambiguous. Meaning: Don't believe that women, or the power of love, can magically make a man stop drinking and abusing. The reality is probably that women stay with men who go on and off the wagon and who abuse, then stop, then go back to abusing again, then stop, and so on. And men stay with women who will have them—because relationships are like that: imperfect, never really resolved, but somehow necessary.
- Film: *Groundhog Day.* Tone: Change. Meaning: Believe that a conceited, self-absorbed man can become a human being if he gets a second chance (and a third, and a fourth, and a fifth . . .) and learns from his mistakes.
- Film: *Crimes and Misdemeanors.* Tone: Irony. Meaning: Ah, life! The bad finally sleep well; the (relatively) innocent toss and turn.
- Film: *The Conversation.* Tone: Metaphysical. Meaning: (1) You can't tell what's going on. (2) It's not possible to remain morally detached indefinitely from the consequences of our actions. (3) Professionals who don't consider the consequences of their trade end up isolating themselves from society.

Get the idea? But it's not that easy. Some modifications are in order. For instance, note how three of the meaning statements above begin with "Believe." This word is like a red flag; sometimes the meaning of a film amounts to wishful thinking. Reality isn't the issue.

My statement of meaning for *My Name Is Joe*, which purposely starts with "Don't believe," feels more real, more true, to me. It tries to break through wishful thinking. And I grant that my theme for *The Mask of Zorro* isn't very serious. But the movie doesn't take itself very seriously either. Maybe a winking movie deserves a winking theme. Or the character of Zorro may have mythic meaning.

Note how three possible meanings are supplied for *The Conversation.* Good films are like this. They suggest more than one meaning, owing to their complexity or subtlety. But you can't really leap from a tone word like "metaphysical" to "It's not possible to remain morally detached from the consequences of our actions." That statement of meaning derives from a different tone, that of *guilt* or *atonement*. *Atonement* is probably better. Also, the third statement of meaning derives from yet another tone—*arrogance*. When you find that right word to describe tone, you are halfway to meaning.

What was said for *Devil in a Blue Dress* is incomplete, since it does not expose the film as a cop-out. Denzel Washington gets off the hook and lives, turning potential noir tragedy into mere melodrama. And concerning *Alien:* Often the meaning in a film is hidden, buried, slipped between the frames. Thus the dominant tone of *Alien* is not manipulation, but good, old-fashioned dread, as befits a monster film. The resolution of *Alien*, when Ripley acts so bravely to shoot the creature out into space, strikes a blow for can-do feminism, which is a far different kind of meaning than what was initially supplied. To repeat: A good film suggests more than one meaning.

Genre Movies

Often the search for meaning starts with the most commonplace movies, namely those popular types of movies that film theorists call "genre" movies. Movie genres include the thrillers, romantic comedies, war movies, sci-fi films, and goofy kid flicks that probably account for 85 percent of all movie production. However, when film writers call these popular and recurring movie types *genres*, they imply a theory you might want to know about. Basically it is this: The popularity of recurring types of movies has more to do with their appeal to certain deep-seated psychological and sociological issues that viewers bring to them than simply with effective storytelling.

Viewers are usually not aware of these deep connections. Thus they view genre movies on two levels, on the surface level of story and on a deeper, preconscious level having to do with who they are and what they believe the movie means for society. Genre movies give viewers permission to entertain their most embedded fantasies, fears, and even hostilities. In the light of day, people put such notions away. Often they are unthinkable. But in the darkened movie theater—perhaps because all this does take place in the dark—with a genre movie to open them up, the deep stuff in them rivets them to the movie as much as the story does. Let's see how this works with a few well-known genres.

Crime Movies

There were genre movies during the silent era, but it might have been Warner Brothers' *The Public Enemy* (1931) that inaugurated the era of sound-movie genres. In this movie, James Cagney plays a cocky prohibition gangster who pushes a grapefruit into a woman's face and doesn't let nobody pull no shit on him. He goes down at the end, to be sure, but he goes down courageously, with class.

10.1. *The Public Enemy.* James Cagney, one of the first in a long line of screen tough guys who affected the behavior of millions of men worldwide. Warner Brothers.

This movie came out just as the reality of the Great Depression was setting in, and it was a big hit. Genre theorists today feel that *The Public Enemy* appealed to viewers who secretly longed to be rid of straight society (which was going to hell anyway) and to be outwardly lawless, swaggeringly independent. But if you were to ask these people at the corner drug store if they wanted to be gangsters, they would have looked at you funny.

Even today the gangster is nearly always pictured in movies as a romantic and colorful figure who packs a lot of power with his gun. Just think of the characters in *Pulp Fiction* (1994). So many of these characters are meant to be *cool*—there is no other way to put it. Consider how the nonstop verbal confidence of Samuel L. Jackson might appeal to viewers of all races who go, "Hey, it's okay to be mean *and* good with words." Jackson reinforces fast-talking hip-hop music. Consider how cool Bruce Willis is in the film, putting away those perverts in the pawn shop. He does it himself. He doesn't run to the police because in the world of Pulp Fiction there are no police. Real men get it done themselves. The cops are corrupt and lazy. It's a world beyond civic protection where smarts and bravery get you through, not dialing 911. It's a metaphor for life—that's how so many viewers probably *feel* about *Pulp Fiction*, down deep. Please, this is not to say anything so banal as that the characters of *Pulp Fiction* are bad role models so we should suppress the movie. No, viewers allow this deep and cynical meaning to wash over them in the dark, then go out and resume being 7-Eleven clerks, shoe salesmen, and high school chemistry teachers, for the most part.

The Dark Three

Here I roll three genre movies into one: the horror film, the monster film, and the slasher or splatter film. They often overlap and borrow features from each other. Their popularity says unkind things about Americans as film viewers. Film theorists have proposed that monster films are really about deep, bad things going on inside of us. We subconsciously believe ourselves to be monsters. We feel guilty about this or that. We see the screen monster thrashing around, causing incredible loss of life and property. Through it, we confront our own monstrous inner selves. When the monster in the movie is finally vanquished, we perceive it as our own just punishment. We leave the theater the way we walk away from a confessional, feeling good, purged, saved and sanctified. If we die, we will go straight to heaven.

Or maybe we don't feel so penitent. These dark genres may have special significance for men, one part of the theory goes. The inner demons aroused by the screen monsters may in fact represent men who have abused, mistreated, and otherwise marginalized women over the centuries. Movie monsters could represent to men a wet dream of omnipotence, an unbridled pillaging of a society that has not given them the breaks they think they deserve. Or slasher movies might appeal

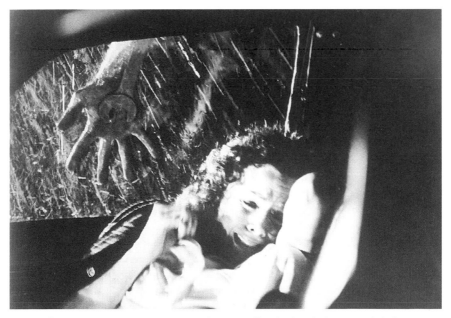

10.2. *Halloween.* The medium of film seems just naturally suited to the horror and slasher genres. How familiar it all is—dark, rain, menacing hand, blunt object, woman, entrapment, abject fear.

to men who secretly want to get back—*really* get back—at women for all the stuff they have put them through. Please, none of this is consciously perceived or expressed. Women don't leave theaters saying to their mates, "See? That's what I've been telling you. You're just like Godzilla." And men don't for a minute think about taking butcher knives to their wives when they get home. All this happens somewhere in a low, inexpressible part of the brain stem. The overall effect has been judged to be salutary: the subconscious enactment opens a safety valve, releasing pressure and forestalling a lot of violence in society, just as dreams are thought to help relieve personal conflict.

Teenpics

I propose that this irrepressible genre splits into three subgenres: compliant, near-rebellious, and self-reflective. Compliant teenpics go along with the American Way of Life. The kids in these films may act rambunctious now and then, but nothing bad really happens. They eventually buy into the adults' program for them. Between 1937 and 1947, Mickey Rooney made fifteen films as Andy Hardy, All-American teenager. In these films, Andy gets in and out of typical teenage scrapes, displaying ingenuity and sweetness, a way with girls, and respect for adults, church, and country. These films were pitched at both teens and adults. The latter never felt threatened. Then in the 1960s came Frankie Avalon and Annette Funicello in a series of innocuous beach movies. Boys loved seeing babes in bikinis for the first time in film history. But the display of nubile flesh was about as far as these films went in questioning the system of repressed sexuality adults had imposed on them.

One of the first rebellious teenpics was *Rebel Without a Cause*, which appeared in 1955. As the title suggests, there was never much of anything for James Dean and Natalie Wood to rebel against except their parents, who are portrayed as failing to understand them. Teens today see this film and ask, "What's the big deal?" But the film was a very big deal in 1955. To rebel against parents was something Hollywood had never really portrayed, much less encouraged. The Disney films always told kids to return home and do what Mom and Dad told them. Actually, there was plenty to rebel against in 1955 if anyone took the trouble to look around. Racism and sexism were rampant, to name just two areas of injustice. But that is the message of near-rebellion teenpics like *Rebel Without a Cause:* Teens are just too dependent and immature to even recognize injustice, much less mount any kind of attack on it. Their rebellion is inchoate.

A teenpic like *Cruel Intentions* (1999) has a related hidden message. The teens in the picture want to wield power in some way, as all teens do. Since they can't do frontal assaults on the greater adult system, they take to manipulating each other. They deflower virgins and get them to fall in love as if it were all a game, with winners and losers.

Since teens can't really rebel against the system, they often take to contemplating their own navels in films about them. *I Know What You Did Last Summer*

10.3. *I Know What You Did Last Summer.* The real reason so many kidpics come out of Hollywood is that 80 percent of moviegoers are under thirty. Now and then these throwaways resonate. Photo by James Bridges. Columbia/Mandalay.

(1997) makes teens squirm. In the story, four recent high-school graduates have been drinking and driving and in general not acting responsibly, when they run over a man and kill him. Instead of taking the dead man back into town and filing a proper police report, as most responsible grownups would do—end of movie—they push the body off a cliff and drive away. This is stupid. But the fact is teens do act stupidly from time to time. They have independence (the car) but not wisdom (hit and run). When they try to cover up their stupidity, they usually cause more trouble for themselves. Sure enough, they are stalked by the embodiment of trouble, someone who knows what happened. He kills them off one by one. On that low, brain-stem level, the stalker stands for guilt-ridden teen befuddlement, which hounds them through three or four pictures. Teens watch this film and on that low level murmur to themselves, *Oh, when am I going to learn to do the right thing?*

TRY THIS

Please do not take the foregoing too seriously. These analyses are merely examples of how I have played with deep meaning in genre movies. *Play* is the operative word here. Try playing this game yourself. What deep psychosocial meaning might reside in the following genres: romantic comedies, love stories, thrillers, Westerns, musical comedies, science fiction films set on Earth, science fiction set in deep space, and films noir?

Subtext

This way of looking at popular movies is similar to genre analysis. A subtext is a hidden agenda in a movie: On the surface the movie tells its story, but on a deeper level there is another concern, or maybe the main concern, that is quite different from the surface story. A sampling follows.

Invasion of the Body Snatchers (1956)

There have been several versions of this horror/sci-fi story. Probably the most famous is the 1956 version directed by Don Siegel. "Pods" from outer space sneak into the bodies of humans as they sleep and turn them into zombies, who then do the bidding of the adult aliens, which is to off-load more pods and spot them under beds so they can wiggle into more humans as they sleep. The eventual goal, of course, is to take over the world. The plot seems pretty lame now, but it was utterly fresh and terrifying to viewers in the fifties. Many commentators read a subtext of communist subversion into this story. Communists in our midst were alleged to have hypnotic powers to subvert people without their knowledge and turn them into mindless dupes of the Soviet Union. In its time, the movie was considered a wake-up call for America.

Home Alone

The subtext of this movie has to do with child empowerment. Eight-year-old Kevin (Macaulay Culkin) is scorned by his family and shut off in his room. In his anger, he wishes his family would just disappear. He gets his wish when the next day the family takes off for Europe and mistakenly leaves Kevin behind. Screenwriter and director John Hughes bends over backwards to make this plot plausible, without a lot of success. But the main thing, and what everyone remembers most about this popular movie, is the pair of burglars (Joe Pesci and Daniel Stern) who try to get into the house, and the ingenuity, aplomb, and cruelty Kevin employs to keep them at bay. Some reviewers have invited viewers to forget about the preposterous surface plot and concentrate on the subtext, which has to do with a child's fantasy of wielding power and exercising intelligence versus adults. This subtext is related to the "Boots" fairy tales in which the youngest of three brothers, invariably called Boots, outdoes his adult older brothers to prevail—for example, to climb the glass hill on his steed and win the hand of the beautiful princess.

Soldier (1998)

Often, detecting subtext can become a kind of game. You take a bad movie and make it interesting and viewable by exhuming a subtext. For example, nobody thought much of *Soldier* when it came out. It's a grim and trite sci-fi shoot-'em-up starring Kurt Russell as a futuristic professional soldier. It's hard to like the character of Sergeant Todd, played by Russell. The guy acts like a robot. He doesn't smile. He has no social graces. In fact, he seems practically autistic. But can he fight. He successfully organizes a band of lost people on a forgotten planet to fight a team of evil exterminators. This movie would be utterly forgettable if the subtext of military roboticization did not invite reflection. You can read this movie as an antimilitary statement: The very thing it seems to glorify, it condemns. Russell's character shows what happens to young men who are militarized: Their souls are stolen, much as the souls of the people in *Invasion of the Body Snatchers* have been sucked out.

Micromeaning

In better films, nothing you see is arbitrarily or accidentally inserted. Every prop, color, texture, window, view through the window, person in the background, cat on the sofa, or wailing of a siren has been deliberated upon by the director, often in consultation with the cast, screenwriter, cinematographer, sound recordist, set decorator, and lighting technician. It takes hours to dress a set for a take, move people into it, rehearse lines, rehearse movements, and finally roll film. It takes so long because, in the mind of the director, every element that offers itself for photography has meaning: She may not call it "meaning"—she just knows the details work for her and for the film, individually and collectively.

Below is a description of the first scene of a movie called *My Brilliant Career*,

10.4. *Singin' in the Rain.* Subtext: What does the rain really mean? What most moviegoers forget or don't want to remember about this scene is that Gene Kelly has just come from seeing Debbie Reynolds home, and she did not invite him in.

which was directed by the Australian Gillian Armstrong in 1979. The film has to do with the unpromising pre-publication life of Australian writer Miles Franklin, a woman. The setting is a cattle ranch in the Australian outback at the beginning of the twentieth century. We first see a ranch house in an extreme long shot in a prairie-like setting. Inside the house is a young woman, Sybylla, played by Judy Davis, who is alone and deep in thought. Through narration and reading her journal out loud, she tells us that she feels destined to be an artist of some kind. She writes: "This is the story of my career." Then she thinks a bit and inserts "brilliant" before "career." The ranch house is plain, even rather bleak. The exterior needs paint. At first we see Sybylla from the outside in—that is, through windows and an open door as she paces the living room and walks up to windows, reading as she walks, composing aloud, finally sitting at a table to write.

Then, gradually, the sound of the wind comes up. Before, only Sybylla's voice had been heard. The wind gets louder. A branch of a tree, bending and fluttering in the wind, is reflected in the glass of a window; in the same frame we see, through the window, Sybylla at a table, deep in thought. Then the camera angle is reversed. We are now in the house. We see Sybylla in the foreground and the window in the background. We also see, through the window, a ranch at work: men and women rounding up cattle, closing gates, working to tie things down before a gathering dust storm. We hear a female voice call out to Sybylla several times, but she doesn't seem to hear. Finally, on the fourth or fifth call of her name, with the wind now a fury, Sybylla is roused to get up, close the windows, and go out, closing the door behind her.

Virtually every detail of this scene is meaningful:

Details	Meaning
Sybylla alone in ranch house.	Sybylla is different, out of place, a fish out of water, not a member of the ranch-work team.
The shots from the outside in.	Sybylla's world is narrow, isolated—books, thoughts, words, and writing. This is almost like looking inward to her psyche.
Unpainted exterior of farmhouse.	These people have practical values that are not friendly to art.
No ambient sound; only the sound of Sybylla's thoughts.	Sybylla has screened out the outer, real world.
Sybylla reciting, then writing, "My 'brilliant' career."	This is an ironic assessment of Sybylla's chances for success in such a setting—so she's not totally naïve.
Gradual mix-in of wind.	The outer world starts to impinge aurally.

Agitated tree limb reflected in window.	The outer world now impinges visually.
Agitated limb composed with Sybylla lost in thought at the table.	Sybylla is oblivious to the outer world.
Reverse angle: Sybylla in foreground, ranch hands seen through window, scurrying.	View of outer world widens. Now Sybylla's obliviousness seems a little ridiculous.
Edited sequence: from inner to outer.	Sybylla's artistic inner world must eventually yield to the practical, unkind outer world.
Sybylla finally comes around, hastens to door, closing it behind her.	Outer world wins. Sybylla's artistic inner world in jeopardy. Closing of door symbolizes the closing off or protecting of her fragile inner life from the harsh outer life.

Here is another description of a scene from *Cabaret*, a film directed by the famous Broadway director Bob Fosse in 1972. The film is set in Germany during the 1930s. Two young men, one British (Michael York) and one German (Helmut Griem), take refreshment at an outdoor wine garden in the countryside. It's a warm sunny day. A boy of fourteen or fifteen rises and begins to sing a German folk song, "Tomorrow Belongs to Me," in a sweet tenor. He is blonde, handsome, winsome. The other people present pay attention to him, apparently enjoying the song and the boy's rendering of it. Then the camera pans down to reveal a swastika on the arm of the boy. His expression changes gradually from innocence to determination. A long shot of the boy is symmetrically composed: An aisle leading to the little platform on which the boy sings is positioned in the middle of the frame from foreground to background, while the others' seats go off in rows perpendicular to the top and bottom of the frame. A dog gets up and walks diagonally away from the boy, crossing the aisle. One by one the people listening rise, seeming to snap to attention; many of them, especially the younger ones, also begin to sing. Their expressions are fanatic, militaristic. The boy singer starts to look fierce. There is a cutaway to an elderly man, still seated, who looks away and shakes his head. Finally, near the end of the song, the boy is captured in low angle as he raises his arm in the Nazi salute. Michael and Helmut get up—they have remained seated throughout the serenade—and leave.

Analysis of micromeaning:

Details	Meaning
The setting is rural.	National Socialism, or Nazism, has so pervaded Germany that it has reached the countryside.

The singer is a boy.	National Socialism has so pervaded Germany that even boys embrace it. Also, the boy's innocence embodies the innocence and gullibility of the entire country.
The folk song, "Tomorrow Belongs to Me."	The title suggests the aims of the Third Reich to rule the world and also the association of National Socialism with mythic roots of Aryan supremacy.
The swastika on the boy's arm.	The association is made explicit.
The boy's expression changes from innocence to fanaticism.	The fanatical, perverse nature of National Socialism finally comes out. Even children have been brainwashed.
The listeners snap to attention.	Support is widespread and robotic.
The listeners take on the same obsessive, depraved, scary expression as that of the singer.	Something about National Socialism turns ordinary citizens into mindless hatemongers.
The symmetrical composition of aisle, chairs, platform, and singer.	The symmetry suggests the control of people's minds with militaristic precision.
The cutaway to the old man, who looks away.	Some do not agree, especially old-timers who remember the carnage of World War I, and could even have participated in it.
The dog walking away.	Beats me—but it must mean something. You have to go to a lot of trouble to have a dog walk through a shot. It's two hours of work for half a dozen people.
The final salute of the boy.	The whole thing has been a ritual display of support for National Socialism.

Frankly, few film scenes are packed with as much micromeaning as are these two scenes. They might even strike you as contrived, for all the weight they have to bear. A movie scene doesn't really have to work this hard. Here is a scene from *Toy Story 2* with just a single significant detail. One is enough to spin out the meaning of the entire scene.

- Background: Woody, a toy cowboy, has been snatched away by a toy collector who wants to sell him and the other toys that were featured in a now-classic, *Howdy-Doody*–type TV show of the 1950s. The collector plans to sell the whole ensemble to a rich Japanese.

- The scene: Woody is locked in an upstairs room of the home of the toy collector along with the other toys from the TV series. Woody says no. He doesn't want to be sold. He wants to go home to his owner, a kid named Andy. Woody steps to a ventilation duct, opens the grill, and looks inside, getting ready to split. Then an old prospector toy, who acts as a spokesmen for the others, says, "You go back to your home and your Andy will soon dump you. You'll end up rotting in some landfill." This gives Woody pause; he stops to think. He looks down the duct—and there's the significant detail: The point-of-view shot of the duct is rendered dark, with an infinite regression of repeated rectangular frames marching off to nothingness, getting smaller and blacker.
- Meaning: This is one of the most meaningful point-of-view shots in all of film history. The dark duct is death to Woody—death, obscurity. These are key words of the philosophy of existentialism that undergirds the film.

Symbols?

If you wish, you may regard such a detail as a *symbol*, which is anything in a film (or in a novel or in real life) that has more significance for what it stands for than for what it literally is. The wind in the opening scene of *My Brilliant Career* is more than just wind; it's a symbol of how the outer world impinges on Sybylla, forcing her out of her self-absorption. But Sybylla's going outside is also a symbol—for hav-

10.5. *Sunset Boulevard.* Satiric set dressing. The boudoir as trap. The exaggerated cupids and ornate headboard perfectly suit Gloria Swanson's flamboyant, theatrical personality. William Holden knows better but he is helpless. Paramount.

ing to join the real world. And closing the door behind her—she closes it to keep the dust out of the house, yes, but the closing can also be a symbolic act of protecting her vulnerable inner world. Also, as I have suggested, the point-of-view shot in *Toy Story 2* of the infinite regression of the frames of the darkened duct was probably meant to symbolize Woody's eventual fate: landfill nothingness.

Maybe this process can be carried too far. If you look for symbols everywhere, all the time, in all the details, you could become too preoccupied intellectually and fail to simply enjoy the film on an affective level. You need a balance. For this reason, it might be useful to simply call these details *meaningful*. Credit the director and other film professionals with designing and dressing sets or contriving action in ways that pretty much always mean something, and leave it at that. Or reserve symbol-watching for only the most interesting props or bits of action, and otherwise just enjoy.

Intrusive symbols are something else. They so obviously cry out for interpretation that you can't ignore them. As props, they do not occur naturally or blend with the story. They call attention to themselves. Sometimes they feel contrived and arty. You have to stop everything and figure out what they mean before you can get back to enjoying the movie. Here are some examples of intrusive symbols in films:

- The black monoliths in *2001: A Space Odyssey*
- The work space that is only four-and-a-half feet high in *Being John Malkovich*
- The use of color in *Pleasantville*
- The impertinent use of the color blue in *Blue*
- The rain of frogs at the end of *Magnolia*

TRY THIS

Next time you rent a film that you consider thoughtful in its working out, play a scene over a few times and take note of its details. Which props, colors, movements, and textures—or anything else about the scene—seem meaningful? Meaningful how? Would you elevate any of these details to the status of symbol? If so, what do the details symbolize?

Macromeaning

This kind of meaning is at the other end of the scale from micromeaning. You deal with micromeaning prop by prop and detail by detail as you watch a film. You deal with macromeaning later, after closing credits roll. You might experience what I call the Fridge Response: You go to a movie and find it interesting, then go home and open the fridge for a snack, then pause with the fridge door open, cool air pouring over your feet. You think, "What the hell was that film about?" Here are some takes on macromeaning.

Metaphor

Some film experts write about "symbol" and "metaphor" pretty much interchangeably. However, I have noticed that most reserve the term "metaphor" for the film as a whole. They say, "*The Godfather* is a metaphor for American capitalism"; or, "The sinking of the *Titanic* is a metaphor for the demise of the Gilded Age"; or, "*Frankenstein* (*Young*, *Son of*, *Bride of*, *Return of*, *Meets Abbot and Costello*—the story had been made thirty-one times by 1995) is a metaphor for the consequences of bad science."

Thus a few movies, without really straining to do so, embrace important institutions of society or significant periods of history via overarching metaphors.

Epic

As chapter 7 suggests, epic films sweep up big chunks of the history of peoples, together with their hopes, dreams, and fears. Epic films are often very likeable. They are big and showy; they splash period costuming and detailing all over the

10.6. *Frankenstein.* The classic confrontation of scientist and monster. Or maybe science is the monster. Note details capable of micromeaning: the rocks, the fog, the distance between the two, the expressions, and the torch. Ah, the torch! Why not a flashlight? Why is a torch better? Universal.

screen; they have soaring musical scores and large casts. The best of them are almost certain to get Oscar nominations.

Changing Times in Gone With the Wind

Gone With the Wind straddles the American Civil War. Before the war, the South was a genteel, innocent, slave-based society. Rhett Butler (Clark Gable), Scarlett O'Hara (Vivien Leigh), and the rest of the plantation crowd could afford to be genteel and innocent—though Rhett knew better. The women fluttered their eyelids; the men rushed off cluelessly to war. Then Atlanta burned, the South fell, and the old way of life was, well, gone with the wind. Southerners' lives were forever changed. Many people fault this film as racist, and this is certainly true, but that particular criticism isn't any fun. See the movie again as a piece of Americana circa 1939.

Packaging and Promotion in The Right Stuff

This is a big, three-hour movie about the dawn of the American space age. Like *Gone With the Wind*, it splits in two. The first half of the film is about the training of American astronauts and early failures, the second half is about triumph and ballyhoo. I could have written about this film in the previous chapter with the greatest of ease because it strikes an interesting mix of tones in the way it treats heroism: In some places the heroism is authentic; in others it is knowingly faked or shown to be co-opted by national purpose. The scope is certainly epic. You learn a lot about America in the 1960s by tuning in to this film—that is, if you don't mind viewing history through the particular satiric filters of Tom Wolfe, who wrote the novel, and Philip Kaufmann, who directed the film. As a nation, we certainly deserved the prestige brought by the achievements of daring men like Alan Shepard, John Glenn, and Gordon Cooper. But Wolfe and Kaufmann also had a lot to say about how these and other astronauts were packaged and promoted, just like Cadillac El Dorados with their swoopy fins. *The Right Stuff* won five Academy Awards.

Subculture as Epic in American Me *(1992)*

This heartfelt film has enough hopes and fears for any epic. It's just not a mainstream epic. Instead, it's about life in the Latino barrio of East Los Angeles, and one man's rejection of a white, middle-class lifestyle. The man is Edward James Olmos, who also directed. Soon he is immersed in gang life, with the usual tragic consequences. No Academy Award nominations.

Journey as Epic in El Norte

This is the Latino equivalent of *The Grapes of Wrath*, an epic film in its own right. Just as the Joad family hopes for a better life in California, so do Rosa and Enrique, forced to leave their native Guatemala for political reasons. The journey is hard enough. The brother and sister are hopelessly innocent and are exploited at every turn. But Los Angeles, their destination, is even tougher. The journey is as bitterly ironic as that of the Joad family. The story of Rosa and Enrique is the story of all U.S. immigrants seeking to improve their lots. Nominated for Best Screenplay.

Myth

In chapter 7, we briefly looked at characters who embody myths in the sense of representing our enduring, seldom-questioned assumptions about society. Now we look at how myth pervades films and provides important narrative framework. Here are five films with mythic resonance.

Film	Myth
The Mask	Inside every nerd, there is a real man, confident and resourceful, just waiting to pop out.
The Fugitive	Doctors will honor the Hippocratic oath even while on the run from the law.
Shane (1953)	The day of the gunfighter in the Old West must eventually make way for family and community.
Pocahontas (1995)	By her example of respecting nature and living close to it, Pocahontas may turn John Smith and the society he represents away from values of rapacious colonization (lots of luck).
Field of Dreams (1989)	Ah, baseball! It's magic. It has power to heal just about anything—rifts between fathers and sons, the bitterness of aging writers, an entire nation grown cynical.

Each of these films invites us to think wistfully (or maybe the proper word is "wishfully"). In *Shane* Alan Ladd happens to ride into a certain valley in Wyoming in the 1860s at a most propitious moment. Cattlemen and farmers have been squabbling over land, and matters have come to a head. The leader of the cattlemen has hired a black-clad gunman to intimidate the farmers. But the cattlemen—who have no women, family, or community—are doomed to lose, mythically speaking. The tide of history is not on their side. The story follows a kind of domestic manifest destiny: *Family will triumph.* Blonde, light-struck Shane makes it happen, by killing the gunman who wears the black hat. But Shane, who is himself a temporarily retired gunman, must also pass into history, just as the cattlemen do. At the end, he rides out of the valley and into history—mythic history.

Pocahontas embodies, in cartoon form, all of our myths about indigenous peoples and nature. They are perceived to be the guardians of the pure and good. Caucasians (Europeans and Americans) act to despoil the pure and corrupt the good.

And baseball, the most mythic of sports, America's pastime, speaks of leisure, timeless afternoons, the rat race set aside, Casey at the bat, Maguire and Sosa. The sport evokes a nostalgic, pastoral America dominated not by modernist "team-

10.7. *Pocahontas.* This film is in a long line of Disney films about young woman around whom wild animals willingly cluster. Why? More on nature on pages 166–71.

work" but by larger-than-life loner heroes, cracking home runs, scrambling after grounders, shagging flies in a vast, frontier-like outfield. Anything baseball touches must be renewed. This is the point of *Field of Dreams.*

Countermyth

This is my term for myth gone bad—the negative, flip side of myth. Myth is always positive and hopeful, but Americans aren't stupid. They hope and expect only so long and so far. When the hoped-for does not materialize, they smarten up. They may become bitter. They tune out the myth or reverse it.

The entertainment industry, notably Hollywood and rock 'n' roll, cashed in on the national souring of dreams that may have set in on a large scale after Vietnam and Watergate. For example, as a people, we used to believe in the FBI and the local cops. We revered J. Edgar Hoover, the longtime director of the FBI, nearly elevating him to the status of a god. We *believed* in Jack Webb as Sergeant Friday, the coolly efficient, incorruptible police guy on TV's *Dragnet.* Not only was Friday incorruptible; nobody ever even made attempts to corrupt him. Society just didn't do things like that.

Then the press stopped protecting Hoover and revealed him to be a strange bird who wanted Martin Luther King, Jr., locked up as a Commie. In the 1960s, a phenomenon called *police brutality* was discovered and given a name. Cops were accused of beating African-Americans with nightsticks. Rampart precinct cops in

Los Angeles were revealed to have planted evidence on suspects, thus sending them to prison. The result of so much bad press was that many people lost faith in law enforcement. Accordingly, we got movies like *Serpico* (1973) in which good cop Al Pacino risks his life resisting corrupting influences among his fellow cops, and *The French Connection* (1971), which despite its exciting story about the NYC narcotic department's efforts to stop drugs from entering the city, is probably more interesting for its portrayal of Popeye, a vicious, snarling, can't-be-stopped narcotics officer played by Gene Hackman. Popeye is the new countermythic cop, obsessive to a fault, amoral and scary. He suits the times.

Countermythic cop films are still popular. Cops like this give Harrison Ford a very bad time for most of *The Fugitive*. One recent countermythic cop film—*L.A. Confidential* (1997)—took a pair of Oscars. The Dirty Harry films are also countermythic, but it's not the San Francisco police force or the FBI that is tainted; it's the whole damn society, which Harry Callahan finds soft on criminals. You don't deal with psychopaths, you shoot 'em. There was a large audience for films with an attitude in 1971, when the first *Dirty Harry* film came out, and there is a large audience for films like this now.

10.8. *Dirty Harry.* As Dirty Harry, Eastwood became a national icon, or honored figure—the countermythic, reactionary hero who saves society from topless dancers, liberal judges, hostage-taker negotiators, punks, and sociologists. To Eastwood's credit, he has often broken out of the redeemer role to play a wide range of characters, including those that aren't very redeeming. Warner Brothers.

Here are some film metaphors, film epics, films based on myth, and films based on countermyths. See them, detect tendencies.

- FILM METAPHORS: *2001: A Space Odyssey, All that Jazz* (1979), *The Color of Money* (1986), *The Duellists* (1977), *Glengary Glenn Ross, The Third Man.*
- FILM EPICS: *Ballad of a Soldier* (U.S.S.R., 1959), *Battleship Potemkin* (U.S.S.R.), *The Bicycle Thief* (Italy), *Pather Panchali* (Bengal), *Amadeus* (1984), *The Blue Kite* (China), *Easy Rider, Reds* (1981), *Elizabeth* (United Kingdom), *How Green Was My Valley* (1941), *Lone Star* (1996), *Nashville, Stagecoach, The Seven Samurai* (Japan), *The Wild Bunch.*
- FILMS BASED ON MYTHS: *Beauty and the Beast* (France, 1946), *Citizen Kane, Bonnie and Clyde, Dark City* (1998), *The Gold Rush, Gallipoli* (Australia), *Meet John Doe, Scarface, Tender Mercies* (1983), *Terms of Endearment* (1983), *Knife in the Water* (Poland, 1960).
- FILMS BASED ON COUNTERMYTHS: *The Apartment, Blade Runner, Kids* (1995), *Mad Max* (Australia, 1979), *Mildred Pierce* (1945), *The Road Warrior* (Australia, 1981), *The Last Picture Show, Slaughterhouse Five* (1972), *Blade Runner, Batman, The Crow* (1994).

Theme

I've touched on the subject of *theme* often in the book, lingering longest in chapter 6 on what I called "the conflict of theme." But more needs to be said before the book can be closed. Simply put, theme is supreme meaning. If myth and countermyth are about expectations, good and bad, theme is about truth—with a lowercase *t*—truth, that is, as seen by screenwriters and the directors. What could be more important?

In Movies

You can look for theme in any motion picture, even a good-time movie like *Back to the Future.* This flick tells a terrific story about a teenager played by Michael J. Fox who goes back to 1955 on the twin missions of bringing his future parents together and making them feel better about themselves so that when they all get back to 1985 (the present), the McFly family will shake its dysfunction and become closer and stronger. On the surface, the story doesn't seem capable of much weightiness. So why go searching for truth in material like that? But if you dig deeper into the movie, you realize that *Back to the Future* isn't about time travel or the invention of the skateboard. No, it's basically about *family*, and we can relate to that.

If then you take family to be the rock-bottom, deep-down *subject* of the film, then you are just a short distance from articulating a theme or two. Examples are:

- Bad experiences in the past may develop eventually into personality problems that can lead to dysfunction in families.
- With early intervention, personality problems can be avoided and families thereby strengthened.
- Kids do care—not just about their own existence, but about the emotional well-being of their parents.
- Kids aren't dumb. They do have the capacity to see what's wrong with their parents and take action to help them.

With themes like these, you get double the viewing. You enjoy the movie as story *and* idea. Also, as I suggested a long time ago in the Introduction, you transform a mere movie into a *film*.

In Films

Other motion pictures are more obviously thematic. They start out as *films*—their *filmness* is built right in. *Citizen Kane* is like this. Right from the start, when producer-director Orson Welles undertook the project for RKO Studios, he aimed at seriousness, at art, at something thoughtful and intellectual, and so did his co-screenwriter, Herman Mankiewicz. The story is based on the life of media czar William Randolph Hearst. I have written about the film's photography in chapter 1, its tragedy in chapter 6, and its point of view in chapter 7. It's a complex film because it offers a multiplicity of themes. Here are some examples:

10.9. *Citizen Kane.* The greatness of this film doesn't just jump off the screen and into your lap. Even though the film is sixty years old, it strikes many viewers as strange, different. You have to go to it. However, since you are nearing the end of the book and have completed a number of "Try This" sections, you ought to be well equipped to take it on. RKO/Turner.

Subject	Theme
Reality	is multifaceted, subjective, ultimately unknowable.
Wealth	isolates he who possesses it, turns him into a selfish, power-seeking monster. (We knew this. This is more countermyth than theme.)
Materialism (or the acquisition of material things)	ultimately corrupts the possessor.
Materialism	ultimately becomes meaningless, even an addiction: the more one acquires, the more one wants; the more one wants, the less one relates to any one "thing."
American liberalism	in time betrays itself, loses its ideals. Becomes a plaything in the hands (or psyches) of the very rich, to be acted upon with a wink.
Money	Can't buy happiness. (We knew this too: another countermyth.)

  TRY THIS

See *Citizen Kane*. Trace these various subjects, themes, and countermyths. There are more.

Arriving at Large Meaning in Two Contemporary Films

You can get addicted to ferreting out themes like this. It's not a bad thing to get hooked on.

Being True to Yourself: *American Beauty* (1999)

American Beauty is a fine fix. Here's how we might arrive at its theme. First, that subject of theme. What is the film *about*? Let's settle on *the midlife crisis* for now. From such a subject might flow this theme: When a middle-aged man finds himself in a stultifying marriage and a dead-end job, he has to do something seriously different to save his soul.

What suburbanite Lester Burnham (Kevin Spacey) does is this: He stops pretending. He tells his boss what he really thinks about his job (writing dumb advertising copy) and gets fired. That's fine with him. He also starts speaking frankly to his held-in, unfaithful wife, Carolyn (Annette Bening), and feels good about that. No more phony life for him. Also, he allows his repressed sexuality to emerge and starts fantasizing about his daughter's cheerleader friend, the beauty of the title. Considering all this, maybe a better theme subject is *authenticity*, or just being true to yourself.

10.10. *American Beauty.* This film, which was produced independently, ought to have had a modest playoff, thence to obscurity. But thanks to Steven Spielberg, who talked his colleagues at DreamWorks into getting behind it, the film got good promotion, grossed over a hundred million dollars, and won a clutch of Academy Awards. When this happens, Hollywood executives scramble to find something "the same but different" to get out next year. Invariably the imitations feel inauthentic. (Also see photo 1.12.) Photo by Lorey Sebastian. DreamWorks.

Meanwhile, the teenager next door, Ricky (Wes Bentley), is a kind of loner video artist. He and his family have just moved in. His father is a spit-and-polish retired colonel; his mother has silently suffered her husband's domination. Ricky tapes the various goings-on at the Burnham household from his bedroom window. He tries to meet Lester's daughter Jane (Thora Birch), but her friend Angela, the cheerleader (Mena Suvari), advises her against getting mixed up with him, calling him a "weirdo." For her part, the cheerleader comes on as totally experienced in matters of sex. Where is this going? Ricky is authentically his own person. For example, he tapes the wind playing whimsically with a swirling paper bag. He is sensitive to beauty in the commonplace. Soon Jane realizes that her friendship with the cheerleader has robbed her of authenticity; she starts seeing Ricky, whose realness of self appeals to her.

One more person needs to get real, and that is the cheerleader. Lester finally gets her in bed and is about to do the deed when she breaks down, frightened. She admits that she has had no sexual experience at all. She has been all talk. Lester sympathizes and backs off. He respects her honesty—that is, her finally being real.

Maybe then you realize that *the midlife crisis*, as a theme, just does not stretch far enough. You need a broader or more fundamental theme subject. So you settle on authenticity—being true to yourself. If so, these themes might accordingly flow:

- When people stop putting on a show, they can reach within themselves and pull out something real, genuine, authentic.
- Achieving authenticity makes a person feel terrific. It's like removing a tremendous burden from the soul. You feel truly free.
- Being authentic has its risks: You can never really go back to the old phony life. You must disavow your phony friends, get out of town, start all over again.
- Being authentic is more than just risky, it can be fatal. Dangerous people perceive authentic people as threats.

As the last theme suggests, Lester pays a high price at the end of the film for being true to himself.

Listening to the Heart: *Welcome to the Dollhouse* (1995)

This film is also about suburbia, but it's much darker than *American Beauty*. It starts off as a very funny film about a girl, Dawn (Heather Matarazzo), about thirteen, whom everyone at her middle school despises. Dawn is the classic nerd. People play mean tricks on her. Her family members seem indifferent to her social isolation and loneliness and do nothing to nurture or protect her. In fact, they treat her like a second-class family member. It's not surprising then that Dawn herself starts treating other people shabbily.

Soon you stop laughing. This is serious business. Dawn leads a wretched life. Todd Solondz, who wrote and directed, has a very grim view of suburbia. It's a waking nightmare. There is no love or life or spirit or soul anywhere in sight. None of the kids learn anything at the school—not surprising because none of the teachers know the first thing about teaching. The kids are spiteful and hateful.

Analyzing *Welcome to the Dollhouse* thematically might proceed like this. First, a thematic subject: *cruelty*. Or, maybe it's *the suburbs* or *the outsider*. These are all good impulses, good starts. And from these starts, some themes:

- For *cruelty*: People are cruel. That goes for young people and adults, including parents and teachers. (Duh. Can't we do better than this?)
- For *suburbs*: Life in the suburbs is a nightmare. (What else? Say more.)
- For *the outsider*: Life is a nightmare for the outsider whom people of all ages treat cruelly. (Closer.)

The film haunts you. You can't just set it aside. Something about mere theme-grubbing bothers you. It's incomplete, only part of the story. You think it's fine to

10.11. *Welcome to the Dollhouse.* Nerdette Dawn, alone, perplexed, her locker bearing hateful graffiti. This independent film is more pessimistic than American Beauty, and no Steven Spielberg came to its rescue. Still, it made a little money, which has encouraged other independent filmmakers to make their own quirky visions, even dark ones. Photo by Jennifer Carchman. Sony Pictures Classics.

read a book like this to learn how to detect themes in films, but this kind of analysis lacks something. It doesn't help you get to the bottom of *Welcome to the Dollhouse* in a *human* sense. So you the see the film again, this time with an open heart. On this second viewing, you are struck—actually *moved*—by a certain fact of the story, namely, that Dawn doesn't seem to be aware that she is being shit on. Her particular misery makes her condition doubly poignant to you. Your head had intellectualized you out of this awareness. Theme cheated you.

This new heartfelt bearing really starts to get to you during the last scene of the film as Dawn's class takes an end-of-the-year trip to Disneyworld. (Disneyworld—you find yourself thinking about just *that*.) En route, on the bus, the class starts singing the school song. At first Dawn is reluctant to join in. You (and your heart) don't blame her. The two of you want her to rebel, get away from that school, get off the bus, start her own life far from her cruel classmates and indifferent parents, away from the suburbs. But you realize she's just too young and dependent for that, and you are saddened.

Finally, though, Dawn does starts to sing. But she sings in a faint, spiritless monotone. She doesn't smile and isn't animated as her exuberant classmates are. What can possibly be going through her mind? Maybe by now she doesn't even have a mind. She looks at her knees as she sings. She reminds you of the brain-washed Lawrence Harvey in *The Manchurian Candidate* (1962). Maybe by now the system has completely taken over her mind and quashed her soul beyond recovery. She's been turned into a pod person, like the people in *The Invasion of the Body Snatchers*. Or maybe she still does have a mind but it's in a state of utter, profound depression. It can't express itself. Maybe then the rock-bottom, down-deep, can't-get-no-more-basic theme of the film, *discovered more with the heart than with the head*, is that of *total victory*, total control, by the 'burbs. To sing, as Dawn finally does, is to give up all resistance, to capitulate.

Such a hopeless vision! You think about yourself in relation to the film. No, it wasn't totally hopeless. You have learned a thing or two about the melancholy of nerdness as a result of letting your heart have its way. You are a better person. There is hope for *you*.

Triangulation

At the end of the book, making these grand statements about a film I love very much, I am inclined to put into perspective all the techniques and ideas I've discussed, though I have to be selective here. I am glad that *Welcome to the Dollhouse* doesn't have any intrusive symbols to deal with, because, personally speaking, I don't like those symbols very much. But I do like Dawn's costuming, naïvely colorful and sweet, and very sad somehow. We know she is out of it by what she wears. Is the costuming then a symbol? Naw. It's just a carefully selected detail. It pleasures me to contemplate its meaning.

I am reminded now of how far the American film scene has come during the couple of decades I've been following it. *Welcome to the Dollhouse* could not have been made thirty-five years ago. The corporations (including Hollywood), which were just starting to gain the total power they now have, would have been aghast. They'd complain. *You can't shoot that screenplay,* they'd tell you. *It makes suburbanites look viscious. We need to keep everyone happy so they'll be in a mood to buy our Rocket 88s and Hoffman EZ-View TVs.*

It's hard enough for the contemporary indie filmmaker to find an audience, especially since one-time principled independent distributors like Miramax have sold out to the likes of Disney, and festival organizers are now looking for the merely *slightly* quirky independent film that will cross over and do big business. So it's a miracle that Solondz got his cheerless film made and shown. Maybe the current prosperity has allowed that to happen. But I worry about the fate of courageous filmmaking when the economy goes bad and everybody gets practical and stingy.

Way back in the Introduction, I suggested that *filmness* may be a joint product of two things, thoughtful content and a thoughtful viewer. Determining *meaningfulness* may work something like this, too, only I believe this is finally a three-way transaction among film, head, and heart. The film first informs your head but, if you allow it, finally ends up down in the heart. The heart wants to lighten the heavy ideas the head has wrought, make them softer, pliable, just plain human. The head isn't sure and says, *Come on. We gotta see that film again.* So off it goes to the video store. The heart affably goes along.

About the Author

J im Piper has taught film study and filmmaking at Fresno City College in California for over thirty years. He still makes films—short, noncommercial films. He has taken awards in little festivals that accept personal films in places ranging from Palo Alto, California, to Brno, C.S.S.R, only it's not called C.S.S.R any more. He has lived through, and not just read about, huge changes in the American Cinema, and he remembers those pre-multiplex days when you could go around the corner to an art film theater and see a foreign film. He has published three books, two English texts, and a filmmaking book way back when video was just a Hershey bar in Sony's hip pocket. He has been a contributing editor to a nationally circulated filmmaking magazine, and he likes to put together free, EZ, big-screen video festivals for the community. He resides in Fresno with his wife Carol, his stepson Kyle, three cats, two dogs, and seven fat goldfish in a pond.

Index

ALLWORTH PRESS
NEW YORK

Books from Allworth Press

Making Independent Films: Advice from the Filmmakers
by Liz Stubbs and Richard Rodriguez (softcover, 6 × 9, 224 pages, $16.95)

Producing for Hollywood: A Guide for Independent Producers
by Paul Mason and Don Gold (softcover, 6 × 9, 272 pages, $19.95)

An Actor's Guide—Your First Year in Hollywood, Revised Edition
by Michael Saint Nicholas (softcover, 6 × 9, 272 pages, $18.95)

The Health and Safety Guide for Film, TV & Theater
by Monona Rossol (softcover, 6 × 9, 256 pages, $19.95)

Casting Directors' Secrets: Inside Tips for Successful Auditions
by Ginger Howard (softcover, 6 × 9, 208 pages, $16.95)

Promoting Your Acting Career
by Glenn Altermann (softcover, 6 × 9, 224 pages, $18.95)

Writing Scripts Hollywood Will Love, Revised Edition
by Katherine Atwell Herbert (softcover, 6 × 9, 160 pages, $14.95)

The Screenwriter's Guide to Agents and Managers
by John Scott Lewinski (softcover, 6 × 9, 256 pages, $18.95)

So You Want to Be a Screenwriter: How to Face the Fears and Take the Risks *by Sara Caldwell and Marie-Eve Kielson* (softcover, 6 × 9, 224 pages, $14.95)

Writing Television Comedy
by Jerry Rannow (softcover, 6 × 9, 224 pages, $14.95)

Selling Scripts to Hollywood
by Katherine Atwell Herbert (softcover, 6 × 9, 224 pages, $12.95)

The Screenwriter's Legal Guide, Second Edition
by Stephen F. Breimer (softcover, 6 × 9, 320 pages, $19.95)

Writing for Interactive Media: The Complete Guide
by Jon Samsel and Darryl Wimberly (hardcover, 6 × 9, 320 pages, $19.95)

Please write to request our free catalog. To order by credit card, call 1-800-491-2808 or send a check or money order to Allworth Press, 10 East 23rd Street, Suite 510, New York, NY 10010. Include $5 for shipping and handling for the first book ordered and $1 for each additional book. Ten dollars plus $1 for each additional book if ordering from Canada. New York State residents must add sales tax.

To see our complete catalog on the World Wide Web, or to order online, you can find us at *www.allworth.com*.